BLACK PERFORMANCE AND CULTURAL CRITICISM
Valerie Lee and E. Patrick Johnson, Series Editors

The Queer Limit of Black Memory
Black Lesbian Literature and Irresolution

MATT RICHARDSON

THE OHIO STATE UNIVERSITY PRESS
COLUMBUS

Library of Congress Cataloging-in-Publication Data
Richardson, Matt, 1969–
The queer limit of Black memory : Black lesbian literature and irresolution / Matt Richardson.
p. cm.—(Black performance and cultural criticism)
Includes bibliographical references and index.
ISBN 978-0-8142-1222-6 (cloth : alk. paper)—ISBN 978-0-8142-9323-2 (cd)
1. Lesbians in literature. 2. Lesbianism in literature. 3. Blacks in literature. 4. Gomez, Jewelle, 1948—Criticism and interpretation. 5. Barnett, LaShonda K., 1975—Criticism and interpretation. 6. Adamz-Bogus, SDiane, 1946—Criticism and interpretation. 7. Brown, Laurinda D.—Criticism and interpretation. 8. Muhanji, Cherry—Criticism and interpretation. 9. Bridgforth, Sharon—Criticism and interpretation. 10. Kay, Jackie, 1961—Criticism and interpretation. 11. Brand, Dionne, 1953—Criticism and interpretation. I. Title. II. Series: Black performance and cultural criticism.
PN56.L45R53 2013
809'.933526643—dc23
2012050159

Cover design by Thao Thai
Text design by Juliet Williams
Type set in Adobe Garamond Pro and Formata
Printed by Thomson-Shore, Inc.

9 8 7 6 5 4 3 2 1

For My Mother
Ruthel Monk Richardson
1939–2007

CONTENTS

ACKNOWLEDGMENTS

This book has taken years to complete and a village of support, including the financial support of the University of California, Santa Barbara Dissertation Fellowship in the Department of Feminist Studies, University of California Presidential Postdoctoral Fellowship, Woodrow Wilson Foundation and the University of Texas at Austin (UT) Dean's Fellowship, and research support from the Warfield Center for African and African American Studies and the Department of English at UT.

I am grateful to my dissertation committee, who supported me throughout the dissertation stage of this process: Ula Taylor, Norma Alarcón, Chris Nealon, Paola Bacchetta, and Ruthie Gilmore. I give special thanks and honor to the scholars who guided me early on in my career, but who have since passed on: Barbara Christian, VèVè Clark, and Albert Johnson. I know they are watching over me.

I appreciate the feedback and support of a long list of colleagues at UT in the African and African Diaspora Studies Department, the English Department, the Warfield Center for African and African American Studies, and the Center for Women's and Gender Studies, but especially Omi Oshun Joni Jones, Lisa Moore, Ann Cvetkovitch, Jennifer Wilks, Meta DuEwa Jones, and Kristen Hogan. I would like to thank all of the graduate students at the

University of Texas who have assisted me in this project: Eric Covey, Yvette DeChavez, Michelle Mott, Jared Richardson, Stephanie Rosen, Corinne Greiner, and Connie Johnson. I could not have done this without the help of my colleagues and friends Mireille Miller-Young, Marlon Bailey, and Xavier Livermon. They have read many drafts of this work and have devoted countless hours to supporting me both academically and emotionally. I have been honored to receive generous feedback from Jafari Allen, Jennifer DeVere Brody, Marianne Hirsch, Adrienne Davis, LaMonda H. Stallings, Jeffrey McCune, Felice Blake, Zakiyyah Jackson, Sharon Patricia Holland, Frank Wilderson, and E. Patrick Johnson. I would also like to thank Ifalade Tashia Ashanti, who guided me through difficult roads. This book would not be the same without them.

The one scholar who has touched this work more than anyone else besides me is Omise'eke Natasha Tinsley. Without her as an intellectual role model and interlocutor as well as commentator and loving supporter, this book would never have come to fruition.

I am grateful to my mother, sister, and nephews—Ruthel Monk Richardson, Sydney Matthews, Kevin Matthews, Michael Matthews, and Marcus Matthews. They have seen me through every inch of this book, from the first day of graduate school to publication. I thank them for listening to me and praying for me every day.

A special thanks goes out to Baia Tinsley for filling my days with laughter, joy, play, and love.

Listening to the Archives

Black Lesbian Literature and Queer Memory

The Museum of the African Diaspora (MoAD) is a recent structure that has emerged as a monument to Black memory. Opened in San Francisco in December of 2005, the museum is literally positioned between archives. Located near Union Square, the museum stands across the street from the California Historical Society, and a few doors down from the San Francisco Gay, Lesbian, Bisexual, Transgender (GLBT) Archives. Each one of these institutions holds pieces of Black history, but there is no single structure that houses a satisfactory story. For a Black queer subject like me, standing between these institutions brings into stark relief the fractured and incomplete nature of the archives. It makes me aware of my own desires for a place in the archive, especially in the archives of Black memory.

Walking through the doors, I feel a sense of anticipation; I want the museum to be as beautiful and expansive as its name. Sun streams into the lobby from the clear glass windows that make up the building's outer wall. Unlike most other places in San Francisco, Black people are working in the museum. The first thing that catches my eye is the writing on the walls above the gift shop. The walls speak, asking the visitor to engage in a collective practice of remembering, imploring us to not forget our past and to honor our ancestors. Inscribed on the walls, the words "reinvent," "remixing possibilities," "transform," and "creativity" yell to me as I make my way across the lobby. These are the properties that Black queers bring to the Black experience. We reinvent our bodies, renaming ourselves according to the genders we create, regardless of anatomy. We remix the possibilities of Black kinship, making family across boundaries not determined by blood. We transform Black culture through unique local and diasporic practices. I am excited. With these concepts guiding the museum, I anticipate queers to be central to, or at least a significant part of, its representation of diaspora. The entrance to MoAD stands in opposition to the rotunda at the National Archives. That room tells a story of national beginnings from the perspective of the colonizer; the imposing figures of the founding fathers nobly stand in peaceful contemplation of the beautiful nation they built. But it is a story fraught with lies, deceit, betrayal, hypocrisy, genocide, forced labor, and rapacious violence—all obfuscated by an illusion of order. MoAD, in contrast, is about diaspora, privileging a perspective of origins outside the nation-state, locating Africa as the Black homeland and emphasizing continuity. Though it is important to note that recent scholarship has focused on Black diaspora as a practice of shared discontinuities and processes of imagination,[1] I feel some comfort in this vision of connected histories and shared beginnings, and I want to belong to it despite my critique of this perspective.

The museum's permanent collection is a set of exhibits that puts African dispersal into a global context. It sets the tone for the museum itself, situating its priorities in relation to remembering the story of slavery and colonialism from the perspective of four themes: origins, movement, adaptation, and transformation. The front wall of the building is a glass window that allows one to see outside from the staircase, which leads to all the floors of the museum. Next to the staircase is a three-story photograph of the face of Africa, or more precisely, the face of a little African girl. This photograph is the literal face of the museum; because of the glass wall, it is visible from the street and transforms the front of the building into an impressive tableau. The original photograph was taken by Chester Higgins Jr. and incorporated into a photomosaic titled "Photographs from the African Diaspora," a composite of over two thousand individual photographs. The mosaic is a significant archive of Black memory and is a permanent part of the museum.[2] The pictures line the staircases between the museum floors. They are beautiful; they move me with their sheer force of evidence in numbers. Each one touches an affective punctum that is temporally situated through the setting, clothes, hairstyles, and other visual aspects of the subjects.[3] Each photograph tells a story—mothers and daughters, men in military uniform, weddings, funerals, spiritual ceremonies, Black men with children, men and women dancing, children at play, men and women at work. They tell me a story that I already know, one of pride and joy, resistance and endurance, family and love. The photographs also talk back to the ever-present narrative of the broken Black family, which is challenged and reconstituted in many forms on the museum wall. There is a phonic materiality to the visual. I think of Fred Moten's insistence on the photograph that screams as part of a mournful/political practice.[4] I am reminded that the purpose of the project is to provide what Hirsch and Spitzer call "points of memory" or "points of intersection between past and present, memory and postmemory, personal memory and cultural recall."[5] They are included in the infrastructure of the museum in order to make an argument or a point about Black memory.[6] The photographs argue for closure on the enduring questions regarding the inherent pathology of the Black family; they yell that the accusations are untrue, that Black families do exist. Representation of a normative resolution to the question of Black familial pathology requires the suppression of any echo of queerness. In this context queerness would be unmelodic, improvisational, unpredictable, and irresolute.

On the second floor, there are several sections that make up the permanent exhibit at MoAD. There are more objects in the permanent collection that speak to me, to all the visitors, about the normative Black subject. At the top of the steps, leading into the second floor, is an installation on adornment. It has three figures: a man, a child, and a woman. The placards next to the figures describe the role of adornment in culture, but to me the story they tell is about gender. In the installation, the faces of the figures separate from the torsos and morph into different ones. The torsos also change every few seconds, mixing the traditional with the contemporary, the urban with the rural. This fragmented Black body is put back together in gender-appropriate terms. Difference, multiculturalism, and diversity are celebrated in the facial morphing. Asian, African, and white European faces join those of African descent, celebrating a mixed-racial heritage, clearly eschewing racial purity. However, there is no male face with lipstick, for example, or faces that challenge gender binaries at all. Apparently, there is no place for gender variance in this diasporic social imagining. There is a queer limit to how we understand our history and ourselves.

In MoAD the photographs and the figures together tell a narrative that binds the body to normative genders and to heterosexuality. The heterosexual matrix, as Judith Butler has explained, is the logic that links biology to gender presentation/expression and sexual object choice. The expectation is that these qualities—anatomy, gender, and sexuality—predict each other through a linear progression.[7] The visitor experiences this logic first by way of the images on display in the photomosaic. Then, figures at the top of the stairs remind us of the proscribed biological basis of the familial and communal representations and again offer us a resolution to the accusations of Black familial pathology and gender aberrance in the biologically based nuclear family.

Further down the hall from the figures is an interactive set of stations where a visitor can take an auditory and visual tour of Black musical history: gospel, blues, jazz, hip-hop, reggae, and more. I notice myself creating my own version of a queer story in the existing cacophony of sounds and images. As Cheryl Dunye so eloquently states at the end of *The Watermelon Woman,* "Sometimes you have to create your own history."[8] There is a queer materiality to Black musical performance that is missing from the exhibit. Where is Sylvester on the soundtrack? Ma Rainey's "Prove It on Me Blues"? Joan Armatrading? Or Luther Vandross? The richness of Black queer performance disappears, and with it goes the expansive potential of embodied knowledge.

Queers threaten mainstream Black political and cultural narratives of racial uplift and achievement, respectability and civility.[9] The MoAD permanent exhibit is connected to a larger diasporic aim to resolve the trauma caused by dominant positioning of Black people as sexual deviants who have "incomplete, deviant and ruptured" families.[10] Black queer people, as Evelynn Hammonds suggests, are dangerous to the collective, for we are a reminder of the accusation of sexual deviance and gender aberrance that we have fought so long to deny, decry, and defend against.[11] The wall provides evidence of the nuclear family; the figures tell a story of clearly defined and bifurcated genders; the musical archive exists without any queers. It is a call to remember our past, a gesture to history, and an entreaty for the future, but one that does not figure the queer in the Black past or, by extension, the future. As I look upon the permanent exhibit, it becomes clearer and clearer that I am the "constitutive outside" of what is understood, celebrated, and remembered about Blackness.[12] As the exhibit is careful to demonstrate through images from around the world, it is clear that the imperative of normativity is not located solely in the United States but is a condition that spans the diaspora.

As I ended the process of writing *The Queer Limit of Black Memory,* I returned to this beginning and realized, finally, that I had written the book to trace a (narrative) mosaic of Black queerness that would have cracked the walls of MoAD that afternoon. In this volume I have gathered novels and short stories that point to what is irresolute and irresolvable about the Black relationship to normative definitions of gender, sexuality, and family. Here, "irresolute" takes on the connotation of something unfixed, with movement and potential, while "irresolvable" refers to how Blackness remains structurally positioned as "Other" in dominant understandings of the human, which, as Sylvia Wynter argues, cannot be resolved through respectability and civility.[13] Unfortunately, the politics of respectability and civility structures Black memory in mainstream Black representations and institutions (such as MoAD) toward a narrative of resolution and normativity. I wrote this book taking Hortense Spillers's call to "insurgent ground" seriously, and in that spirit, I argue for an embrace of the messiness of Blackness.[14] MoAD: in these pages, I imagine that these letters can also stand for the Messiness of the African Diaspora, in all of its queer glory.

Black people have a fever for the archive.[15] At the time of this writing, construction is underway for a Smithsonian National Museum of African American History and Culture.[16] Even this will not break the fever—a dis/ease manifest as much in the physical structure of large institutions as in the conventional and familiar narrative of memory reified through the archive. Achille Mbembe defines the archive first in terms of "a building, a symbol of a public institution," and then the "collection of documents" that are housed there. He concludes that "[t]here cannot therefore be a definition of 'archives' that does not encompass both the building itself and the documents stored there."[17] This "entanglement of building and documents" is exactly what I have endeavored to underscore: it is at the root of Black expectations of recognition of collective past and present struggles that culminate in official state resolution of grievances.[18] In addition to the authority and recognition that is associated with archives, their creation is also a method of defining the collective. As Mbembe argues, the institution has an "architectural" power that produces an "inescapable materiality" and an instantiating imaginary.[19] Ultimately, the archive is no more than a

> montage of fragments [that] creates an illusion of totality and continuity. In this way, just like the architectural process, the time woven together by the archive is the product of a composition. This time has a political dimension resulting from the alchemy of the archive: it is supposed to belong to everyone. The community of time, the feeling according to which we would all be heirs to a time over which we might exercise the rights of collective ownership: this is the imaginary that the archive seeks to disseminate.[20]

For disaffected people, the autonomous creation of physical institutions becomes an important alternative to the distortion of their histories at the hands of the dominant group. For once, the dominated has control over the historical timeline and the "composition" of documents used to represent this history. In the MoAD example, the photographs make a literal photographic composition, and the music display is an aural one. Together, all of the displays in the permanent exhibit create a feeling of collective ownership of the past and an image for the future.

As a departure from the institutionalization of the national archives, and even MoAD, I consider a different archive. This archive consists of a group of novels and short stories that are a diffuse, mobile, and decentralized set of literatures written by Black lesbian-identified authors from around the diaspora. These literatures project a range of embodied queer practices and identities into a past seldom collectively recalled Black departure from sexual and gender norms as a method of resistance to oppression. The group of texts examined here creates a counternarrative of history wherein multiple forms of deviance—sexual and gender variance, for example—are part of a repertoire of everyday acts of pushing back against the overwhelming epistemic violence that situates Blacks as nonhuman Other.[21] The novels and short stories are artifacts of denied memory and performances of the "strategic absences" (68) and revised tropes of popular history, particularly representing those who are "intentionally missing, hidden or not saved" by archiving institutions.[22] As José Muñoz and Diana Taylor have noted, although there is an inherent relationship between the repertoire and the textual, embodied performance is often "banish[ed]" to a subordinate category of "ephemera" in relation to the supposed stability of the materials in a traditional archive.[23] In contrast, the texts gathered here acknowledge the profound impact of performance in constituting Black queer memory, pointing toward the centrality of embodied knowledge.

Standing in MoAD, I seemed to be at an impasse of desires. The desire to be recognized as part of Black memory is antithetical to the Black desire to be considered "civilized," and nonpathological (normative).[24] One way to resolve this impasse is to represent the queer as normal as possible—as homonormative and transnormative.[25] Another strategy is to remind Black people that Black culture and history are already imbued with queerness. While there has been some documentation and discussion of Black gay male history and representation, Black lesbians and transpeople have not received as much academic attention.[26] For the Black lesbian writers who have taken on the challenge of re-remembering the past, the Enlightenment framing of Blacks as the sign of sexual excess continues to affect Black collective memory. Black lesbian renarration of the past explores the "curious tension[s]," to repurpose Gates,[27] between Black desires for normativity that are enacted through politics of respectability and civility, and the realities of queer experience that are central to Black cultural life; between "authentic" Blackness and the "inauthentic" Black queer; between historical evidence and queer imagination; and between bifurcated gender categories and expansive queer gender identities. These tensions are worked out through queer vernacular epistemologies, or forms of expression, that comment on and resist the oppression of queer sexualities and genders, as well as create queer kinship networks, communities, and alternatives to diasporic displacement.[28]

Irresolvable Genders

> It was to be the peoples of Black African descent who would be constructed as the ultimate referent of the "racially inferior" Human Other . . . the negation of the generic "normal humanness," ostensibly expressed by and embodied in the peoples of the West.
>
> —Sylvia Wynter "Unsettling the Coloniality of Being"[29]

Why Black lesbians? In some ways, this question is at the heart of the matter. Historically, Black has been inextricably tied to the queer—the lesbian in particular. According to Sander Gilman, the dissection of Black women's reproductive bodies in the nineteenth and early twentieth centuries led to the refinement of the distinction of the lesbian as an inherently deviant group with genitalia as excessive as the mythical Hottentot apron.[30] The Black female body has historically been irreconcilable to white society in relation to notions of womanhood. Even as Black women reconstructed the category to reflect their own needs, they were simultaneously subject to brutal scrutiny under the scientists' knife.[31] According to Evelyn Brooks Higginbotham, race provides gender's "power to mean."[32] An extension of Higginbotham's argument recognizes that Blackness obscures the meaning of biological sex as well. Nineteenth-century anatomists looked for the definitive proof of Blacks as the "missing link" between apes and humans through the dissection of Black women's bodies, with special consideration of their genitalia, "locat[ing] racial difference through the sexual characteristics of the female body," namely, a fascination with an imagined phallus in the form of an elongated clitoris to match the lengthened labia majora.[33] The Black becomes the aporia between sex and gender such that the two never meet in any fashion that would satisfy the dictates of normative heterosexuality. The supposed lack of physical distinction between the sexes was thought to indicate a low moral character[34] and to manifest in a morbid sexual appetite that included homosexual attraction. As Sharon Holland has observed: "It appears that the words *lesbian* and *black* are forged in blood, in physiognomy, and ultimately in racist science."[35]

This historical legacy leads gender to be a categorical conundrum in this book. As a category, woman is particularly vexed, as is Black women's connection to that category. To claim a stable gender is a battle in a context wherein Black humanity is a perpetually open question or an unresolved debate, and part of what remains unresolved is Blacks' ability to inhabit the gender categories given to us by chattel slavery and colonialism. To claim a stake in gender is a deeply embedded political statement of Black humanity. As I have argued elsewhere, mainstream Black communities consider claiming non-normative genders to be tantamount to race treachery.[36] The actual experiences of Black sexual degradation took place in a field of violent epistemic debasement that defines the Black as an object of sexual aberrance; in this case the "sexual" takes on both biological and carnal registers. Black people are not violable under this episteme, for we are all walking, pulsating libidos, living for sexual encounters. Black bodies are unknowable under the schema of a two-gender system and therefore must be dissected for scientific investigation and comparative study. In this context of extreme violence, it is no wonder that Black people repress the memories of the epistemic violence of gender and sexual misnaming, as well as the physical violation that this epistemic framework makes pervasive. It is Black women's vexed relationship to womanhood that has catalyzed Black lesbians to write most consistently about Black transgender experiences.[37]

Black lesbian authors contribute to the category of the "queer," especially in their representation of gender diversity, but also in their insistence that Black culture is inherently non-normative, which is why deviance along gender and sexual lines is so threatening—it exposes the futility of our claims to rights and inclusion based on shared normality.[38] Roderick Ferguson has placed women of color feminism (and Black lesbians as central to this project) as providing a major alternative to neoliberal normativity. He states that "women of color feminism attempted to dislodge interpretations of racial domination from the normative grip of liberal capitalism."[39] Furthermore, he argues that women of color feminism is an epistemological, social, cultural, and political formation that challenged the "normative hues" of oppositional movements, including civil rights, women's and Black power movements.[40] My analysis of the fiction in this book shows that Black lesbian writers are beneficiaries of and contributors to a reconceptualization of Black resistance to include gender variance as well as sexual transgression and the epistemological frameworks that forge those practices. As C. Riley Snorton has pointed out, Black lesbian feminism is a tradition that is based on a racial critique of gender categories. The work of early Black feminist writers and activists paved the way for a reimagining of Black embodiment along gender lines.[41] It is therefore no surprise that literature by Black lesbians gives an unprecedented accounting of the sexual and gender diversity of Black communities. They contest what Rinaldo Walcott calls a "narrative of coherency" about Black gender[42] and instead represent Black embodiment as unlimited and imaginative: butches/studs, straight transmen, femmes, bigender folk, women-loving-women, transwomen, drag kings, gay men, bisexuals, feminine transmasculine/masculine transfeminine people, and gay-attracted transmasculine people.[43] For Black people to claim gender at all is brave given the array of violences enacted physically and epistemologically to strip us from gendered being. Thus to claim such an assemblage of creative interpretations of the self is also dangerous in its dizzying audacity and flagrant noncompliance with the terms of our dehumanization.

Negated by the Negated: Disremembering the Queer

> Everybody knew what she was called, but nobody anywhere knew her name. Disremembered and unaccounted for, she cannot be lost because no one is looking for her, and even if they were, how can they call her if they don't know her name? Although she has claim, she is not claimed.
>
> —Toni Morrison, *Beloved*[44]

This quote from *Beloved* introduces us to the condition of the disremembered that *The Queer Limit of Black Memory* addresses in relation to Black queerness. Morrison reminds us that we cannot remember those we do not miss. In many ways this book is about the dead—both those who have physically passed on from this material plane of existence, and the figuratively "dead." The figuratively dead are those who have never been recognized as fully human to begin with, the dispossessed and disremembered. My discussion of the "dead" is in conversation with many different scholars, including Frantz Fanon, Saidiya Hartman, Hortense Spillers, Sharon Holland, Abdul JanMohamed, and Orlando Patterson. What these scholars have in common is an acknowledgment that "some subjects *never* achieve, in the eyes of others, the status of the 'living.'"[45] For these purposes, "living" is having available to oneself a full range of subjectivity and citizenship; and the status of nonliving reflects that "residual subject relations" set in motion from slavery and colonialism are still active in the dominant imaginary, remaining uninterrupted by the formal ends of those systems.[46] I am particularly interested in the ramifications of Black figurative death on Black queers, especially gender-variant people. I contend that Black queers are, in many respects, dead to Black memory and that this literature is an archive that pays respect to the ancestors and to the "dead," creating a way to grieve those who have gone unclaimed.

Loss, particularly the loss of homeland, dispersal, and rupture of subjecthood, are critical elements of the diasporic condition, which itself is embedded in the Black experience. Part of the constitution of Blackness is negation and displacement. Institutions like MoAD are created to remember the loss, but even there, Black queers do not figure into the collective memory. The Black queer falls even deeper into the abyss of negation because we are not even part of the memory of loss. We are not grieved by the collective; our claims are rejected as inauthentically Black and "un-African." We are disremembered and unrecognized by our own—negated by the negated, dissociated from Black memory.[47]

According to Freud, dissociation occurs as a result of intrapsychic conflict. The ego actively represses memories of traumatic events in order to "protect itself from experiencing the painful affects associated with them."[48] This reflex to self-protection re-emerges on a collective level with the process of dissemblance, wherein Black women do not reveal details about their sexual lives out of their distrust of the archives.[49] The insidious, poisonous violence of the idea that Blackness represents sexuality and gender gone wrong has affected the Black collective unconscious to such an extent that it is an act of self-care *not* to know its own members. Trauma situates Blacks in a peculiar predicament in relation to the past, such that dissemblance is necessary to keep certain events of violation hidden and unspoken. I further contend that part of the effect of trauma is not only to keep elements of the past hidden but also, as an added measure of self-protection, to *disremember* them—to erase them from collective memory. The Black collective unconscious, as Fanon saw it, is bombarded by the values of the colonizer to the extent that it turns to self-hatred. The result is that the Black queer is the "phobogenic object," the anxiety-producing mnemonic that signals to the unconscious that it must protect itself from remembering.[50] A phobogenic object that threatens to unearth the amnesic defenses created through repression, the queer becomes dead to Black memory.

One of the consequences of the stealing of Black bodies and cultures for the transcontinental slave trade is that Black people are profoundly concerned with historical memory, or how historical narratives live in collective memories of the past. Given centuries of grotesque distortion of Blackness in every form of representation (history, law, literature, philosophy, film, public media), for Black people, one of the only available resources of historical documentation is memory. Two beautifully poetic essays, Saidiya Hartman's "Venus in Two Acts" and Omise'eke Natasha Tinsley's "Black

Atlantic, Queer Atlantic," are useful guides through the choppy waters of making use of fiction as an alternate archive when collective memory falters. As Hartman suggests, for certain Black subjects the formal archive is a "casket," a grave, a "death sentence, a tomb, a display of the violated body, an inventory of property . . . [and] an asterisk in the grand narrative of history."[51] Telling a story about lives (and deaths) of abject people is a process of insurgent counterhistory and reclaimed memory. The pathway to the thoughts and the "picture of the everyday life" of the forgotten is a route forged through the imagination of those looking for them.[52] When the formal archive fails and (collective) memory is a catacomb of the worthy dead, or what Judith Butler calls "grievable life,"[53] then "sometimes [one] has to create [one's] own history."[54] I have stated elsewhere that any picture of the quotidian that reveals so-called deviant behavior is excised from any formal accounting of lived experience as a measure of self-protection for the individual and for the collective "self." Therefore, Black women and Black queer people have a reasonable distrust in the archives.[55] The desire to "retriev[e] what remains dormant"[56] and "[listen] for the unsaid,"[57] leads to the impulse to find recourse in different sources of knowledge. In this case, the archive of knowledge is found not in a particular edifice or set of official documents, but through the fictional accounting of a dispersed set of practices, discourses, and feelings available to the imagination in order to utter the "unspeakable."[58] The Black lesbian fiction analyzed in this book is a method of addressing the violence of excision from Black memory and of Black queer self-articulation. It is also a history counter to humanism, creating, as Omise'eke Natasha Tinsley describes, a "new geography . . . of sexual, gendered, transnational and racial identities" and a "queer, unconventional and imaginative archive" of resistance.[59]

In this volume, I look at acts that both resist the dominant oppression and simultaneously entangle the protagonists in forms of domination. I offer this as an expansion of Cathy Cohen's definition of resistance that emphasizes that "political resistance is the intent to defy laws, interactions, obligations, and normative assumptions viewed as systematically unfair."[60] In addition, I want to stress that I do not want to suggest that resistance is always meant to result, or does result, in the overturning or transcendence of current structures. Rather, resistance is simply pushing back against these structures. Blacks who do not attempt to conform to dominant standards of heterosexuality or who dare to define their own genders are clearly moving against the basic conditions of our enslavement and colonization. The boldness of this enterprise is made even more intrepid given that this is an analysis of Black queer resistance imagined from the perspective of dispossessed and disenfranchised poor and working-class communities. As Cohen states, there is potentially much to be gained in Black Studies more broadly by paying attention to those who "are reminded daily of their distance from the promise of full citizenship."[61]

Reconstructing History: Historiographic Literature

> To have one's belonging lodged in a metaphor is a voluptuous intrigue: to inhabit a trope; to be a kind of fiction. To live in the Black Diaspora is I think to live as a fiction—a creation of empires, and also self-creation. It is to apprehend the sign one makes yet be unable to escape it except in radiant moments of ordinariness made like art.
>
> —Dionne Brand, *A Map to the Door of No Return*[62]

As suggested in Dionne Brand's quote from *A Map to the Door of No Return*, Black memory is filled with the fiction of empires. These texts challenge the normative strains of Black memory for its colonized fictions of a past without queers. They enact what M. Jacqui Alexander describes as an "expansive memory" of the past.[63] Expansive memory, as Alexander defines it, is not "bound by the limits of time, enclosed within the outlines of a map, encased in the physicality of body, or imprisoned as exhibit in a museum," nor is it bound, I would add, by definitions of sexuality or the limits of genre.[64] I identify this work as *expansive historiographic* literature, meaning texts that comment on and re-imagine the past, but without concern for historical verisimilitude. Expansive historiographic texts are not bound by the thick description and period detail that historical fiction demands.

My idea of historiographic fiction is partially adapted from literary scholar Linda Hutcheon's term "historiographic metafiction,"[65] which is concerned with the postmodern "incredulity towards realism."[66] Hutcheon's definition of historiographic metafiction accounts for fictional work that resists realist conventions while maintaining a self-reflexivity about the act of writing fiction and the act of writing history. Her definition relies on the interplay between history and parody in order to assert that "both history and literature [are] human constructs."[67] The work that I analyze in this book departs from Hutcheon's definition precisely in its ability to offer commentary not necessarily through parody but through recreations of standard refrains of Black memory. The juxtaposition of historiographic and anachronistic (or expansive) representation emphasizes the temporal contradictions of the texts in their own performance of queering Black time and space.[68] They simultaneously offer reverence toward history and push back against it through rebellious narratives that insist on interfering in the familiar heterosexual and normatively gendered story of the past, creating anachro-nism by centering queers who "don't belong" in the historical narratives as they are currently known. From slave cabins and cane fields to juke joints and jazz clubs, from the neighborhood organizing meeting to the revolutionary assembly, Black lesbian fiction trespasses on the imagined gender and sexual normativity of the spaces of Black self-making—telling their histories with a queer difference.

The fiction analyzed in this volume irresolutely moves "with and against" the normative version of Black memory such as the ones in the permanent exhibits in MoAD. Historiographic fiction performatively[69] queers the temporalities associated with particular historical narratives, often interfering in established timelines.[70] For example, Jackie Kay's novel *Trumpet* refers to Black presence in Scotland during the turn of the twentieth century, well before the 1950s Windrush era, thereby disrupting the conventional narrative of Black migration to Scotland.[71] The texts also blend temporalities, at once recreating the patterns of speech, dress, and other details from a bygone era and mixing them with the vernacular expressions or tone that suggests the contemporary period in which the text was written.[72] Though Laurinda Brown's *The Highest Price for Passion,* for example, is set on a nineteenth-century plantation, its characters approach each other in a blending of nineteenth- and twenty-first-century speech, thereby imagining a language for the contemporary complexities of woman-to-woman sexual desire that has its roots in slavery's ways of meaning.[73]

Vernacular Epistemologies

> For people of color have always theorized—but in forms quite different from the Western form of abstract logic. And I am inclined to say that our theorizing . . . is often in narrative forms.
>
> —Barbara Christian, "The Race for Theory"[74]

These texts situate vernacular modes and folk traditions that have been used to resist racism as queer aesthetic forms. These practices have allowed African diasporic communities to survive despite brutal and rapacious anti-Black violence and socioeconomic exploitation and deprivation. Black lesbian writers use this rich tradition and highlight that vernacular practices have always included explicit commentary on heterosexism and gender oppression. In doing so, they have created representations that not only challenge racist and misogynist hierarchies but also push the boundaries of Black politics to consider forms of sexual and gender nonconformity as part of a Black tradition of resistance to anti-Black oppression. Furthermore, by representing stories of the working-class masses of Black queer people, they establish an archive of Black queer voices "from below" that are very rarely heard anywhere else.[75]

This book thus looks at the impact of Black vernacular culture from a queer theoretical perspective, specifically revising the function of performance, blues, and jazz as structures that enable gender transition and fluidity as well as same-sex desire. I also expand the definition of vernacular culture to include embodied practices of pleasure and erotic desire, arguing that they emerge from specific economic and historical conditions that mitigate abjection as well as create communal bonds, thereby restructuring Black collectivity in relationship to queerness.

By placing texts set in the United States, Canada, the Caribbean, and the UK in dialogue with each other, I figure "vernacular culture" not as belonging to one people but as expanding as diasporic practices. My choice to do so looks to suggest not that all points of the diaspora are the same, but rather that people in each geographic locale interpret, envelope, reorganize, and transform cultural practices in queer ways. Through a process of constructing an archive of "memory, fantasy, narrative and myth," the need for a "law of origin"—for a consistent and tangible "home"—is not dependent on a single physical site that holds the key to authenticity.[76] What's also important is that vernacular cultures do not stop at their reformulation in Toronto, or Detroit, or Grenada, or Glasgow, but continue on, making the circuit again and again to be remade and reconstituted in a never-ending exchange of repositioning, unfolding "beyond the arbitrary closure" it makes.[77] As Dionne Brand suggests in the quote above, self-creation is an art of recreation across and despite the boundaries of empire.

The Black queer ancestor is an unimaginable figure in mainstream diasporic memory. That she does not exist is a fiction of domination, an effect of trauma that has made her illegible even in alternative archives. To speak of her, one has to be creative and seize the means of archival production while pointing to her absence in written history and in memory. Black lesbian writing, then, is a practice of historical commentary, a trespass against demands of evidence, finding recourse and voice through the creation of imaginative counternarratives and embodied practices. *The Queer Limit of Black Memory* tunes into the complicated way that novels and short stories by Black lesbian writers take up the trope of voice and engage with Black-vernacular written performance and phonic cultures, amplifying their voices to resonate with and trouble the established heterosexuality and gender normativity of Black memory. Black feminist writer Ntozake Shange's classic *For Colored Girls Who Have Considered Suicide When the Rainbow Is Enuf* laments the desire to hear a "Black girl's song."[78] In these instances the content of a Black girl's song expands to explore the lives of transgender women, femme gay men, butch lesbians, and so on. In other words, Black lesbians remix what is expected from a Black female voice and sing a decidedly queer song. The practice of remixing is a task that requires new epistemes. As Sylvia Wynter argues: "the re-writing" of the subject "must necessarily entail the un/writing of our present normative defining of the secular mode of the Subject."[79] This book considers Black lesbian deployment and development of vernacular practices and discourses as a basis of knowledge for the revision or "un/writing" of the normative Black memory, which has been especially challenged in these texts through the representation of gender-variant or transgender characters. As Karin Knorr-Cetina says in *Epistemic Cultures,* there are cultures that "create and warrant knowledge."[80] I identify the slave narrative, blues, jazz, performance, the erotic, and the spiritual to be Black vernacular sources of knowledge that are critical tools for re-remembering the past.

Epistemology is a politically relevant practice. Black queer literature represents real-world changes in the way that we know things, a shift in knowledge. I underscore fiction and imagination's ability to assert *potential* into systems of knowledge. This is admittedly not the work of the first-hand account. However, the act of reimagining has just as much to do with reminding us that there are those who are being lost in the present, who are slipping out of memory before our eyes and at the tips of our fingers, as it does with populating the past with forgotten subjects. Reimagining is the process of taking something that has already been conceived of and recreating it with new elements, thereby infusing the past with difference. These texts rely heavily on embodied knowledge to attest to the ways that Black experience can be restaged, "heard, remembered, and understood."[81] Reimagining the past gives us the ability to say now what was unsayable then. The "already said" is resurrected into a possibility that could help in reimagining the ever-unfolding present.

Black queer cultures come into being as a result of and despite violence and displacement. Recent works by Darieck Scott and Gloria González-López argue that violence is a productive site of knowledge. Scott asks readers to stop avoiding "uncomfortable questions" in order to examine Black abjection as a form of epistemology, from which he considers how "pain or discomfort" is put to "multifarious uses."[82] In focusing on the point of violation, Scott argues for the "value [in] identifying with violated ancestors."[83] The site of suffering is also a site of release of internalized domination. In "Epistemologies of the Wound: Anzaldúan Theories and Sociological Research on Incest in Mexican Society," Gloria González-López describes the importance of what she calls the collective wounds as an "epistemological location" that she identifies as a space of irresolution that, in "the midst of complex ambiguities, tensions, and contradictions," allows transformation.[84] Reimagining past violences and sites of resistance has the potential to remind those of us in the present to be aware of those falling around us: falling into violence, falling into mass incarceration, falling into despair. It could help us to remember what it is about the moments of erotic pleasure and creativity that are such valuable sources of knowledge.

Archives: Using New Epistemes, Revising Traditions

What are queer versions the Black past? If Black people living during and around the time of the diaspora were to listen to Black queer voices, what would they hear? The texts that I discuss in this volume reenvision Black poor and working-class communities through a politics of improvisation as opposed to a politics of respectability. In jazz, the improvisation solo moves with and in contradistinction to the melody. In similar ways, these texts work with and against the politics of respectability and normative gender categories to create an irresolute revision of those traditions.[85] They deliberately rework the beloved tropes of the neo-slave, migration, and diasporic narrative—replacing the assumed normative genders and heterosexuality associated with these genres with main characters that are queer, bodies that do not conform to their biological function, pleasures that come from unexpected places, and sexualities that eschew the homo/hetero binary.

Slavery is the door through which this analysis of expansive historiographic fiction enters. Through readings of four contemporary works about slavery, generally known as neo-slave narratives—"Louisiana, 1850" by Jewelle Gomez, "Miss Hannah's Lesson" by LaShonda Barnett, "The Champagne Lady" by SDiane Adamz-Bogus, and the novel *The Highest Price For Passion* by Laurinda D. Brown—I consider the neo-slave narrative as a form of vernacular epistemology, which foregrounds the role of desire and pleasure in literary and historical narratives of female sexual abjection. These texts reimagine the psychosexual dynamics of the plantations, especially the sexual servitude between female slave and slave owner (who, it is too often left unsaid, *can also be female*); they expose the intimate nature of bondage and comment on racial passing as a gendered practice. These works are particularly significant given the centrality of slavery in African American literary scholarship and the lack of attention to issues of homoerotic desire in the peculiar institution. I analyze the focus on woman-to-woman sexual relationships in slavery as part of the authors' attempts to recuperate agency for the Black female slave. Using these short stories, I posit that representations of sexual relations between Black and white women in slavery function as a way to reimagine Black women's resistance to racial and sexual abjection. The mulatta (often depicted as "tragically" not white enough and eschewing Blackness) shows up in many of the narratives of same-sex desire represented in this volume. In the neo-slave narratives I have gathered here, the mulatta is depicted as an "undead" personage situated between the social death of slavery and liberal subjectivity.[86] She is a figure that represents the potential of Black femininity, yet she refuses heterosexual resolution and is transformed into a complex figure of sexual agency.

The mulatta figure also emerges in *Her* through the main character, Sunshine/Kali. In Cherry Muhanji's revision of the migration novel, the characters' embrace of irresolute genders and sexual relationships provide them with a method of resistance to abjection. *Her* also introduces the blues as an epistemological practice embodying Black queer memory, both as a queer aesthetic form and as a counterpublic space wherein Black sexuality and gender identity are reimagined through performance. Muhanji's novel constructs a blues of mobility, repetition, and improvisation that infuses bisexual, lesbian, and gender-transgressive narratives with both a Black cultural foundation and a queer predilection for boundary crossing. The novel's main female character, Sunshine, has a male alter ego named Kali. Sunshine/Kali uses the blues to enact a gender transformation in the middle of the novel and to subvert traditional expectations of the "tragic mulatta" trope. This second chapter of *The Queer Limit of Black Memory* (like the third chapter) expands on previous scholarship that has documented how African American women blues singers of the early twentieth century used the blues to express female masculinity and desire for other women.[87] I suggest that in Black lesbian fiction, the blues functions as an epistemological framework through which (trans)gender practices are reimagined for transfeminine as well as transmasculine people, thereby expanding the ways in which Black femininity and womanhood are imagined and understood. As a novel, *Her* is a theoretically sophisticated text in its formulation of African American migration involving multiple points of transformation. Movement happens on a number of levels as Blackness is represented as a dynamic and living cultural and political practice that is evidenced in the characters' literal and symbolic transitions across boundaries.

Throughout the texts, the characters' processes of transition are documented through performance, commenting on history through the vernacular. For example, the reinscription of the blues in a queer context in *Her* both revises the migration genre, including the traditions that form its foundations, and reinterprets the historical archive to foreground the influence of performance in the formation of Black queer communities. The third and fourth chapters of this book also centrally locate performance as a practice of vernacular epistemologies and as a space that allows for nonbinary gender identities to be affirmed and for variant sexual desires to flourish. As Jill Dolan argues, performance "provides a place where people come, embodied and passionate, to share experiences of meaning-making and imagination that can describe or capture fleeting intimations of a better world."[88] However, instead of enacting what Dolan calls a "radical humanism," these texts question Enlightenment humanism as a framework for Black queer self-fashioning.[89]

Sharon Bridgforth's two published books—*the bull-jean stories* and *love conjure/blues*—as well as her currently unpublished play, *delta dandi,* are set in unspecified African American rural southern communities, resituating the blues and the juke joint as a "queer space"[90] in the heart of African diasporic spiritual traditions. As Bridgforth stated in our 2009 interview, she considers herself a griot (historical storyteller) illuminating and retelling familiar stories, but with the forgotten queer subject at their center. My chapter devoted to her work demonstrates the ways that the divine is embodied in her texts, marking the text's aim to archive ancestral memory in the body of the reader/audience/performer as well as its meditation on how the written word can itself become an embodied and divinely inspired performative instrument.

In both Bridgforth's work as a whole and in the novel *Her,* the early and mid-twentieth century are remembered respectively as times when rural and urban Black communities created counterpublic, working-class places where performing the blues meant expressing sexual and gender fluidity not only for the performers but also for the audience members.[91] These authors reimagine the blues space as providing a respite from the racial exploitation of industrial and agricultural labor by offering a place where Black queer people could have their own gender identities and sexualities without fear of condemnation. The blues and the spiritual work in partnership in Bridgforth's plays and texts as interconnected epistemologies that make it possible to queerly reenvision transatlantic flow of ancestral memory.

Scottish author Jackie Kay's 1998 novel *Trumpet* is an occasion to consider Black migration on a larger scale through the cross-Atlantic circulation of culture, specifically jazz, and its contribution to the construction of gender for diasporic Black communities. *Trumpet* is a fascinating example of the diasporic narrative, a text that explores the past, present, and future effects of the transatlantic transit and trade of African bodies. The novel's main character is Joss Moody, a Black transgendered man born in Scotland of a white mother and an African father. The novel resists resolution; the revelation of Joss Moody's female birth causes a scandal that rocks the world of Moody's wife and son, disallowing the narrative to rest comfortably in normativity. *Trumpet* is set entirely in Scotland and England yet continually challenges the notion of a Black subjectivity bound to the nation-state through its use of jazz as a diasporic signifier that ties Black (queer) people together across the diaspora.

Dionne Brand's 1996 novel, *In Another Place, Not Here,* tells another story of diaspora through woman-to-woman sexual desire. It is a lyrical and haunting narrative of the brief but significant relationship between a sugar cane worker and a revolutionary activist during the final days of the Grenadian socialist regime. The text asserts their belonging in the memory of the Caribbean and in the revolutionary consciousness of the Black diaspora. Struggles for national liberation are the backdrop to the story of the two women's desperate search for "home" and belonging. The disappearance of Black queer subjects from the diasporic memory of resistance compounds the loss already felt from the irrevocable robbery of "home" and "homeland" suffered through slavery. The novel suggests that an alternative to searching for "home" in a physical location is in the belonging that can be found in another's arms. The love between the two main characters is the basis for an epistemology of the erotic that serves as a channel for a change in consciousness for the cane worker, Elizete. She finds the erotic to be a life-saving gift that flows through her and opens her to experiences other than violent exploitation. Meanwhile, her lover, Verlia, chooses the path laid out by revolutionary rhetoric, only to find that it is not expansive enough to move her from alienation to belonging.

Each of these examples looks inward to Black queer experience to reconstitute Black collectivity, acknowledge the generative power of Black queer resistance strategies, and archive the disremembered creativity and multiplicity of Black sexual and gender identities. This work speaks back to real-life consequences of disassociating queerness from Black conscious memory. Returning to Morrison's poignant assertion that the forgotten go unclaimed, we see that these authors resituate the queer into Black memory in a context of Black queer death ungrieved. If no one remembers our names, then who will grieve our deaths?

My reading of the fictional texts suggests that there are many more lives to grieve than previously realized.[92] A politics of civility and respectability would demand that Black people claim a collective mourning, which, according to Freudian definition, is a signal that resolution is possible and that Black grief and perhaps even Black anger and discontent will finally come to an end.[93] However, grief is a productive affect that resists amnesia.

The Queer Limit of Black Memory concludes with a meditation on the effect of the dissociative process in which the Black queer is repressed in Black collective imagination. One consequence is the inability for Black people to grieve queer death on a collective scale. On October 28, 2009, President Barack Obama signed the Matthew Shepard and James Byrd, Jr., Hate Crimes Prevention Act of 2009 into law. The symbolic force of Matthew Shepard, killed in a homophobic assault in 1998, standing as emblematic of queer death next to James Byrd, killed in a racist lynching in the same year, representing Black death, demonstrates the extent to which Black death and queer death are considered mutually exclusive in the broader imagination and for Black people in particular. However, our deaths do not go completely unnoticed. As *The Queer Limit of Black Memory* tells us, Black queer people find creative ways to remember each other and to grieve for ourselves when others do not. In our grief we create an ever-expanding archive of Black queer innovations in Black experience, resistance, and self-making.

CHAPTER 1

Desirous Mistresses and Unruly Slaves

Neo-Slave Narratives, Property, Power, and Desire

Archiving the Unrecoverable

Slavery is the African American "primal scene."[1] It is the condition in which the memory of an African presence in the Americas is born. True to the Freudian context of the term, it is under these circumstances that Black sexuality in the Americas is first constituted, creating the enduring memory of sexual subjugation. Capture, transport, enslavement, and subjection begin the story of Black subjectivity and sexuality, but they are not the end. It is not only the bare acts of brutality but also the memory of resistance that are crucial to, in this particular instance, African American subject formation. It is therefore appropriate that we initiate this excavation of fictive reconstructions of Black memory at the beginning, with four neo-slave narratives that imaginatively revisit slavery as a site of African American women's resistance.[2] African American lesbian authors wrote these works about Black female slaves in the southern United States and their sexual relationships with white women.[3] The neo-slave narrative is its own form of vernacular epistemology, a literary genre written in order to create knowledge despite the historical erasure of the experiences of the abject in the formal archive.

The work I analyze here suggests that there is tremendous knowledge to be gained from investigating the small pleasures that are possible even within the confines of the coffle. "Miss Hannah's Lesson," *The Gilda Stories, The Highest Price for Passion,* and "The Champagne Lady" reconsider how resistance to slavery is remembered, as they situate woman-to-woman sexual relations and pleasure as disruptions to abjection. Pleasure and exploitation, desire and domination exist simultaneously in these retellings of slavery. Black lesbian neo-slave narratives reorganize the political discourse of Black women's internal lives and gesture toward the other side of the sexual veil, where an "unspeakable" queerness resides. They depict the unimaginable and the unrecoverable in order to insert sexual agency into the memory of Black women's sexuality in the "primal scene" of slavery. These narratives unfold at the place where the discourses of the lesbian and the Black meet. If, as I argued in the introduction, part of the epistemic trauma of the nineteenth century is that these two figures are permanently comingled, then representing woman-to-woman sexuality in slavery is a direct way of exposing the wound.

However, these are not entirely liberatory representations, but depictions of instances of irresolute resistance. They invite an examination of what Saba Mahmood describes as "uncoupling agency from the progressive goal of emancipatory politics," a task that has implications for contemporary, real-life LGBT politics and critical race scholarship.[4] Scholars such as Saidiya Hartman and Darieck Scott examine the uneasy relationship between slavery and pleasure. Hartman argues that a product of slavery in the nineteenth century (and, by extension, the contemporary memory of the period) is the placement of "terror and enjoyment" into an overlapping relationship with each other in order to "dissimulate the extreme violence of the institution and disavow the pain of captivity."[5] Scott also looks at the point of terror and enjoyment, but in relation to fictional depictions of the rape of Black male bodies. He argues for a hermeneutics that would allow for the "transformation of the elements of humiliation and pain" to find the pleasure (and therefore power) in abjection.[6] Historian Mireille Miller-Young urges scholars to consider the "complexities and ambiguities of black women's experiences of pleasure and danger, exploitation and disenchantment."[7] In order to look at these complex intersections in the fiction, my discussion of pleasure is different from my analysis in a later chapter concerning the erotic. In "Uses of the Erotic: The Erotics of Power," Audre Lorde defines the erotic as the "irreplaceable knowledge of the capacity for joy" and the satisfaction made through interconnectedness with others.[8] Lorde makes a distinction between the erotic and experiences that she considers to be "plasticized" sexuality or "sensation without feeling."[9] In this chapter, I follow the "sensation" of pleasure of the orgasm and the vexed emotions surrounding it in order to argue that the representation of slave women's pleasure simultaneously resists some relations of domination and sustains others. As Sharon Holland points out, Lorde assumes that the erotic is a "means to undo difference, rather than facilitate its entrenchment."[10] I demonstrate how desire and domination as well as pleasure and protest are in irresolute tension with each other, but often missing from the Black memory of slavery.

As a form of resisting relations of domination, the neo-slave narratives analyzed here depict Black women slaves as having sexual choice as opposed to being an empty space for the desires of others. The dynamics of enslavement require Blacks to be an extension of the master's will and desires, which makes a structural distinction between person and property. In the realm of imagination, these narratives restore Black female slaves to memory as desiring sexual subjects, thereby reordering on the plantation, as Sylvia Wynter says, the "the mode of Desire."[11]

Clearly, these authors represent an imagined space for Black women's enjoyment of their bodies outside the confines of realism. Even though *The Gilda Stories* is the only avowedly supernatural text in this chapter, all of the works take on the challenge of expansive historiographic fiction, as I am defining it, to transcend the boundaries of realism. They depict a version of the enslaved female body that can experience pleasure without being transformed into a liberated subject. These nonrealist representations of slave women's experiences make use of the neo-slave narrative as a creative epistemology or a "new science" of "self-making/modeling/figuring" that proposes a reinvention of Black female subjectivity that is not imagined by enlightenment humanity.[12]

I read the project of reordering memory through the texts themselves, but my interpretation is also informed by informal interviews and public presentations in which all four authors have revealed that they are students of Black history and that their stories come from a particular desire to engage with Black history and/or to write Black lesbians into history in some way.[13] Adamz-Bogus's "The Champagne Lady" is part of an unfinished collection of short stories titled *Hatshepsut's Legacy,* after the gender-bending Pharaoh of Ancient Egypt.[14] LaShonda Barnett's "Miss Hannah's Lesson" is the only short story in her collection, *Callaloo and Other Lesbian Love Tales,* set in the past.[15] Jewelle Gomez was a guest speaker in my "Contemporary Black Women Authors" class at the University of California, Berkeley, in 2004, where she said that she did extensive historical research to write *The Gilda*

Stories. Finally, on a panel titled "Why We Write" at the 2009 Fire and Ink Black LGBT Writers Conference in Austin, Texas, Laurinda Brown spoke of the historical research she conducted in preparation for writing *The Highest Price for Passion.*

The influence of Black history on these stories does not rest in their thick description of the nineteenth century but in their approach to representing Black women's sexual lives in slavery. The texts reflect the historical breakthrough of the 1980s and 1990s during which feminist historians reinterpreted the evidence from planters' logs, diaries, travelers' accounts, and slave narratives to begin to construct accounts of Black female slave resistance through the body. They indicate work stoppages, deliberate acts of incompetence, abortion, contraceptive practices, feigned illness, and infanticide as strategies by which Black women's limited control over their own bodies interrupted the flow of labor in domestic and field settings.[16] Given that actual Black slave women's internal desires and sexual practices are irretrievable in the archive, the texts I analyze here insert lesbian desire as a way to imaginatively give slave women characters some modicum of choice and control over their destinies. These works put a lesbian twist on historical research by representing embodied resistance through affection between women. Therefore, love, sex, and pleasure become forces that push back against the absolutely negating system of brutality and death. As in Gayl Jones's novel *Corregidora* (1975), or in the controversial work of artist Kara Walker, the legacy of slavery is represented through a comingling of pleasure and brutality.[17] Their proximate representation of satisfaction and release actually gives us a glimpse at the limits of the sexual, where the abject finds momentary reprieve. Far from representing any resolution to systems of domination, the texts I analyze here open up a problem seldom acknowledged: a Black woman finds some relief in a field of constraint through sexual relations with a female member of the master class.

The neo-slave narrative is generally a genre associated with the representation of resistant counternarratives to dominant versions of history. Bernard Bell's now-classic study, *The Afro-American Novel and Its Tradition* (1987), directs attention to the overall struggle for freedom in African American literature in general and in the neo-slave narratives he describes.[18] Several scholars have focused their political genealogy of the neo-slave narrative on the new politics of the mid-twentieth century. Although all agree that Black identity is rethought through the neo-slave narrative genre, they each emphasize different influences on reshaping and reclaiming Black memory of slavery. More recent scholarship has tended to situate neo-slave narratives in relation to either Black nationalist or feminist politics. Araf Rushdy's *Neo-Slave Narratives: Studies in the Social Logic of a Literary Form* (1999) argues that slavery has been revised in light of shifts in political consciousness that stems from 1960s and early 1970s Black Power movements.[19] In *Black Women Writers and the American Neo-Slave Narrative: Femininity Unfettered* (1999), Elizabeth Ann Beaulieu argues that women-authored slave narratives are a literary outgrowth of "both the civil rights movement and the feminist movement."[20] Similarly, Angelyn Mitchell's *The Freedom to Remember: Narrative, Slavery, and Gender in Contemporary Black Women's Fiction* (2002) identifies Black women's writing as "liberatory narratives," based in antiracist and antisexist oppositional politics.[21] In her book *Black Subjects: Identity Formation in the Contemporary Narrative of Slavery*, Arlene Keizer emphasizes that the "contemporary narrative of slavery" (3) is a "touchstone for present-day meditations on the formation of Black subjectivity."[22] Furthermore, Keizer observes that the "rebel slave came to symbolize black agency within the slave system, and the theme of resistance structured most African American and Anglophone Caribbean literature about slavery."[23] I build on this earlier work by situating neo-slave narratives in relationship to Black lesbian feminist writing and politics and to the queer "contradictions inherent" in resistance.[24]

In these narratives, resistance is imagined through desire and pleasure, in contrast to the strategies which most scholars highlight that emphasize a commitment to heterosexual marriage and monogamy.[25] These texts represent slave women not only as mothers, daughters, and wives but also as lovers of other women. The Black female protagonists recall the Black female slave body outside of the reproductive function, where the slave reproduces the master's labor force by using her literal biological reproductive capacities to figuratively reproduce slavery. The stories introduce Black women's non-reproductive pleasure as a method to subvert the sexual use-value of Black women's bodies, usually called upon to satisfy the needs of white manhood as well as Black manhood, in whatever limited patriarchal privileges exist between slave men and women in the community of slaves.

As opposed to relating mostly with men, in these stories the slave women protagonists satisfy their (sexual) needs through demonstrating solidarity with and desire for white women. Cheryl Clarke foregrounds this proposal in her 1981 essay, "Lesbianism: An Act of Resistance."[26] Here Clarke identifies Black women's sexual relationships with white women as a tool for healing a history of violence and inequality. Clarke uses the master/slave relationship to signify women as "slaves" to male "masters," which she specifies as the "white capitalist man."[27] She says, "If we, as lesbian-feminists, defy the taboo [of interracial sex], then we begin to transform the history of relationships between black women and white women."[28] However, as Clarke does, in this chapter I analyze texts that relieve white women of culpability for their support of, investment in, and benefit from the brutalization and exploitation of Black bodies. Despite the authors' intentions to construct tales of healing, their white female characters still represent white privilege and racial domination, thereby exposing how unruly texts are creating meanings that "slip past" the author and are "populated with meanings that [she] could not imagine."[29] My analysis of these stories questions the union of "lesbian" with a transracial sisterhood and instead examines how the term "lesbian" often obfuscates the mechanisms of domination and discipline inherent in relationships between owners and owned. Although these stories endeavor to demonstrate through the representation of interracial relationships that lesbian desire is an act of resistance, they also demonstrate the opposite—that domination and white supremacy still proliferate in same-sex couplings. I argue that the recourse to romantic love, marriage, and coupling in these stories also represents a tragic misrecognition of white domination that is mistaken for love. This is a valuable lesson that extends into considerations not only of the past but also of the current and future potential for political coupling with white queer women. If we are to take the past seriously in our contemporary evaluation of white women as political allies, as Cheryl Clarke suggests, then Black lesbian neo-slave narratives provide a unique and fertile archive to speculate on these previously underexplored relationships.

In *The Gilda Stories* and "Miss Hannah's Lesson" the affective discourses of slave-master "family," "friendship," and "love" displace the direct forms of violence that create the very category of the slave. In fiction there is an imagined history in which white women join in the fight against capitalism, exploitation, brutality, and imperialism, with desire as the catalyst. The literary maneuver of a fantastical interracial lesbian sisterhood is reflective of present-day desires for a racially integrated and harmonious LGBT movement. "The Champagne Lady" and *The Highest Price for Passion,* on the other hand, are more ambivalent about the place of the white mistress. The Champagne Lady herself is not entirely white and therefore displaces the myth of white purity, implicating white women in a history of racial subterfuge in order to protect the property of their own whiteness. Anger at white women's culpability in the commodification and denigration of Black women pours forth in the texts as the Black women protagonists situate themselves in relationship to a failed sisterhood.

The mistress–slave couplings that do take place in each story represent a "different geometry" of Black women's sexuality.[30] These representations allow for a consideration of interracial sex that is not about Black women collaborating with the white master against Black men. They are an opportunity to consider sex for Black women slaves as more than just a "sorrow song," as Omise'eke Natasha Tinsley suggests.[31] What if, however, these new geometries do not offer comfortable conclusions but show us the depth of Black sexual irresolution? With regard to the possibility of Black women's pleasure in the confines of slavery, Black feminist scholar Hortense Spillers states that whether the "captive female and/or her sexual oppressor derived 'pleasure' from their seductions and couplings is not a question we can politely ask."[32] She goes on to question if "'pleasure' is possible at all under conditions that [she] would aver as non-freedom for both or either parties" and doubts that "sexuality as a term of implied relatedness" is "appropriate, manageable or accurate to *any* of the familial arrangements under the system of slavery."[33] Historian and literary scholar Saidiya Hartman's assertion that the slave's pleasure is subsumed under the master's right to use and enjoyment underscores Spillers's doubt.[34] What are we to do then with neo-slave narratives that capture a vision of Black women slaves in orgasmic release? Can there be an epistemology of pleasure?[35] Both scholars' doubts speak to the extent to which even imagining women slaves as experiencing gratification, even momentarily, is such a vexing proposition that it goes beyond the limits of how the human is imagined.

The Girl, a Slave

The Gilda Stories leaves any pretense of realism behind in the world of the Gothic vampire novel. As a piece of speculative fiction, *The Gilda Stories* takes the opportunity to explore an extrahuman condition. The novel's runaway slave protagonist, the Girl, is transformed into a vampire, but more importantly her predicament extends the discussion of white identification as a condition of compounded alienation and is a metaphor for the "ultimate slave" as "undead."

According to Orlando Patterson's exhaustive comparative research on slavery worldwide, *Slavery and Social Death* (1982), there is a "perverse intimacy in the bond resulting from the power the master claim[s] over his slave. The slave's only life [is] through and for his master."[36] It is this "perverse intimacy" that defines social death itself, for the slave is stripped of all claims to a previous line of ancestors and thus is alienated from his/her culture and familial lineage. "Desocialized and depersonalized," the slave is introduced into the community of the master as a "nonbeing."[37] Patterson discusses slavery as a "highly symbolized" domain of human experience, wherein the captive is reduced to a liminally alien nonbeing.[38] The slave is constructed as socially dead through a series of rituals that mark natal alienation: rejection of former kinship, change of name, imposition of a "mark of servitude," and assumption of a new status in the household.[39] The pattern of bondage depicted in the Black lesbian short stories follows these guidelines in the form of an interracial "queer" kinship model that stresses the ability to create "family" bonds across race. The fact that captivity demands the obliteration of Black kinship situates the protagonists as isolated and in need of family, which the mistress provides. They are "marked" by whiteness corporeally and through rituals of conversion to white identification through education and training in womanhood.

According to Patterson, the "ultimate" slave is one that tests the boundary of the category of slave.[40] Even given slaves' constrained existence, these stories portray slave life at the limits of its definition in which the Black female protagonists seem to have some control over their conditions. On the surface, they are prized close associates of their masters, taken care of and even "loved" by their owners. They appear to wield power in their environment and over their masters/mistresses. At the same time, in these neo-slave narratives, the protagonists are "living surrogates" of their masters' will and extensions of the body of the owner. This is consistent with the slave and neo-slave narrative traditions, which in part portray the ultimate slave as an extension of the owner's person.[41] Proximity to power is what gives a slave power, albeit "a very peculiar and perverse form of power."[42] The ultimate slave, or "undead," is also reimagined in gendered terms, which this nonrealist set of texts presents as Black women who claim gender categories of femininity and masculinity. To be Black and female is to be "denied 'feminine' qualities" even in lesbian contexts.[43] Therefore, the trope of the mulatta still provides a pathway to legible femininity and, in this context, to the flexibility of gendered being. This reimagining of the slave's relationship to power and to humanism makes the neo-slave narrative central to African diasporic fiction, allowing for a break in our now-familiar understanding of slavery, or what A. Timothy Spaulding suggests is the reclamation of "authority over the history of slavery and historical record."[44]

The Gilda Stories takes authority over history starting with a reordering of power relations. In the novel's universe, Black displacement from the human family is an opportunity to join the ranks of the "undead" by miscegenation, specifically by mixing human blood with vampire blood. The process of blood mixture and introduction into vampire culture and community gives the protagonist a variety of "extra-human" powers, including the ability to be a masculine dark-skinned Black woman in the nineteenth century. The main character does not start out with this empowered relationship to gender and Blackness; rather she must be acculturated and transform these relationships.

In the beginning, the protagonist does not have a name, only a gender, having shed her slave name after she escaped slavery in Mississippi. Referring to her as "the Girl" indicates her alienation, rootlessness, and separation from family and community (a community she finds with the women of Woodward's brothel). Gomez's designation of the runaway slave as simply a gender is theoretically poised against Hortense Spillers's assertion that the slave is "ungendered flesh," consolidated together as laboring bodies for their owners' accumulation.[45] "Girl" suggests that she is nothing but a gender, the open potential for other people's desires. It also indicates perpetual immaturity, a designation that is not surprising given the slave's condition as an eternal "child" in relation to the parental figure of the slave owner. More importantly, it implies that the process of the commodification of flesh has distinctly gendered dimensions, suggesting that a runaway "girl" slave is an embodiment forged by distinct relationships to power. Her namelessness signals that in a patrilineal economy of subjectivity she is ultimately without kin, without a mother to name her, or a father to give her a surname, or owners to designate her slave appellation.

The novel shares Clarke's reliance and trust that white lesbians are natural partners in the resistance to racial oppression and that Black and white women (and all queers in general) have a common enemy in straight white male power. The queer kinship model in *The Gilda Stories* positions a multiracial cast of characters as part of the same familial order. The novel assumes that the "Other" status of being white and queer automatically ameliorates racial privilege and power, breaking the racial contract of white supremacy and social dominance. Critics have suggested that the novel's multiracial queer kinship provides a model for the displacement of white patriarchal power without considering the white female connection to racist power relations.[46]

Throughout the novel, when the Girl recalls her early years as a slave she remembers and speaks only of her mother; her thoughts are filled with the embodied memory of her mother. Before the arrival of the vampire, Gilda, the Girl relies on her mother's African ancestral wisdom to guide her. Her mother is the bearer of African memory: "The legends sketched a picture of the Fulani past—a natural rhythm of life without bondage" (10). The mother constructs Africa as the antithesis of U.S. slavery and bondage. It is the land of abundance and acceptance, "the home across the water that her mother sometimes spoke of as having fresh bread baking for everyone, even for those who worked in the fields" (11). Africa is a site of nurturing and nourishing, the eternal "motherland" passed down from mother to daughter. This nurturing portrayal of African life contrasts starkly with the brutality and deprivation of the plantation.

In a reversal of supposed Black animality and inhumanity, The Girl starts off in the novel as a runaway slave who is convinced that whites are subhuman monsters. She states that she is "not ready to give into those her mother had sworn were not fully human. . . . [Whites] ain't been here long 'nough. They just barely human. Maybe not even. They suck up the world, don't taste it," her mother says, inverting the script of European enlightenment narratives of progress by positioning white people as atavistic vampires "suck[ing] up the world" in a frenzy of rapacious colonialism and slavery (11).[47] Even as she sleeps in a barn, her mother's memory provides her with comfort and the fortitude to resist danger on an unconscious level:

> The Girl slept restlessly, feeling the prickly straw as if it were teasing pinches from her mother. The stiff moldy odor transformed itself into her mother's starchy dough smell. . . . At other moments it was the crackling of the brush as her mother raked the bristles through the Girl's thicket of dark hair before beginning the intricate pattern of braided rows. . . . The Girl clutched tightly at her mother's large black hand, praying the sound of the steps would stop, that she would wake up curled around her mother's body. . . . In sleep she clutched the hand of her mother, which turned into the warm, wooden handle of the knife she had stolen when she ran away the day before. It pulsed beside her heart. (9)

A white male rapist lurks at the edge of her nightmares, in the prickling of the straw and the moldy odors that emanate from the barn. However, the only "property" she has is her mother's teachings of her own distant memories of freedom. The Girl incorporates the "natural rhythm" of a distant, but not disappeared, Fulani past into herself, transforming the "prickly straw" and "moldy odor" into her mother's loving, "teasing pinches" and the "starchy dough" smell of her body after baking biscuits for the white slaveholders. The "teasing pinches" and the internal sound of the "crackling of the brush on her hair" before braiding act as warnings from her mother's spirit to clutch her hand. The Girl's mother has a prominent place in her memory, passing on, even beyond death, tools that she needs to survive. Her mother's touch rests in the core of her body, becoming her heart, and she uses it as a tool of resistance.

In her half-consciousness the Girl senses the presence of a white male rapist, a recognizable figure of white supremacist and misogynist domination. To the Girl he is a "beast from this other land" whom she kills, slipping the knife her mother gave her into his chest. "She entered him with her heart which was now a wood-handled knife" (11). She does not mind his blood, which covers her body. She considers it "a cleansing" of the world, "the death of a beast and her continued life" (12). The white male bounty hunter is the epitome of white supremacist denial of Black female rape.[48] He interprets her "unswerving gaze as neither resignation nor loathing but desire" (11).

"He rubbed his body against her brown skin and imagined the closing of her eyes was a need for him and his power" (11). Black women's supposed infamous proclivities for bestial and overabundant sexual excesses fuel the bounty hunter's projection of "need" and desire for him. He "anticipat[es] her submission to him, his head swelling with power and the thought of invading her" (11). At this point she can recognize his efforts to possess her. The Girl's eyes "were wide, seeing into both the past and the future" (11). She can see into the past and the future of white male sexual exploitation and violation of Black women. The Girl successfully negotiates power in the form of white male lust and the threat of sexual violence by evoking her mother's wisdom.

Gilda, a white woman who appears just after she has killed the bounty hunter, interrupts the Girl's freedom. Gilda is simultaneously a savior and another "mistress." When faced with power in the form of white woman-hood, the Girl cannot recognize its danger, and her psyche is invaded. The vampire enters her mind: "The Girl loosened her grip on the knife under the persuasive touch of Gilda's thoughts" (13). Gilda takes "possession" of the Girl immediately after she has freed herself from the rapist. One act of unsuccessful penetration is followed by the successful penetration of her mind. However, when Gilda finds her, she stops being able to see into the past and future; in fact, she becomes "unseeing" (12). At the sight of Gilda, the Girl is "seized with white fear. The pale face above her was a woman's, but the Girl had learned that they too, could be as dangerous as their men" (12). Quickly, though, she forgets the lesson her mother taught her: to recognize that white women are part of the system of degradation and domination and not to assume they are natural allies.

The Girl's time at Woodard's reveals the unfreedom embedded in perceived freedom. The Girl's status as a "free" person is tenuous and elusive. In order to evade the slave-catchers and bounty hunters, she has to remain confined to Woodward's, the brothel that Gilda owns. Her movement is restricted, but not her labor. Gilda speaks her instructions directly into the Girl's mind, "You don't have to tell me anything. I'll tell you. You just listen and remember when anyone asks: You're new in the house. My sister sent you over here to me as a present. You've been living in Mississippi. Now you live here and work for me" (17). The Girl steps into a form of bondage similar to what she has risked her life to escape. She is immediately set to work for Gilda and cannot leave without being escorted by a free (white) person. She exists in limbo as "property of another order,"[49] neither "free" nor formally enslaved.

At Woodward's, the Girl's longing for her mother is part of her longing for an Africa that "[recedes] more with each passing year" (10) after her mother's death. This slippage of memory coincides with the Girl's absorption into the life of the brothel, away from any other Black people except the few employed as servants. Gilda replaces the main character's slave mother and becomes her redeemer, her mother/lover. The fantasy genre allows for Gomez to literalize what are otherwise symbolic dynamics. The displacement of Black filiation in the creation of white lines of kinship happens through the actual exchange of blood between vampires as the novel's protagonist, a runaway slave, becomes a literal member of the "undead." Gilda looks into the Girl's eyes and sees what she wants to see, her own needs reflected back at her. "Gilda saw herself behind those eyes. . . . Gilda saw a need for family that matched her own" (16). The Girl instantly becomes a "willing" subject to Gilda's desires for expanding her kinship network. As a "free" person, the Girl acts as a loyal servant, owing her status solely to Gilda's kindness in taking her in. Gilda could easily declare the Girl her property, but she does not have to.

Scholarly criticism of the book celebrates Gilda's replacement of the Girl's mother, citing their relationship as indicative of "multiple vectors of kinship"[50] that deny racial hierarchy and valorizing the text as imagining "horizontal lines of kin."[51] In fact, the text asks us to see the two as equals very early on, even though it offers evidence to the contrary. Part of the invitation to white kinship that Gilda poses is her convincing the Girl that she is involved in an even exchange of power. The Girl says, "This woman, Gilda, could see into her mind. That was clear. The Girl was not frightened though, because it seemed she could see into Gilda's as well. That made them even" (17). Though she can "see" into her mind, the Girl's vision is limited to what Gilda lets her see. The Girl is susceptible to the "affective erethism"—Fanon's schema of racial alienation—that presents vertical relations of power to her as horizontal lines of kinship.[52]

The Girl's memory of her mother's teaching becomes a distant dream in the "lost empires" of her mother's stories. By the end of the chapter, Gilda displaces the Girl's mother, rebirthing her as a member of her "undead" clan. In order to be a part of her new family, the Girl must essentially give up her memories of white brutality under slavery. The Girl looks toward and imitates Gilda, "matching her words to the rhythm she had heard in Gilda's voice, just as she often imitated her walk when no one watched" (22). Gilda asks the Girl to "put aside the faces who've hunted you, who've hurt you" (44) and replace them with love. The Girl simultaneously takes Gilda as an alternative maternal figure and grieves her Black mother. As soon as Gilda speaks of love, the Girl discovers that she "loves" Gilda and her native American partner Bird, feeling "the loss of her mother, new and cutting" (42). In fact, the moment of pleasure derived through blood/sexual exchange also reanimates the Girl's attachment to Blackness.

The Girl is reborn through pleasure as Gilda holds "the Girl's head to her breast and in a quick gesture opened the skin of her chest. She pressed the Girl's mouth to the red life that seeped from her" (46). This is simultaneously a gesture of maternal breast-feeding and a sexual offering of her breast, producing a "rising excitement that was unfamiliar to [the Girl]" (45). Gilda introduces the Girl to a physical sensation of pleasure that was previously unknown, except the "trance of sensuality" she felt during the only opportunity her mother had to give her a bath (12). The vampire extracts a song from the Girl's memory as she "soap[s] and rins[es] and massag[es] the Girl into restfulness, drawing out the fear and pain with her strong, thin hands as she hummed the tune from the Girl's childhood" (47). Gilda replaces the original experience of pleasure, the feeling of "intimacy" and "sensuality" the Girl felt from her mother's "large Black hand" (9) with her "strong, thin hands" (47).

However, becoming a vampire is not a simple (de)racialization process. Her "mixed blood" also is a catalyst for her century-long allegiance to Blackness and Black queer community building. It is Bird's repetition of this exchange of blood that "complete[s] the circle" (47) of the transformation ritual, leaving the Girl with more than Gilda's maternal offering. Mary-Louise Loeffler emphasizes Bird's role in the Girl's metamorphosis, crediting her with the Girl's "inscription into the matrilineal tradition of lesbian vampirism."[53] I suggest that this blood rite also relieves the new Gilda of illusions of freedom and humanity, which, because she is a runaway slave, are not available to her.

Before transformation, the Girl naively assumes that the lack of shackles translates into unencumbered freedom. As in "Miss Hannah's Lesson," *The Gilda Stories* has a Black female character that introduces an alternative reading of their collective situation as Black (freed) slaves, but again she is dismissed as ignorant and close-minded. Bernice, a Black servant at the brothel, "look[s] more like her mother than anyone the Girl had met since running away, but she seemed like a sister too" (26). Bernice shares the wisdom of experience with the Girl when she asks about the possibility of manumission, counseling the Girl to be vigilant about her freedom. The Girl's response is to naively assert, "We free already Bernice. Won't mean so much over here you think?" (26). However, Bernice reminds her "[T]hey's whole lot of us ain't free, just down the road. . . . It's not the war, it's the freedom we got to keep our eye on" (26). The Girl responds that she "remember[s] how to do that" (26), but her memory fades and her "sight" fails to recognize how much her own restrictions of movement challenge her designation as "free."

The Girl's transformation into the new Gilda ushers in her reconnection with Black communities. As Spaulding asserts, as the new Gilda she traverses the twentieth century seeking connection with different African American communities and social protest movements.[54] Scott Bravmann points out that Gilda's inclusion in vampire society is contested along racial lines by some white vampires.[55] As a member of this "undead" family, the Girl/Gilda has gone "up" in social status. She has superhuman powers that enable her to travel unharmed, and she is provisionally welcomed into the company of her white gay "extended family" in San Francisco. This new-found mobility and invulnerability leads Alexis Pauline Gumbs to assert that the vampire is a "figure of queer Black feminist survival . . . agency and power."[56]

Despite these few exceptions, critical reception of the book often emphasizes an undifferentiated queer community in the past and invites analogies that occlude the reality of racial violence between queers in the past and the present. One critic concludes from the novel that the Girl (now Gilda) is offered "the safety to come out of that other 'slavery' she experienced in Louisiana, a closeted lesbian identity."[57] Some critics identify the white women in the novel as bystanders to the slave system of violence. Shannon Winnubst's analysis of *The Gilda Stories* understands the Girl's resistance to her white male perpetrator as the novel's radical disruption of white male maneuvers to remain innocent and hidden from historical rape. For Winnubst, this straight white male desire to portray himself as "innocent" is a "fantasy that both protects and constitutes this reality, the reality of the violent and violating straight white male body."[58] *The Gilda Stories,* she says, "usher in new ontologies" as "same-sex relationships . . . drive a stake in to the heart of this straight white male ontology."[59] Apparently, as "that same straight white male rape[s] black slaves in the kitchen, mixing with their blood, . . . their white wives [sleep] in their conjugal beds upstairs."[60] This fantasy of white female innocence that sleeps quietly while the master rapes obfuscates the reality of the violent and violating white female body.

Actual slave narratives identify both the mistress and the master as torturers and sexual violators. The mistress's phobia that the slave will "take her place"[61] beside the master as his immediate subordinate, thereby displacing and reducing the white woman to the position of Black female slave, sends her into jealous fits. This fear leads mistresses to persecute Black women. In the classic slave narrative by Harriet Jacobs, *Incidents in the Life of a Slave Girl,* the mistress, Mrs. Flint, is not innocently at rest but is anxiously somnambulant, visiting Jacobs's bedside late at night to "penetrate" her ears, using the words she imagined her husband might say. She reenacts her husband's sexual stalking ostensibly in order to "test" Jacobs's response, but this can also be an enactment of her own desires. The fear that Jacobs will take her place becomes an act of consumption: "I want you so that he can't have you." Nell Irvin Painter suggests that Sojourner Truth's *Narrative of Sojourner Truth* also contains veiled evidence of sexual abuse by her mistress.[62] A representational focus on white male phallic brutality creates a construction of a universal "master," leaving the history of the mistress's potential for sexual exploitation undertheorized as well as positioning her as a vehicle for Black women's sexual release. In the next short story as well, "Miss Hannah's Lesson," the mistress stands irresolutely both at the center of the protagonist's pleasure and at the center of her captivity.

Mistress-Lover-Friend

Several of the neo-slave narratives analyzed here revisit the plantation household from the perspective of light-skinned slaves, in the tradition of the mulatta trope. Colonizers demand mimicry as homage to their dominance,[63] and in "Miss Hannah's Lesson," the relationship of the main character, Sarah, with her owner's daughter, Hannah, centers on her ability to mimic white femininity and therefore be deserving of respect and dignity. The extent to which light-skinned characters are successful in their approximation of middle-class, white feminine gender is part of how they "pass" for "white" and "pass" as acceptable love objects for whites.

Traditionally in Black women's literature, the existence of the mulatta as a desired being demonstrates that racial differences are superficial and fictional. Her presence says that there are no innate boundaries of intelligence and refinement, only ones that white-supremacist culture creates for Blacks.[64] The mulatta's emulations of white feminine womanhood can be read as an interruption in the racial schema that blurs the boundaries of race. In the retelling of the story of slavery, Black women have also maintained the tragic mulatta trope as a way to articulate desire through the assertion of the characters' proximity to whiteness. Black lesbian authors use the trope as a means through which "to explore not only the . . . questions of race, racism, and racial identity, but complex questions of sexuality and female subjectivity as well."[65]

In "Miss Hannah's Lesson," the young protagonist, Sarah, clings desperately to the "useful fiction" that love with her white mistress, Miss Hannah, can save her from the "tremendous heartache" of slavery and give her access to the elusive experience of pleasure and joy.[66] "The idea of being sold to another plantation or the thought of being married off with the sole purpose of producing more slave-hands horrified Sarah. Eighteen years on this earth had given her strife and tremendous heartache. The only joy she'd known was in Miss Hannah's presence" (33). In this example, for a slave woman, heterosexual penetration is a business transaction for her owner. Sarah recognizes herself as an instrument of her master's wealth—a laboring slave and a living factory for future generations of slaves, regardless of who "fathers" any of her potential offspring.

Sarah's conflict between exploited sexual labor and the promise of pleasure are not mutually exclusive. Rather, she makes what Saidiya Hartman describes as "a deliberate calculation" to "love" Miss Hannah, which "intensifies the constraints of slavery and reinscribes her status as property, even if figuratively property of another order."[67] The deeper Sarah falls for Miss Hannah, the more demands are placed on her body, even as she seems to be gaining freedom. For example, Sarah is subject to Miss Hannah's caprices of power play and the erotic fantasy of role reversal. Miss Hannah slips Sarah "fresh buttered biscuits from breakfast" (32) as if they were a gift; however, they are actually the same biscuits that Sarah prepared earlier, but was not allowed to eat.

Frantz Fanon's *Black Skins, White Masks* is of fundamental importance in producing a vocabulary for unpacking how Black women's fictional texts have positioned interracial same-sex relations as liberating for Black women. His discussions of the Black psychic incorporation of whiteness as a strategy to mitigate the annihilating forces of racism continue to be crucial in theorizing Black interiority. Black people's consciousness is taken over by white psychogenesis, creating a neurosis of inferiority and lack. In his discussion of interracial relationships, he postulates that Black people find it fruitless to "blacken, to negrify the world," and instead, afflicted Blacks must "bleach" their own bodies and minds.[68] Fanon describes this as a heterosexual dynamic; however, woman-to-woman relationships do not escape the vicissitudes of anti-Blackness. Sarah's "love" for Miss Hannah is a tricky business. Fanon defines "true, authentic love" as the act of "wishing for others what one postulates for oneself," which "entails the mobilization of psychic drives basically freed of unconscious conflicts."[69] One conflict that must be in alignment is that "the person [he] loves will strengthen [him] by endorsing [his] assumption of [his] manhood."[70] Black female slaves cannot make a "gift of themselves," as they are always already the sexual "gift" to white power.[71] However, in the commingling of beauty and virtue that haunts Black female existence, they must be made into "proper" gifts through the mastery of European language and culture *and* in the acculturation to acceptable female gender.

Sarah must then submit to Miss Hannah's erotically charged fantasy of a teacher/student relationship imbued with French lessons, where she must indulge Miss Hannah's desire to play the "teacher" of a gifted "student." The lesson opens the story and linguistically enacts the slippages between white desire and domination:

Comment vous appelez-vous?
Je m'appelle Sarah
Où habitez-vous?
J'habite à Dubbonnet. J'habite près de Baton Rouge.

[What is your name? My name is Sarah. Where do you live? I live in Dubbonet. I live near Baton Rouge.] (32)

In this verbal exchange, an exchange of position also takes place. Miss Hannah uses the formal second-person "*vous*" to address her slave, which linguistically subordinates the speaker to the person being spoken to. Miss Hannah's ability to "play" with structural power dynamics in her private scenes with Sarah marks her ultimate authority and ownership of Sarah. Sarah's answer that she lives in Dubbonnet suggests that she has an autonomous living situation in a town or province near Baton Rouge, Louisiana. However, Dubonnet is the name of the plantation and the surname of Miss Hannah, a site of bondage and a reminder of Miss Hannah's position as heir to the Dubonnet wealth, of which Sarah is one piece. Every part of the French lesson transmits a serious "lesson" in the coupling of pleasure and domination for the white female slave owner. Through the manipulation of one slave, Miss Hannah lives out her fantasy of relinquishing power through the use of the formal "*vous*" without putting her privilege in jeopardy; she also indulges in the construct of having a "partner" whom she can converse with and a supplicant whose only access to joy is through her presence. The biscuit, which is not a "gift" but a product of Sarah's own exploited labor; the French lessons, which are really erotic games of power; and the partner, who is actually a slave mistress, all consolidate Sarah's condition as an abject object of white female power and manipulation.

Another interpretation of the term "*vous*" in the French lesson is to consider it a second-person plural address (from the French verb "*appeler*") to the collective Black condition that Sarah represents. Sarah is "called" to acknowledge her place as a hybrid form of "both person and property" in order to act as a placeholder for Miss Hannah's desires.[72] Miss Hannah desires Sarah's desire—for her, to be her, and to admire her. The command to mimicry requires that it is never complete, that it is always the "same, but not quite . . . a complex strategy of reform, regulation, and discipline" designed to simultaneously keep the colonized and enslaved subject to a white ideal and to reassure the slaver that she is superior to the copy.[73] Sarah's "lesson" is also a rehearsal for the future so that Sarah knows the proper way to address her white superiors. Miss Hannah provides the model that Sarah knows to follow. Far from being a simple "love tale" as the subtitle to the book states, "Miss Hannah's Lesson" demonstrates "a social relationship of dominance" based on race despite the fact that the story takes place between women.[74] The dissonance between mutual love and chattel slavery's asymmetrical property relations is negotiated and resolved psychically through Sarah's acceptance of the invitation to the mastery of white language and gender offered by Miss Hannah.

"Affective erethism" manifests and is negotiated according to biological sex, and it is heavily reliant on heterosexual dualisms.[75] According to Fanon, both Black men and women strive for white inclusion and acceptance; however, sexual difference produces different psychic drives: Black women want to whiten the race by having children for white men, and Black men become obsessed with "mastery" on various levels. Black men are obliged to prove to white people that they are worthy of human consideration through the "mastery of the cultural tool" of language.[76] Facility with written and spoken colonial languages becomes the primary way in which the colonized Black male can gain status among whites. If one cannot whiten the skin, then cultural whitening is an alternative, providing elevation "above his jungle status in proportion to his adoption of the mother country's cultural standards. He becomes whiter as he renounces his blackness, his jungle" (18). By "becoming white," he can engage in an agreement with his white patriarchal superior to have access to white womanhood. Once he has demonstrated that he is no longer a savage, but a student and a scholar, then he can obtain white authorization to "take [his] sister" and become elevated from being a "genuine" Negro.[77] He is particularly driven to "prove that he is a man" through the sexual conquest of white womanhood, which is an act of "revenge" against white male exclusion.[78]

The Black women protagonists in these stories cannot participate in the gentlemen's agreement between the white patriarch and his Black male subordinate that Fanon describes. For them, the mechanism by which the invitation to whiteness occurs is also through the acquisition of language and (white) femininity. Wherein Fanon's Black male student is given a white female by his white male associates under the terms that he is "no longer a Negro," Sarah's body, and the bodies of her other fictional counterparts, are already available to any white person. The best circumstance Sarah wishes for is to be *chosen by* her white mistress, whom she hopes will offer her "something akin to freedom" within the constraints of captivity.[79] She has this arrangement under the condition that she must approximate white womanhood in exchange for recognition of their "beauty and virtue," within the discrete moments of recognition from their white owner.

Fanon's discussions of Black female "seductions" to whiteness involve the absorption of white culture and proving one's whiteness through sexual liaisons with white men. The elevation comes from the acceptance by white manhood, which functions as the arbiter of humanity. This ontological Black female unconscious "asks nothing, demands nothing, except a bit of whiteness in her life."[80] The Black woman must demonstrate that she "possess[es] beauty and virtue, which have never been black."[81] She desires "lactification," or the whitening of the race.[82] Unlike for Black men, the future of the Black race and its phenotypic range depend on her. Women symbolize the fate of the nation, its boundaries, and its reproduction.[83] The term "lactification" takes its root from lactose. The term suggests that "mother's milk" has been corrupted. Her mind and her body have been taken over by whiteness, even in terms of the use of her womb, which, in turn, allegedly causes the physical and psychic decomposition of the race. For Fanon, there is "honor" in being the "daughter of a white woman" because it suggests agency and choice of affection.[84] To be the child of a Black mother and a white father means that one has been "made in the bushes,"[85] and is the product of white patriarchal privilege to coerce any female-bodied person into sex. White women are granted the ability to participate in a "giving" of themselves to Black men, "not a seizing" of their bodies through rape.[86] However, Fanon implicates Black women in their own coercion. Not only do they have to submit to white phallic violence, but they are also vilified as engaging in a "nauseating phenomena" of collaboration with white masculinity to eradicate Blackness from its "pit of niggerhood."[87]

However, Fanon did not imagine desire between women. White identification comes with a promise to Black women that they can obtain enough self-possession to participate in a "giving, not a seizing" of themselves as white women can. This promise "seduces" these Black lesbian narratives into fantasies of love and agency with white women. The assurance that woman-to-woman "relationships" with white women will secure a pleasure outside patriarchy lures the characters into an imagined reciprocal bond between themselves and their white female owners. The women in the stories readily accept the promise of joy and pleasure, as misery and negation are associated with Black female sexual relationships with other Black people. The only thing that can come of such relationships is to maintain one's status as "worthless," to sink deeper into the "pit of niggerhood." As Fanon quips, "X is black, but misery is blacker," meaning that although a woman may be

Black, she will only find more misery with a Black man, especially if he is dark-skinned.[88] Negotiations for acceptance take place through her sexual use-value. She cannot enter into a "gentleman's agreement" that Black men of class aspirations have with white men for their sisters, so she must be able to attract men/people of status to her. Under the system of slavery, Black women's bodies are colonized for the "sexual, productive, reproductive, creative prerogatives and energies" of others.[89] Omise'eke Natasha Tinsley has taken Fanon to task for this omission, noting the possibilities of "fluid" desires and sexualities[90] that are strategically deployed to contest the limitations of heteronormativity. Heterosexuality becomes the assurance that she will be a Black "hole" for men's use, Black or white. Furthermore, as Audre Lorde suggests, one Black woman is a reminder of another's status as socially dead. In Lorde's essay "Eye-to-Eye," she argues that Black women are often unable to have solidarity with each other because they are mirror images of each other's pain and exclusion, or social death.[91] Within these constraints, interracial lesbian desire functions as an imagined release from racist patriarchy. The "romance" with desiring whiteness appears to be an opportunity to join the world of the "living."

From the beginning of the story, Sarah is convinced that her psychic and emotional bondage could be relieved by Miss Hannah's recognition and reciprocation of affection. Sarah's faith in Miss Hannah's emancipating gaze of mutual desire is at the heart of how the invitation to white identification ushers in Black self-hatred and annihilation instead of liberatory pleasure. Convinced that Miss Hannah's nominal recognition is "the only joy she'd known" (33), Sarah rejects her communal ties to other slaves. The narrator says:

> [Sarah's] devotion to Miss Hannah was far beyond the understanding of the other house nigras and field hands. Sarah once overheard Clara, the main cook for the Big House say, "It's not natural for dat gurl to enjoy the company of a white woman so much. She acts like a hungry newborn baby and Miss Hannah is de only one wid da tit to feed her. She never talk wid gurlz her own age or her own kin'. Cuz she pretty wid long hair she tellin' dat gurl she white. Sarah fool enuf to believe it." (33)

What is startling about this passage (besides the Black dialect that Sarah does not share) is that it is the only time when a Black voice intervenes in the text's own romanticism. Clara's statement suggests that Sarah has replaced her Black mother with Miss Hannah in a violent psychic evacuation of her Black self. Through her relationship with Miss Hannah, Sarah goes through a developmental shift in identification, displacing her Blackness in a process of "affective erethism" leaving her "unable to develop black self-love."[92]

Clara's warning that Sarah is a "fool" to believe that she is white, meaning to cast her identifications with Miss Hannah in rejection of the rest of the slaves, goes unheeded. Sarah's "desire to exist in the gaze of the Other"[93] is what David Marriott describes as "black alienation and psychic dispossession," meaning the violent intrusion of white unconscious that displaces a conscious Black identity.[94] In order to participate in Miss Hannah's sexual fantasy of teacher–student, "lover–friend" (42), Sarah physically turns Miss Hannah toward a "broken piece of mirror" so that they both can be reflected at the same time and "Sarah [turns] to face Miss Hannah . . . then she [lifted] Miss Hannah's hand and placed it on her own caramel-colored face" (33–34). This dual gesture of facing the mirror and then each other is an act of doubling. The two become twins; with the positioning of Miss Hannah at her side, Sarah literally and metaphorically turns away from the "house nigras and field hands" (33) to identify instead with Miss Hannah.[95] Sarah exists in a limbo of alienation, confined to the small cell of her cabin, isolated from the other slaves and completely at the mercy of her mistress. The Black maternal figure (in the form of other Black women who give advice) is eviscerated and replaced by the white lesbian figure. The mirror itself is fractured; the apparatus of scopic identification is fundamentally flawed, symbolizing the distortion of Sarah's "view," possessing the right, freedom, and privilege to love herself as white. Sarah's act of "specular alienation"[96] is part of the conversion to whiteness that allows Miss Hannah to make her a "property of another order" and claim the sexual desires as well as the pleasures of her slave in her inheritance of property.

Like Clara's statements of the psychic evisceration of whiteness on Sarah's mind, the text includes another interruption of the lesbian romance narrative in the form of Sarah's unconscious dreams. Sarah begins her sexual life as the male Dubonnet's sexual commodity that he "rents" to a business associate, a shrimper from New Orleans. As her relationship with Miss Hannah becomes more overtly sexual, Sarah has a dream: "She was in the kitchen of the Big House and Miss Hannah entered dressed like the shrimper. She kissed her as the shrimper did" (38). Miss Hannah manages to gain exclusive rights over Sarah's body by threatening to reveal the family secret of father–daughter incest. The narrator reveals that several years prior, Mr. Dubbonnet had raped his virgin daughter "after an evening of debauchery," impregnating her with a "sibling-child" (39). The narrator further reveals that the child was spontaneously aborted, leaving Hannah barren and unwanted by the surrounding white community, as "no man or woman came near [her]" (39). After the baby's death, she has leverage over her father, who values his own honor. She threatens to tell "the entire state of Louisiana" about the incest, which would cause him to "lose [his] respect if people understood why [she has] never been asked to marry" (39). Miss Hannah essentially threatens her father with a form of social ostracism, suggesting that the incest taboo is strong enough to break the contract of white patriarchal dominance. As a result, Miss Hannah inherits Sarah from Mr. Dubbonnet. The transfer from Mr. Dubbonnet to Miss Hannah does not fundamentally change Sarah's condition of enslavement. She is transformed into "property of another order" that prevents her from being subjected to the shrimper's lusts. However, Sarah's dream that the two are dressed the same reveals that Miss Hannah and the shrimper occupy a similar structural position in relationship to Sarah, regardless of how much Miss Hannah "protects" her from physical labor or lavishes gifts on her. It is Miss Hannah's relation to the patriarchal transmission of property, however, that determines the difference between the two.

"Miss Hannah's Lesson" is extremely forgiving of white womanhood, positioning Miss Hannah as a victim of white male domination and authority, similar to the position of Black women slaves. Miss Hannah is the legitimate heir to the family wealth, and, as such, when Mr. Dubbonnet transmits ownership to her, he also releases her to fully enjoy her property, sexually or in any way that she chooses. Clarke, Hartman, and the text assume that it is the patriarchal distribution of property relations that secures the subjection of Black women. "Regularity of sexual violence" and "the reproduction of property" are categories that differentiate the bonded and the free.[97] However, Miss Hannah's regular subjection to incest by her father and subsequent impregnation does not break the master–slave contract. Miss Hannah's sexual abuse by her father is juxtaposed with Sarah's story of being "rented" to the shrimper, as if the social, political, and legal condition of slavery is analogous to childhood sexual abuse, rendering the two women equally disenfranchised and therefore equals. "Miss Hannah's Lesson" and *The Gilda Stories,* which we will come back to later in the chapter, attempt to circumvent patriarchal kinship by corrupting it with female inheritance or by breaking its line of succession. However, despite their focus on woman-to-woman relationships, these texts demonstrate that white female authority depends on efficiently seizing and inverting power from the male patriarch.

In the fantasy of fiction, the slave women "author" their own sexualities. Lesbian relationship affords them "choice," "agency," and alternatives to white patriarchal power by their sexual agency. However, even in the context of a fictional world that operates on a fantasy of white female altruism, aspects of the material relationship of Blacks as white property emerges. In

"Miss Hannah's Lesson," part of the full use and enjoyment of the slave as property is the production, reinforcement, and support of white masculinity in white male and female-bodied subjects through the process of sexual domination of Black women. The racist construction of gender holds Black women as the Other of white female identity, allowing white women to explore gender categories and stretch the boundaries of "acceptable" behavior. Sarah's structural predicament of enslavement makes it imperative that in order to qualify as a "favored slave" (38), she must fulfill Miss Hannah's gender requirements, leaving Miss Hannah able to create her own gender identity in relation to Sarah. At a moment when the fantasy is in danger of breakdown because of Sarah's lack of facility using eating utensils, Miss Hannah "spits" at her that she "is not an ape" (34) and proceeds to teach Sarah to "eat properly and sit and walk like a true woman" (35). It is the very fact that Black women are not included in the category "true woman" that makes Miss Hannah's request especially cruel, reinforcing her own mastery and rejection of the category.

Miss Hannah's violent reaction is indicative of the gendered, sexual, and racial stakes tied into creating Sarah as a near-white cultured lady, the kind of woman that Hannah is forbidden from outwardly courting in upper-class white society. Her white masculinity depends on Sarah's correct application of white femininity, even if she has possession of it only in the slave cabin. Lurking behind Miss Hannah's claim of "love" lies the painstaking process of the consumption of Sarah's body and mind for her own self-making. Convinced that their sexual desire and intimate friendship can leap the divide between owner and slave, Sarah proclaims them "lover-friends" on the last page (42).

The end of the story places Miss Hannah and Sarah together in her cabin for the consummation of their relationship. Barnett's description of the sex between Sarah and Miss Hannah positions Sarah's pleasure as resisting the dictates of white patriarchy: to have exclusive use of her body regardless of her desires. Sarah anticipates that Miss Hannah will "insert her fingers like the shrimper does," but she is surprised when Hannah "[kisses] her on the piece of flesh that [tingles] . . ." (41). As Sarah is on the receiving end in the sexual dynamic (meaning that she is being acted upon by Miss Hannah), the text enacts an interesting reversal of what Black slaves traditionally receive from their mistresses. Instead of punishment, scorn, abuse, or a work assignment, Sarah receives pleasure. Sarah's sexual encounter with Miss Hannah is a momentary interruption in the overwhelming debasement of slavery. Her time with Miss Hannah opens the possibility of using her own body for herself in a field of constraint, even within the context of her intimate relationship.

As anodyne as the text is in relation to Black and white women's connections, certain aspects of the slave paradigm are not overturned. According to the text, Sarah's pleasure does not "free" her materially, nor does her emotional relationship with Miss Hannah translate into emancipation. As symbolic mother/lover and child, the two are locked in an embrace outside the reach of Mr. Dubbonnet, the bond between mother and child existing beyond the limit of discourse but not outside the reach of bondage and domination. Through Sarah and Miss Hannah's relationship, we observe how the oedipal is structured through property and ownership, masquerading as affection and mutuality. In Miss Hannah's arms Sarah finally arrives at a "pleasure she had never known before" (41) in her nonpenetrative sexual experience; Sarah's orgasm is "beyond words" (32).[98] It is not something that she is able to "freely explore" (41). Despite the text's insistence that the two characters "[melt] into each other" (42) at the moment of orgasm, it is still a sensation that is under Miss Hannah's control.

Miss Hannah frees herself from the bonds of patriarchal domination by negotiating for custody of a Black female body, thereby taking the place of Sarah's father as controller of Sarah's sexual life. The incest subplot does more than simply provide the white female character with an opportunity to empathize with Sarah. Having failed the test of maternity and patronymic succession, Miss Hannah is free to find pleasure in her own body without worry of a compulsion to marry and have children. Miss Hannah's failed maternity frees her from the bonds of heterosexual demands where "the vagina and the jouissance" of (white) women are negated, giving them only one option "of gaining access to the symbolic paternal order" through "childbearing and procreation in the name of the father."[99] Of course, this theorization of the maternal is the site where psychoanalytic feminism fails to account for race and the fact that Black women are refused the maternal function[100] and therefore have no entrance into the "socio-symbolic community."[101] As a result of her power over her father's sense of honor, Miss Hannah demands that Sarah is freed from her sexual labor with the shrimper. Ostensibly it seems as if Miss Hannah is acting on Sarah's behalf, but it is really her own sexuality that she has freed. Unlike Sarah, she is allowed to choose her partners, and by taking control of her pleasure, she is free to pursue it with her slaves. Most importantly, she can potentially *give* pleasure as well as receive it through her slave, as Sarah is only an extension of Miss Hannah and her desires. As an "ultimate slave," Sarah is an extension of the owner's body.[102] Her Black self is evacuated in preparation for the psychic and sexual custody. As a person who has been alienated from her ancestors through the process of enslavement (what Patterson calls natal alienation), her condition is compounded by her isolation from the other slaves. Sarah's interests are identified with Miss Hannah's to use and abuse as she wishes.[103] Sarah must first be made into the white feminine woman that Miss Hannah can never be or have. Their sexual scene, therefore, functions more like an act of masturbation than mutual encounter. The rituals of gender/racial conversion have assured that a white woman has taken Sarah's place. Therefore, even in this alternative universe, giving pleasure is still an impossible and unknowable experience for a Black woman. She can feel pleasure only under the condition that it is part of Miss Hannah's gratification. Sarah's transformation from just another slave to a piece of "property of another order" marks her transition from being dead to "undead." If the condition of slavery is one of social death, then the creation of an ultimate slave is the making of an existence as property and person that is heightened to a point of psychic crisis, a crisis resolved through white identification. Sarah is "possessed" by Miss Hannah, both in the sense that she is counted among her material possessions and in the sense that she is psychically occupied by Miss Hannah's desires.

The white women in *The Gilda Stories* and "Miss Hannah's Lesson" are benevolent sisters poised to help their Black counterparts through their privileged position. Their education and their privilege with the master are metaphors for the fact that in the present, "lesbian" is an identity that allows people to make a plea for justice and rights. Part of how that is possible is its association (along with the term "gay") with whiteness, making the ability to demand lesbian rights part of the privileges and properties of whiteness.[104] But their attempts at claiming the privileges and pleasures of that property do not survive the test of race. By making "lesbian" synonymous with "white," the stories suggest that interracial desire provides access to the property of whiteness through lesbian claims for individual liberation. In this way the white characters are idealized vehicles for Black women's quest for social and political agency. In these stories, white women fulfill the fantasy of white allies who assist Black women in their struggle against structural racism. However, when analyzed, the texts reveal that they are still working in their own racial self-interest. In contrast, the remaining stories I analyze represent structural racism more explicitly. Slaves' vulnerability to the violations of sale, upheaval, and sexual relationships with whites is portrayed as much more manipulated than and beneficial to the desires of the whites who surround them.

Passion's Price:
Subversive Irresolution in
Representations of Interracial Relationships

Both Laurinda Brown's 2008 novel *The Highest Price for Passion* and SDiane Adamz-Bogus's ca. 1985 short story "The Champagne Lady" owe a debt to the nineteenth- and early twentieth-century novels *Clotel; or, The President's Daughter* by William Wells Brown (1853), *Iola Leroy* by Francis Ellen Watkins Harper (1892), and *Contending Forces* by Pauline Hopkins (1900) because they share plot elements: a light-skinned heroine passes for a white woman and illegally marries a white man; she bears his children, who also live as white people (often slave owners themselves). Inevitably, tragic circumstances intervene in their arrangement, and the white patriarch dies, leaving the children of the union to fall into bondage.

The Highest Price for Passion puts a twist on the sentimentalism and plot conventions of early neo-slave narratives. In this novel it is the daughter of the white plantation owner, Miss Annie, who falls in love with a young slave, Josiah. Despite the fact that she is married to a brutal slave owner, Miss Annie consummates her love for Josiah and gives birth to twins: a son, Quincy Josiah, and a daughter, Amelia, while her husband is away fighting in a conflict along the United States–Mexico border. Miss Annie hides her pregnancy and Amelia's birth from her husband. She sends Quincy Josiah to the North and hides Amelia, along with other runaway slaves, in a cave a few miles outside the plantation. Miss Annie explains their peculiar situation to Amelia, comforting her with a promise that she is "not a slave because [her] mother was never a slave" (113).

Similar to "Miss Hannah's Lesson," the text absolves the plantation mistress from responsibility or culpability with respect to the institution of slavery. Like Stowe's Little Eva from *Uncle Tom's Cabin* and Georgiana in *Clotel,* Miss Annie is the virtuous daughter of a rich planter who believes in the humanity of her slaves. She says to her friend Lizzie, "They are people just like we are, my friend. They breathe like we do, they hurt like we do, and they love like we do, too" (72). Immediately after this statement, Miss Annie acknowledges her financial benefit from and social investment in slavery through her marriage: "slaves [are] supposed to obey their masters because that [is] what the Bible instruct[s]" (73). The novel quickly moves from Miss Annie's courtship to her marriage, with no contemplation of the limited choices that would have been available to her as a white woman in the antebellum South. Amelia confronts her mother about her investment and participation in slavery through her marriage. She says, "Since you are his wife, does that make you a slave owner, too?" (112). Miss Annie answers vaguely, "In theory, it does, but in reality it does not" (112), denying her part in upholding and benefiting from the institution. Miss Annie's relative power in relation to her husband is foregrounded years later when he discovers that she has given birth to Black children; he subsequently slaps "her in the face with all his might, and, before she could hit the floor, he slap[s] her again" (115). He beats her repeatedly, calling her a "nigger-loving whore" (116). Miss Annie's declaration that she does not believe in slavery, coupled with the abuse she receives from her husband, situates her in the text as a sympathetic figure and distances her from the structure of white supremacy and ownership that separates her from her slaves. As a result of the husband's rage, Miss Annie is shot and presumed dead, and Amelia is sold into slavery. Amelia's eventual capture is a classic plot device, used in both *Clotel* and *Iola Leroy,* wherein the light-skinned heroine is forced into bondage despite never having been a slave. However, despite such plot similarities, *The Highest Price for Passion* departs from the tradition in many ways, including its focus at the end of the novel on a secondary white female character: Miss Annie's friend Lizzie.

The first half of the text revolves around Miss Annie's young-adult romance with Josiah and the bond between Miss Annie and her mother, and it partially reflects on her friendship with Lizzie. At first, Lizzie is not much more than a bigoted foil for Miss Annie's abolitionist sympathies. This changes once she is reintroduced later in the novel as an embittered middle-aged woman, trapped in a marriage with a man who physically repulses her. Lizzie's return in the novel finds her impertinent to her husband's authority; she is demanding, independent, and unwavering in her place as mistress of her own plantation. As a result of defying her husband and forcing her way onto a purchasing trip, Lizzie is in the position to personally bid on Amelia at a slave auction. The text's ambivalence toward interracial relationships comes from Lizzie's cold dedication to slavery. Not having shared her friend's sympathy for the condition of slaves, Lizzie develops a sudden interest in Amelia (whom she renames Passion)—a puzzling and intriguing part of the text.

Lizzie says,

"Everything else was a blur to me. I do not know what life was before that moment. My heart's rhythm had started over, and, despite the rain, the sun burst wide open with brilliance. Before me stood something not from this world, something too beautiful for any man to ever destroy. It was beyond beauty for me. It was something I'd never in this lifetime seen. All loves I had known, at that point, never mattered to me because it was clear to me that I had never known love. There was nothing left in my soul . . . A hush fell upon the room where for me, passion entered." (184–85)

Lizzie's declarations of love go hand-in-hand with the insistence that her love object is an object in the basest sense of the word. The entire passage uses "it" to refer to Passion (Amelia), demonstrating the contradiction between her feelings and her structural relationship to Passion. Words like "true love" become suspect when she cannot bring herself to admit to Amelia's humanity. Lizzie's inner thoughts highlight the contradictions between feeling love and buying another person. While the other stories focus on the fantasy of love, *The Highest Price for Passion* centers on the concomitant existence of love, desire, and property. As Lizzie is wracked with the force of "true love," Amelia is experiencing the brutal humiliation of the auction block: "As he glided his hands across my back, I felt filthier than the dirt underneath my feet, and the feeling heightened when he slide his finger down my spine. Leaning into me as the crowd watched him continue to molest my body before their eyes" (189).

Lizzie's desires for Passion enable the text to portray a queer twist on the jealous mistress. Lizzie kills her husband in a jealous rage and enlists the help of Passion and another slave to bury his body. She is just as brutal as the slave master and jealous of her own husband's affections toward the slave. Brown weaves a commentary into the novel through the character's voice:

"When I saw him laying there with Passion, I can't explain what rushed through me. My feelings intensified when I thought of him touching her. I had seen them many times at night together, and, while my instinct as a wife should have been to be angry with her for imposing upon our lives, I was angry with him for touching and loving on something that was mine. For months I had watched Passion and found I desired her. Having never felt that way about another woman, particularly a servant, I sent my emotions into a hatred toward McKinley for not being the man he should have been to keep me from thinking of her that way." (231)

Lizzie's "instinct" as a white woman to maintain her position as the mistress of the house is overpowered by her jealous rage that her husband has usurped her sexual dominion over her favored slave. In this moment, the text presents Lizzie and McKinley in a "battle of the sexes," or between competing white regimes of power: Lizzie is a strong white female character struggling against female oppression, and McKinley is the white patriarch who is determined to maintain control over everyone in his purview.

The Highest Price for Passion includes a graphic sex scene that focuses on Passion's orgasm but that is told from Lizzie's perspective. Unlike the heterosexual discourses of slave women's seduction that Hartman outlines,[105] Lizzie is neither concerned with Passion's willingness or consent nor interested in Passion's enjoyment, but she is surprised that Passion responds to her touch:

> "For several moments she resisted me. To my surprise, I watched her empty glare become a reflection of ecstasy as she began to move her body in rhythm with the motion of my fingers. Her sporadic gasps turned into consistent moans. . . . Seeing I was not giving up, she eventually gave in and combined the movement of her lower body with my wet forces. In that moment, we no longer existed as mistress and servant but as lovers." (235)

Like the protagonist in "Miss Hannah's Lesson," Lizzie assumes that the moment of orgasm obscures the racial structures that brought them together in the first place. Her assertion that they are no longer bound by the legal distinctions of owner and owned is rendered absurd by Passion's forceful refusal to accept her structural relationship to Lizzie as anything but abhorrent, despite her pleasure during their sexual encounter. Passion describes their relationship as coerced, yet pleasurable, which is in opposition to Lorde's sense of connectedness. Passion says, "I am not going to say I have been comfortable with the things Missus and I do, but there have been times when I did what I need to do to just hear her say that she would set me free one day" (238). Part of the pleasure that Passion receives from Lizzie is based on her enjoyment of the hope of freedom, yet Passion's moments of sexual release are never confused with legal manumission. She clarifies that "[d]espite what she and I shared in bed, it never changed the fact I was her slave, and, until Negroes were free, that was the way it would always be" (240). Unlike Sarah, Passion shares sympathy and desires with other Black people who also share her condition. She attaches clearly her present and future to that of the other slaves, thereby distancing herself from a politics of exceptionalism. Passion yearns for Lizzie's demise and openly argues with her, calling her a liar and disputing her claims of love (241).

Ultimately, the novel suggests that slavery was an institution of passions gone awry. It therefore represents these passions as an entanglement of contradictory desires. The most complex rendering of the relationship between desire/power/resistance and emancipation comes from the poem in the novel's prologue. Written from Passion's perspective about her relationship with Lizzie, the dialect is interestingly inconsistent with the character's voice in the novel. As the daughter of a white woman, Passion (who starts life as Amelia) learns to read and speak in Standard English and only mimics the speech patterns of the other slaves in the presence of whites, as a method of survival (114). It is as if she is two different characters: the relatively educated daughter of the upper class and the oppressed slave:

Straddlin' missus lap with her head pressed against my chest
I hear the voices of the slave catchers
Hooves of the horses beatin' against the earth below
My heart runs with them as she touches my breast.

Missu's hands glide 'cross my skin like molasses
from a tree
She breathes like a bull runnin' wild
Tearin' into my flesh with her tongue
She whispers empty promises to set me free.

Up against her I move with the fire nobody but the
devil put in my soul
I try to fight her but I can't win
With soft kisses against my neck
Missus reminds me who is in control.

With her spirit wrapped 'round me
I feel somethin' that make her feel almost human
to me.
But she give that to me like rations
She say when and she say where
The love starts and where it end.

The only thing I have that is truly my own
Is the name my mother gave me.
Missus asked me if I would bleed for it
Her nails buried in me like the whip
Crackin' my flesh leavin' me scarred forever
Then one night while the devil danced in the
moonlight
Missus, whose skin was both pale and ashen,
Stripped life from me by telling me
My name is Passion.

Passion's slave-self speaks here with a level of irresolution not shown in the other neo-slave narratives. The first three stanzas describe the sexual encounters between Passion and Lizzie. For Passion, their contact is a mix of pleasure and disgust, compassion and disappointment. Far from the diversion and enjoyment depicted in the sex scene between Sarah and Miss Hannah in "Miss Hannah's Lesson," for Passion, contact with the Missus's body triggers the memory of "the voices of the slave catchers." Arousal merges with imagery of torture and fear as Passion associates her heart beating with running from the slave catchers' horses and Miss Annie's nails in her flesh "like the whip." The poem suggests that Passion finds some relief and hope in their interludes, and she is powerless to end them. Lizzie coerces Passion into their arrangement with empty promises of freedom in exchange for her sexual service. Passion's awareness that Lizzie's pledges of freedom are hollow precludes her from also finding their encounters sensual, as she responds to Lizzie's touch and kisses with a "fire" inside of her. With every act of revelry or comfort, there is a concomitant constraint. Lizzie combines "soft kisses" with control, rationing her vulnerability, making full use of Passion as a piece of property: "she say when and she say where / The love starts and where it end." Ultimately, their relationship leaves Passion "scarred forever," both in the sense of Lizzie literally marking her and in the sense of figuratively taking away her name, replacing it with a reminder of ownership.

However, the novel does not completely break from the conventional rendering of the mulatta figure as inherently beautiful and virtuous. Passion appreciates her own physical attributes from completely within a white value system without any self-reflection. She says, "I had grown into a lovely, young woman with piercing blue eyes like my mother and had straight, black hair that waved when it was hit with water. My nose was slightly large and rounded at its tip, and my cheekbones were high like my Mother's were" (111). Passion plays her own part in the melodrama as the saintly, light-skinned defender of the weak as she puts her own self at risk to protect Lizzie's husband, McKinley. "When I tried to help Master, the missus backhanded me and sent me falling to the floor, but I got up and went back to his side" (227). She is protective of anyone who is vulnerable, even a slave owner. As the novel's light-skinned heroine, she maintains her status as morally righteous in the face of the mistress's reprehensible acts.

The novel ends neatly, with all villains getting their due, in the tradition of early neo-slave narratives. Lizzie is disqualified from her husband's fortune due to her duplicity as a bigamist. Passion returns to her mother's plantation after the Civil War and is reunited with her mother and her brother, Quincy. True to the redemptive twists of nineteenth-century neo-slave narratives, Passion's mother, Miss Annie, returns at the end of the novel to have been miraculously saved and taken to the North, where she is reunited with Josiah. Upon learning of the marital fortune of her old friend, Lizzie responds, "I always figured she would marry a nigger," thus clenching Lizzie's role as the novel's unredeemable villain (233).

Lizzie's representation as unredeemable in *The Highest Price for Passion* is emblematic of the differences and anxieties about the present political realities in each text's portrayal of the past. Lizzie's character represents a deep ambivalence toward the ideal of white female solidarity against an overwhelmingly homophobic, anti-Black society that Clarke envisions. As an unrepentantly racist white mistress, Lizzie is neither less desirous of her slave, nor less hopeful that shared intimacy and sexual pleasure will allow her to resist structural inequality at the moment of orgasm, than the sympathetic mistress of "Miss Hannah's Lesson." Interestingly, they both share the fact that they do not free the women that they purport to love. Even though they are approaching it from different perspectives, both stories suggest a history of the limitation of white female alliance. But what are the implications of imagining Black women loving each other in a profoundly anti-Black context? To begin to answer this question, I turn to SDiane Adamz-Bogus's "The Champagne Lady."

"The Champagne Lady"

This story is a departure from the others I have analyzed because it primarily deals with Bastua, the slave *mother* of a lesbian, and it only mentions the daughter in the last two pages. Despite being only ten pages long, it is a dense piece that manages to describe thirty-two years of plot in a compact form. It is the story of Lady, her mother Bastua (a light-skinned slave), her father Andy Colin (a slave owner and a philanderer), and Matt Engleston (Andy's friend and riverboat captain). The beginning is set "in a smoky, but elegant saloon . . . on the edge of the Mississippi River near Bayou Le Batre in Louisiana where trading and gambling gentlemen in the 1800s made stopovers between their travels" (1). Bastua is passed from one white male to another throughout the story. She is originally the possession of an unnamed white male who lost her in a bet with Andy's father. When Andy's father had tired of her, he gave her to Andy to use as he wished. The narrator states that the elder Colin "didn't have much use for Bastua in his old age, and he hoped his son was getting the elder Colin's money's worth" (1). Adamz-Bogus depicts Bastua as a classic tragic mulatta that is ruined for the Black world, never to be a member of the white world if she is abandoned by her white male owners. She is dangerously naive, trusting and loving Andy with delusional abandon. For example, even though Andy is already married to a white woman, Bastua approaches Andy "in full submission, with the assumptions of a new wife, a new wife's rights and promises, stability, and dreams" (3). She is rewarded for her loyalty with a betrayal, as Andy puts her fate in the balance of a wager with Matt. Andy bets Matt about the sex of Bastua's first-born child. If the child were a boy, then Andy would win half of Matt's shares in a steamboat company; if the child were a girl, then Bastua and the girl would be Matt's property. Andy loses the bet and Bastua and her daughter are transferred to Matt's estate, where Bastua passes as a white woman and his wife. Matt's adopted daughter, Lady, grows up not knowing that her mother is a slave. The only ones who know of Bastua's past are her two former slaves and servants, Mama SeeSee and her granddaughter, Belinda. In a postbellum scene evocative of *Iola Leroy* and *Contending Forces,* Matt, the white male protective patriarch, is killed, leaving the story's Black women vulnerable to being exposed as Black and, therefore, to losing their white privilege. At this point the story turns toward an unexpected climax: Lady falls in love with her servant, Belinda, a dark-skinned daughter of a dark-skinned former slave, and the ending suggests that the four women (Bastua, Lady, Belinda, and Mama SeeSee) will create a new future together.

The imagining of Black female-to-female attraction during slavery opens up the possibilities for restructuring Black (historical) imagination. The story's representations of skin-color divides between Black women are indicative of deep-seated separations within Black communities. Literary critic Mae Henderson likens Black divides to Dubois's "veil" as a "division within the race," the boundary "separating the speakable and the unspeakable."[106] By evoking light- and dark-skin color difference in relation to same-sex desire, "The Champagne Lady" represents the collective memories of Black women who love each other as an expression of an "imaginative recovery of black women's history."[107]

Ironically, it is the slave mother's awareness of her place as a "thing" and her suspicion of the white bonds of "family" (queer or not) that may be the crucial difference that opens a space for Black women to meet each other "eye to eye." In "Whiteness as Property" Cheryl Harris lays out the construction of the white racial category as bundle of rights that ensures the bearer "rights of possession, use, disposition . . . enjoyment and the right to exclude others."[108] Still, these rights are not to be equally shared among every holder of whiteness. In "The Champagne Lady" the mere "holding" of whiteness does not guarantee that one can participate in the full enjoyment and manipulation of its use.

At the opening of the story, the rituals of Bastua's conversion into white identification have already taken place through patriarchal succession and incest. She is the mulatta concubine of her owner and father, Andrew Colin Senior. When he tires of her, she becomes the "fast fascination of the younger

Colin [Andrew Junior] and eventually, his mistress" (1). As a trope, the mulatta figure on the one hand separates whiteness from biology, but on the other actually solidifies the white category. Her deployment is dependent on distinct characteristics that are *not* Black. As the quintessential tragic mulatta character, Bastua is "the perfect beauty" sitting like a doll, "silently, polite, trained and lovely to behold" (2). She has more mobility than other slaves, traveling with Andrew Jr., who shows her off to other white men, as he derives pleasure from watching her pass for white: "Andrew love[s] the ruse, the irony, the perversity of it . . . She loved her station as if it were real" (2). Andrew Jr.'s pleasure is the "perverse intimacy" of his power to exercise full enjoyment over his property. Her whiteness is his joy. However, she is aware that his pleasure and her material reality are not the same: "she was still a slave, some thing—not someone—[Andrew Jr.] could do with as he wished—trade her or sell or gamble her away" (2). Andrew Jr.'s pleasure from his absolute power over her makes her a "thing" in relationship to the whiteness that he owns in himself and in her.[109] Paradoxically, the use of slavery as a form of articulating these enjoyments actually reveals that whiteness cannot always be transferred.

Bastua attempts to maintain the illusion of whiteness for her daughter and transfer its privileges to her, but the "fact of Blackness" disrupts the lineage of white inheritance. Through a bizarre turn of events, Bastua becomes the concubine to another white man who allows her to assume the position of the "lady" of the manor. Naming her daughter "Lady" replaces the rituals of white conversion because she is born with an investment in white feminine identification. The infant–mother mirror process is reversed: the mother imbues the daughter with the white feminine ideal that she is denied. Bastua conceals their slave past from Lady, leaving her to believe that she is white. Once established, Blackness (corporeally evident or not) solidifies that one is permanently tethered to slavery; even if given a reprieve, there is always the potential to be captured. The deception is in jeopardy when the legitimate son of Andrew Jr. writes that he is coming to visit, thereby revealing Bastua as an illegal wife to Matt and hence the illegitimate heir to his fortune.

Despite all of the white-affirming dynamics of the rest of the story, the denouement of "The Champagne Lady" generates another set of possible relations between Black women, wherein socially "dead" dark-skinned Black women are desired and claimed by their "undead" light-skinned Black female counterparts. On the very last page of the story, faithful servants Belinda and her mother Mama SeeSee finally come to the big house, suitcases in hand, ready to abandon their passing white mistress. Their loyalty has lasted through slavery into Reconstruction until they, tired of the pretense of whiteness, prepare to leave the plantation at the first sign that the ruse may be revealed. Although the women have been silent throughout the text, the last scene shows their act of defiance.

In an act of desperation, Lady leaps from her chair and begs Belinda to stay with her: "What in heavens name has gotten into you Belinda?" In one brief moment the mulatta character finally acknowledges the dark-skinned women and her dependence on them. These heretofore-silent Black women give the story a denouement that calls attention to their narrative necessity. Silent and rendered to the back of the story, these dark-skinned women are the fictional foils on which white femininity is narratively constructed and maintained. Without their bottomless devotion, the necessary fictional scaffolding of the Big House cannot be maintained. There would be no one to do the work of the household in which the white and passing women live lives of leisure. Without them, there would be no plantation. In a melodramatic turn, Lady's gaze falls on Belinda, whom she relies on to help her interpret their rebellion, her "heart rac[ing]" with "her love for Belinda" (10). In her attempt to understand the new arrangements that would have to accommodate Belinda and Mama SeeSee's bold statement of resistance, Lady "became deathly afraid, an emotion she had only experienced when someone stirred as the two of them were locked in an embrace, a kiss, were naked together in bed" (10). Bastua speaks the final lines of the story: "Sit down Belinda. Have the servants take these bags back to your rooms. You need not run away. We shall face the truth together, face whatever is to come—together" (10). Bastua's invitation to sit down as equals with Mama SeeSee and Belinda is consistent with the endings of novels like *Iola Leroy*, where the light-skinned former slave owner becomes a member of the newly freed Black community. Of course, the convention of the classic neo-slave narrative is that heterosexual courtship and marriage act as a glue to hold together the emergent free Black community.[110] Adamz-Bogus's departure from the heterosexual plot device, and her deviation from white female partnership, open a space to imagine a Black lesbian past and future that is inextricably linked to other Black people.

Concluding in Reconstruction, the ending of "The Champagne Lady" promises that the new Black women who evolve into new relationships with each other and with a white power structure after Emancipation are ready to build their futures together. The fact that Belinda and Mama SeeSee are invited to sit down and work through issues as equals gives hope that skin color does not have to mean an insufferable and insurmountable void between Black women; they can have camaraderie, intimacy, and mutual desire for each other that open the "connections and crosscurrents" for rethinking race, gender, and sexuality.[111]

The end of "The Champagne Lady" is congruent with Audre Lorde's assertion in her essay "Eye to Eye" that Black women "can stand toe to toe inside . . . rigorous loving and begin to speak the impossible—or what has always seemed like the impossible—to one another."[112] Lorde's essay, written alternately in the first person and the second person, shares both a personal testimony and a direct address to a Black female audience that is, in turn, herself. She says, "I loved you. I dreamed about you."[113] Looking desperately for a reflection of self-love in another Black woman's eyes, Lorde envisions the mirror as a gateway to seeing and recovering Black women's self-hatred and externally imposed love of whiteness. She claims that all of the Black and female characteristics that make Black women irresolvably "worthless" and "not acceptable as human" in a white supremacist and misogynistic economy are exactly what would be "suicide" to deny.[114]

These fictional accounts of slavery are, among other things, an archive of Black women's desire for white female political solidarity that includes *giving up* the privileges of whiteness, which would lead to the dismantling of white supremacy. These are also an archive of the grief and anger that this desire has gone unfulfilled over time. In the following chapters, writers turn to other key points in Black diasporic memory, recasting the stories of Black communities and movements with queer central figures, thereby reconsidering the very composition of Blackness. As a vernacular epistemology, the neo-slave narrative urges a reconsideration of the known archive of slavery and of the psychosexual dynamics of the plantation to include the irresolute pleasures between slave women and the mistress. In subsequent chapters, the vernacular provides an opportunity for epistemological revelation. Embodied epistemologies, namely, the erotic and performance, emerge as sources for reimagining the Black body as available for more than endless toil for the profit of others and for connecting Black people within the boundaries of the United States and across the Atlantic. In the next chapter, I explore how novelist Cherry Muhanji uses the blues as an alternative episteme for creating communities and understanding gender identity and sexuality.

CHAPTER 2

Small Movements

Queer Blues Epistemologies in Cherry Muhanji's *Her*

> [Monkey] Dee entered the Chesterfield, went up to the bar for a drink and stood surveying the crowd. Suddenly his attention was attracted by the tip of a silver wing-toed shoe and white silk stockings emptying out from under white satin trousers. But the neck, lifting it like a pink flamingo, dressed as he was in a white coat with a dark pink handkerchief billowing from the breast pocket, a daring silk scarf, with bits of the same pink, draped from his neck. . . . Dee stood . . . forever ready to turn instinctively to him. And only to him.
>
> —*Her* 105–7

n the above excerpt from Cherry Muhanji's 1990 novel *Her*, a gay male pimp, Monkey Dee, turns his attention to Kali—by day a wife and mother, by night a cross-dressing "gay boy." Monkey Dee encounters Kali in Chesterfields, the local gay bar where performers sing the blues, a range of sexualities reign, and gender fluidity is the norm. *Her* is set in a working-class African American neighborhood in Detroit in the late 1950s and early 1960s. The novel's residents are primarily transplants from the rural South, "farmers turned factory workers" who, in the face of segregation and discrimination, have created their own counterpublic spaces, including gay bars where they can practice their newfound Black urban identity.[1] These characters embrace gender and sexual irresolution through the blues, an epistemology that explores gender identity and gives it meaning apart from anatomy or the expected constructions of "lesbian" and "gay" identities. This is especially evident because the main character's masculine gender transformation is *not* attributed to lesbian identification. In Muhanji's novel, Detroit's Black queer community enacts a blues epistemology of gender that communicates a collective sense of possibility despite the continued pressure to define one's gender according to dominant conceptions of the body and identity.[2] In the novel's descriptions of performance, the blues become an embodied and thus highly mobile and ephemeral archive of Black communal nurturing of and support for sexual and gender transgression, a theme that also continues through the next two chapters.

The bars, portrayed in the novel as blues spaces, are key sites for Kali's journey from wife and mother to "boy." Their presence in the text as spaces of queer sexuality and gender transformation also suggests that they are key to a queer understanding of migration. The novel reconsiders the African American Great Migration (1914–45), from the physical movement of southern migrants to northern and midwestern cities to a movement in sexual and (trans)gender possibilities. *Her* troubles the very categories and assumptions of migration as a geographic phenomenon enacted by normatively gendered subjects. Here African American migration becomes a transformative process representative of Black subjectivity in motion, a process that produces gender- and sexual-variant identities that blossom in the bars. It also presents Black queer kinship networks and communities as survival strategies to negotiate the transition to the industrial North and Midwest.[3] *Her*'s insistence on the post–World War II Midwest as a site of Black sexual and gender transformative culture also unsettles the historical narrative of Harlem as *the* privileged center of Black queer culture. *Her*'s focus on gender as a fluid construct in this midwestern urban setting suggests that gender transformation is a fundamental part of the African American migration experience *in general*.

The novel's temporal setting in the late 1950s and early 1960s also produces characters that are invested in the initial formation of a political Black identity based on the demand for civil rights. It portrays the transition from the African American Jazz Age's expressive insight on race relations to the political terrain of the burgeoning civil rights era, which was dominated by a discourse of rights. Muhanji's text suggests that the transition from expressive culture to rights-based culture required that Black people put aside the gender play and public sexual fluidity of the previous era in order to consolidate "authentic" and "appropriately gendered" political subjects.[4]

The novel's plot centers on the "blues people" of an industrial Black neighborhood in Detroit, referenced by its main street, John R. Street.[5] The main character is Sunshine, a young light-skinned woman who marries into a dark-skinned family and who recently arrived in Detroit from Alabama. Amidst hostility from her female in-laws, Sunshine gives birth to a son but is enticed to the street life by the fast cars, dazzling lights, hustlers, and excitement that she sees unfold every night from her bedroom window on John R. Street. Pushed to rage by the intimidating and antagonistic response she receives from her in-laws, Sunshine leaves her husband's home, reincarnating herself as an aggressive and trash-talking alter ego named Kali. Local nightclub owner and formerly famous blues performer, Wintergreen, provides a home for Sunshine/Kali and her child.[6] With Wintergreen's help, Kali begins to explore aspects of gender and sexual play through dressing in men's clothes in order to participate as a gay "boy" in the night scene along John R. Street. In the end, brutally beaten, Sunshine/Kali escapes and asks for assistance from the women on John R. Street. In the course of helping her, the women demand that Kali strip in order to prove that she is "truly" a woman and therefore one of them. At this point, all gender possibility and multiplicity are collapsed into normative representations in a reenactment of the closing of the archives in favor of respectable genders. In spite of the violent reinstating of normative gender at the end of the novel, Muhanji's detailed representation of the gender transgression supported in urban blues spaces of the queer Black community makes her novel unique in the history of African American migration narratives, particularly because it allows for a queer revision of the tragic mulatta, one of the genre's most enduring tropes.

Unsettling African American Migration Literature and Black Queer History

For the African American migrants whom the novel represents, mass migration in the twentieth century came from a political urgency to remove themselves from the oppressive conditions of the South. Popular accounts of African American migrants' motivations for leaving the South argue that the end of formal slavery ushered in a new phase of rural labor bondage in the form of sharecropping, while severe racist violence, epitomized by lynching, skyrocketed. The rise of violence combined with promises of higher wages and better working conditions elsewhere led to a mass exodus from the South. The period of time from 1914 until the 1930s is known as the Great Migration, but Black settlement in the North, West, and Midwest slowed down during the Depression and then climbed again after World War II.[7]

Muhanji (born Jannette Washington) is an African American lesbian fiction writer and scholar.[8] Her experiences growing up in post–World War II Detroit have been the cornerstone of her fiction, including the collection of short stories that Muhanji copublished with Kesho Scot and Egyirba High titled *Tight Spaces* (1987).[9] In African American literary history, *Her* is part of a larger body of work that represents mid-twentieth-century migration from African American women's perspectives.[10] Previous post–World War II migration texts by Black women, like Ann Petry's *The Street* (1946) and Toni Morrison's *The Bluest Eye* (1970), depict the city as sexually dangerous for Black women, precluding any prospect of sexual choice or gender play as part of the survival and coping strategies or as a mechanism for creating community. *Her* contributes to migration literature by reformulating the geography of Black South–North migration in terms of gender transformation and experimentation.

Literary critical readings of African American women's migration novels depend upon a twofold set of assumptions about the Black migrant: that the southern community is the authentic center of Black (women's) culture; and that the city has a destructive effect on Black domestic, sexual, and working lives.[11] In her 1999 book *Who Set You Flowin'*, Farah Jasmine Griffin discusses the migration novel as split into three stages: flight from the violence of the South, confrontation with the urban landscape, and navigation of the urban landscape.[12] In Griffin's configuration, the North is hostile and destructive to the Black migrant, leading to decay, alienation, and dissolution. Borrowing from Patricia Hill Collins, Griffin emphasizes the role of creating safe spaces in African American women's literature as a stand-in for the southern folkways that are invoked through family, the church, and the domestic sphere. The safe space is nurturing, healing, and a retreat—places in the city where "rituals can be enacted to invoke the presence of the ancestor in the North."[13] In the figurative sense, narrative safe spaces are resistant narrative forms, like songs, food, oral culture, and dream sequences.[14] Griffin configures a dichotomy between the city and the South in a way that genders the two geographies: the North is male—hard, uncaring, and unloving—and the South is female—nurturing, caring, waiting, and open for the migrant's return.

Other feminist critics have suggested that it is important to acknowledge the elements of the South that are effective and redemptive, along with the elements of the North that are creative and productive in African American migration literature. Feminist literary critic Madhu Dubey argues that African American literature critics' concerted focus on the southern folk aesthetic brings about a "discursive displacement" of the crisis in the literary representation of the city.[15] She states that "if black community is perceived to be irreparably fractured in the contemporary city, the folk domain of the rural south" is the only domain where Black community can be validated and legitimized.[16] Ann DuCille has also offered that there are many different ways in which to interpret African American literature, reminding us that folk traditions are not the only authentic source of African American women's literature or culture.[17]

As a migration novel that represents the city as a space of growth and potential for Black women, *Her* goes against the dominant memory of travel and migration as a Black male phenomenon. Angela Davis argues that "territorial mobility was a normal mode of male existence" in the post-slavery era, but the blues furnishes an affirmation for women to "keep moving" in their own right.[18] The novel's reliance on a blues epistemology is a reminder of blues women's legacy of travel, movement, and self-recreation in the North as well as the South.

Her also continues to question the perception that the South is the sole wellspring of Black women's culture. In fact, a major contribution of Muhanji's novel is to represent Detroit as a dynamic space for the cultivation of non-normative or non-fixed genders. Several characters are gender variant, from the "passing women" and cross-dressing butch lesbian bar patrons to the transwomen dancing for male patrons.[19] Through the use of the blues epistemology as a source of movement, transformation, and sexual agency, Muhanji's novel troubles the very categories and assumptions of migration as a geographic phenomenon of normatively gendered subjects moving from South to North.

Leaving the "Beloved Community" for Female Company

As a revision of the traditional African American women's migration story, *Her* does not allow for a nostalgic rendering of the South. The novel illustrates the historical literary critical nostalgia for "beloved community"[20] by presenting a complicated narrative of the South and the North that highlights the ambivalence Black migrants feel for each setting. The novel demythologizes the southern rural communities, recognizing that these spaces are rife with internal conflicts and restricted roles for Black women. *Her* also questions the classic literary gesture of representing Black community in the country while chaos and isolation characterize the city. The text raises issues surrounding the kinds of pleasures that are unavailable in the traditional configurations of southern Black female identity. It also speaks to how the South is unsuccessful in sustaining or taming "unnatural" pleasures. By focusing on these elements, the novel reveals how Black female desires are circumscribed by the southern legacy of the plantation economy, which relies on Black women's reproductive labor to sustain itself, even in the aftermath of slavery. As Barbara Omolade observes, "[E]ven after the end of slavery when the white patriarch receded, maleness and femaleness continued to be defined by patriarchal structures."[21]

Sunshine/Kali's mother-in-law, Charlotte, leaves her sisters, Lizzie and Laphonya, on the family farm to follow her ill-fated dream of having a singing career. The only sustained memory of the South comes from Lizzie and Laphonya, two of the novel's secondary characters. Their memories constitute the novel's only representation of southern blues. Unlike most accounts of northern migration in African American literature, in this story the sisters flee not only racist violence but also patriarchal control of their bodies. The "better life" they seek is contingent not only on jobs but also on the sexual and social company of other women. The novel characterizes plantation production as a destructive and "disfiguring" economic and social structure that warps Black women's sexualities and stunts gender development.[22] This repression creates a desperate and incestuous relationship between the two sisters. But when Lizzie migrates to Detroit because she cannot bear the shame of her incestuous relations with her sister, Laphonya follows because she cannot bear life without Lizzie. Together, the sisters leave in search of alternatives to a biological destiny of endless physical, emotional, sexual, and reproductive labor. They journey toward female company, companionship, and connection with other Black women.

The sisters are pressured into sexual relationships with brothers from a neighboring farm. Named after the thirteen original states of the United States, the Jones brothers represent the corrupt promise of America as a nation of self-creation. Lizzie, Laphonya, and the Jones brothers inherit a belief in progress through the cultivation of the land, a sentiment reminiscent of the early promise that emancipated slaves would receive "40 acres and a mule" to begin their new lives. Laphonya recollects their southern life as being primarily concerned with maintaining their land inheritance, which becomes synonymous with restoring patriarchal lines of succession. The future of the Jones farm was thrown into crisis by the lack of available women to bear "chil'rens to carry on they names" (69). Laphonya literally bears that burden by giving birth to thirteen children, one by each of the neighboring farm's thirteen male brothers. Laphonya remembers that "Lizzie and me wadn't about no marryin'. We was a-bout our farm" (67). Preserving Black economic autonomy and kinship is the primary concern of the sisters.

In their recollection of the South, since slavery had disrupted Black patrilineal inheritance, Lizzie and Laphonya were under family pressure to recuperate patriarchal kinship structures by producing children.[23] However,

Lizzie refuses the patriarchal right to her reproduction and denies "being owned and taken by any man, even if he had black skin."[24] Lizzie eschews any sexual encounter except as a means to bear a child, eventually choosing New Hampshire to be the father of her child. Black women within the rural Black community often defied the restrictions on their womanhood and sexuality.[25] For example, when her child dies, Lizzie removes her body from an economy of reproduction, stating, "[S]ince the Lord took the onlyest [child] I had. I ain't gon' bother no mo'" (68). Laphonya remembers, "Each brotha would go and try to convince Lizzie to change her mind. She say no. And I'd say, 'That's my sistah. I'll blow the first fucker's balls off who tries to take it'" (69). In fierce protection of her sister, Laphonya submits to populating the farm with workers who will carry their fathers' names. She becomes the primary sexual sacrifice to the demands of the farm. For Laphonya heterosex is an obligatory act for the purpose of maintaining their way of life; it is devoid of romance and pleasure.

The relationship between Lizzie, Laphonya, and the Jones brothers is the novel's first depiction of Black collectivity, which is contaminated with a legacy of gender dynamics inherited from an enduring plantation system that reduced Black people to laboring bodies and women to the reproducers of those workers.[26] For biologically female people, this labor process multiplies: they are workers in the field and in the domestic sphere, as well as physical reproducers of the labor force. Instead of a glorious "beloved community," the sisters recount a grim tale of serial childbirth through breeding. As noted in the previous chapter (and in subsequent ones), the dominant "mode of Desire"[27] is male use of Black women's bodies sexually, including in the field. There is no room for the sisters to articulate their own pleasure or desire. Laphonya is reduced to the basic physical functioning of her anatomy and the gross mechanics of heterosexual intercourse, while Lizzie cuts herself off from physical intimacy. The demands of the farm lock the sisters into a system of plantation labor in the sense of both the physical work they had to perform and the imperative to produce offspring to cultivate the land. Laphonya recalls how she chose childbirth over farm work, stating, "Farmin' ain't no life fo' no women's. Plowin' fields like a damn mule. . . . I ain't no mule" (68).[28] If she is not a "beast of burden" in the field, her only other option is to be a "mule" of domestic labor. Lizzie and Laphonya continue to operate in a plantation economy where the destinies of their bodies are governed by the dictates of agricultural work. Laphonya's motivation for heterosexual relations comes from a desire to have extra hands to work the farm, not to have male emotional or sexual companionship.

Cycles of reproduction and production are the options that the South offers the Black female body.[29] The environment of the farm circumscribes the sisters' access to other narratives besides work and reproduction. Despite the daunting task of farming alone, the sisters are unwilling to give up the farm: "How could Negroes leave they farm? The onlyest thang to own in the world?" (70). Laphonya asks the rhetorical question, "What was a body to do?" (68). To Laphonya, her body is in service of the land; she becomes like the earth itself, fertile and yielding to the farmer's hands. She cannot fathom that ownership of her body itself is more precious than owning a tract of land.

Laphonya falls into the same pattern of excessive childbirth that entrapped the Jones family's mother. In Laphonya's recollection of the past, she admits to being conscious of her similarity to the Jones family matriarch in her excessive production of offspring, exclaiming, "Well, I be damn! There I was repeatin' Sarah Jones" (69). However, she is unwilling to change her circumstances, believing it to be her fate, until Lizzie's planned escape from the farm threatens to leave her as the sole female presence. Desire for a break in gender roles creates a longing for female company. The sisters suffer from isolation—separated from the possibility of women lovers and cut off from heterosexual pleasures. Laphonya remembers that "[no] other women's would come to where we was stayin' fo' no length of time. They would come but none would stay" (69). As the only women in their closed world, the sisters hungered for female companionship.

Trapped on the farm without other women and faced with mechanical and reproductive heterosexual interactions, incest appears as the only viable option to resist their complete disintegration into sexual abjection. While Laphonya gives birth to thirteen children whom she does not care about, Lizzie and New Hampshire's only child dies at birth. When her breasts are engorged with milk, Laphonya relieves the pressure by sucking out Lizzie's milk. Lizzie and Laphonya's encounter is different from the lactation scene in the previous chapter, where the protagonist is invited to join white kinship. In *Her,* the sisters, already isolated, become enmeshed in an incestuous relationship.

Ostensibly, Laphonya sucks on her sister's breasts because, according to the customs described in the novel, men are not allowed into the birthing house before the quarter moon. For Laphonya the priority is that Black women's space and culture are preserved as inviolable and sacred. Rural women's culture (as represented in the novel) becomes the mechanism by which the sisters enter into a sexual relationship. But the erotics of their exchange in the birthing house haunts the sisters years later, as the two women share the same bed from the time they were children and continue to sleep together into puberty and adulthood and across the country from Alabama until the novel opens in Detroit. Lizzie recalls their sexual history with despair and regret. She accuses Laphonya of never caring "what the Lord say" (73). Laphonya responds by insisting that sisterly bonds supersede the laws of God: "I don't give two shits 'bout ya" (73).

In an effort to reconcile the experience without shame, Laphonya demands that they review the facts of the evening of the stillbirth:

> "What happen when a calf die, Lizzie?" Lizzie didn't say anything.
> "What happen goddammit!"
> "You git another calf to suck," Lizzie said under her breath. (74)

The incident takes place in the exclusive women's environment of the birthing hut, making a safe space for the two sisters to share erotic intimacy without the interference of men. Laphonya demonstrates her dominant role in the relationship as she badgers Lizzie into admitting that the procedure was necessary. To Laphonya, maintaining the integrity of the women's space is part of the natural order of things. She uses the example of the calf to illustrate to Lizzie that what they did was not deviant but part of farm life. Lizzie weakly responds that Laphonya could have gotten New Hampshire to suck out the milk. Laphonya challenges Lizzie's perception that the incident could have been avoided by saying that the birthing house "ain't no place for mens. . . . How we gon' act a fool and disregard everything we know" (74). Laphonya maintains the importance of the sanctity of local women's customs by refusing men's entry into the birthing haven. Laphonya's strict reliance on Black women's traditions is the conduit for her sexual bond with Lizzie. She yells, "You said git another calf to suck not a bull!" (74).

Lizzie's confession that men are inappropriate in the women's space and her acknowledgment of the incident directly contradicts her Christian beliefs, positioning Black southern culture as a powerful guardian that Blacks should respect and remember in the North. Women's folk traditions are no match for the power of Christianity, leaving Lizzie with a sense of debasement and shame. Laphonya reminds her that remaining true to Christian guidelines would have meant working herself to death: "Being good coulda cost ya yo' life" (75). Being good does indeed cost the sisters many hard and lonely years.

By leaving her children behind and traveling to Detroit, Laphonya escapes the restrictions of motherhood. Lizzie maintains her dedication to maternity, living in shame and regret and mourning the loss of her child, even in the North, where she is determined to deny any sexual feelings and refuses all nonreproductive sex. Laphonya, on the other hand, finally gathers the courage to pursue her own gendered and sexual identity in Detroit. Her moving away from the reproductive imperatives of Black plantation and patriarchal forces is a signifier for travel as a mode of freedom for a Black female subject.

If the South is a site of foreclosed possibilities, alternatively, the North is set as the opposite, where gender and sexual identities can be created. In *Her,* space explicitly structures social relations. Movement away from the rural South gives birth to the transformation of Black communities from agrarian, plantation cultures mired in the biological function of reproduction, to vibrant communities of people in control of their own sexualities, enjoying their desires and moving with the ability to define their own genders, at least in the closeness of the Black community. In the North, they find a version of blues culture that is distinct from the blues of the South, which Clyde Woods and others describe as being about resisting racial oppression.[30] In the blues spaces of the North, they find a place where nonconforming gender identities are part of everyday Black communal practice.

Blues Epistemologies of Black Queer Genders

With the influx of the African American population into already overcrowded urban areas came a rise in white anxiety about Black moral degeneracy. Southern migrants were blamed for a wide variety of ills plaguing northern cities, including alcoholism, venereal disease, crime, and "illegitimate" pregnancies.[31] Scholarship on these northern and midwestern communities labeled Black city inhabitants "immoral" and defined Black communities and families as "pathological."[32] The toxicity of the city was couched in term of patriarchal collapse, where Black women develop habits of being too "controlling and aggressive" and Black men are emasculated and absent, which breeds economic failure.[33]

Increasing panic surrounding the "breakdown" of African American families and the rhetoric of family restoration and community building may be part of the reason that representations of African American queer life have been narrowly circumscribed to Harlem and New York and have been set primarily during the period of the Great Migration. The period between the World Wars is also considered to be the peak of the Harlem Renaissance, when a new generation of Black writers and thinkers concentrated on the cultural expression of the bold and unashamed "New Negro" to articulate the terms of social equality.[34] Historians place special emphasis on the 1920s and 1930s in New York as the premier time and location for Black queer life and culture.[35] Because of this historical focus on Harlem blues culture in the 1920s and 1930s, it has come to exclusively symbolize Black lesbian and gender-transgressive cultures transatlantically.[36] *Her* upsets that assumption. While it uses Jazz Age Harlem as an epistemological resource and an inspiration for the continued exploration of Black genders and sexualities, it does not stop there. *Her* goes on to represent interracial bisexual relationships and complicated vectors of gay male desires.

The novel's post–World War II setting provides the opportunity to investigate the interaction between historical and cultural critical interpretations of queer Black culture, providing a context for the novel's heavy emphasis on the blues and blues culture. The development of American urban centers is often theorized as a constitutive element in the rise of gay and lesbian subcultures and gender transgression.[37] For Black women, this assertive stance is most frequently epitomized in the recognition of female blues performers. Audacious sirens such as Ma Rainey, Lucille Bogan, and Gladys Bentley enacted their sexual autonomy onstage, deliberately exploding boundaries of acceptable female public behavior by flaunting their sexualities in live performance and recording raunchy lyrics that flagrantly announced their sexual appetites for both women and men.[38]

The expectations of respectable domestic life are discarded in blues lyrics and in the lifestyles of female blues artists. Assumptions that women's lyrics would be circumscribed to deal mostly with male–female relationships, marriage, child rearing, and romantic love are contested by lyrics and performances that undermine a politics of respectability to make room for the expression of possibility. The queer traditions of great blues artists like Ma Rainey who, with songs like "Prove It on Me Blues," pushed the heterosexual and gender normative assumptions of the genre.[39] As Angela Davis argues, blues by women and women performers, lyrically and in the performers themselves, presented alternative principles of autonomy and movement.[40] For Black women, freedom of movement had a political urgency given the gendered responsibilities that bound women to the domestic sphere, marking a difference between Black male and female conditions. Demands of family and home coupled with the memory of chained and enslaved ancestors make mobility a prized privilege for Black women.

In *Her,* the blues occasions the creation of autonomous Black queer spaces and allows Black women to enact a politics of possibility through gender transgression. The text highlights the assumptions of "real" forms of gender, commenting on the illusion of "natural" gender before queer theoretical suppositions about the discursive properties of gender emerged in academic settings. A cornerstone of the novel's theoretical arc is an elaborate description of both male–to–female and female–to–male gender performance. The text not only expands notions of Black womanhood to embrace female masculinity, but it also challenges the reader to understand male–to–female (trans)femininity as an integral part of a constellation of Black womanhood.

The novel's innovative work of troubling the category of woman invokes the archives of the blues in order to recall the multiply gendered bodies that have existed as constitutive members of Black life.

The reliance on the terms "man" and "woman" for coherence and stability renders Black queerly gendered people virtually untraceable in the traditional archives. Gender-variant people are often misidentified as "lesbian" or "gay," misnamed according to anatomy instead of identity, or forgotten altogether, making it difficult to reconstruct the presence of gender-nonconforming people. The attention to the vernacular or "grassroots archives" of Black queer memory reacquaints the unintelligible with the intelligible. By this I mean that vernacular archives remind Black people of the structural position of Blackness as irresolvable in relation to dominant gender. The blues is the vernacular archive that the novel writes "with and against,"[41] contributing to an archive of Black lesbian fiction that both preserves and transforms the memory of the Midwest in the 1950s and early 1960s as embracing irresolution and affirming gender transgression.

Of course, the North has its own patriarchal traps and residues of slavery, one of which is the domestic sphere and its expectations of maternal fidelity and sacrifice. Another is the virulent antagonism between Black women based on skin-color hierarchies. The novel situates the blues space as an alternative to the drudgery of the domestic and the concomitant gender binaries in heterosexual and patriarchal structures. It is also a space where Black people can reinvent and heal old wounds of jealousy and hostility structured by racist paradigms that created a light- and dark-skinned split between Black women. The novel suggests that blues is a language *and* a practice that can facilitate the emergence of Black queer subjectivities and release them from legacies of slavery.

The novel's main protagonist, Sunshine, wants to break free of her bonds to the domestic sphere—as a wife and the mother of her "pretty brown" son—and enter into the leisure and "play" spaces of urban Detroit. Sunshine was instructed by her mother to reject working-class Black people as beneath her and to aspire to bourgeois status. Sunshine's first chance of escape came in the form of marrying Brother, the son of former Alabama dirt farmers Miss Charlotte (Lizzie and Laphonya's sister) and King Solomon. Her mother-in-law, Charlotte, compels her to find satisfaction in her domestic life and be satiated by her wifely duties of reproducing and raising another Ford Motor Company worker. Both options mean she must find pleasure in capitalism, either as the wife of the bourgeois capitalist of her mother's dreams or as the mother of the factory worker. Sunshine wants to escape the prison of domesticity and maternal obligation, feminine expectations, and matrimonial sex. It is not the rhythm of the Ford factory that propels her but the beat of the informal economy of the street. Sunshine/Kali is attracted to the bustle, language, tempo, and pulse of John R. Street and away from the deluge of domesticity and reproduction. Neither her worker husband nor her new infant son interests her. She is attracted to those who sell their bodies and peddle hope (numbers runners), to industrial workers like her husband and his family. During the day, Sunshine watches John R. Street bustle with workers still connected to their southern roots, symbolized by a figurative "umbilical cord . . . steeped in memory deep inside the psyche" that acts as symbolic "lashes and other chains" (40), tying these workers to the drudgery of labor. The "dislocated aunts went to the right with their leather shopping bags . . . and store bought shoes with the sides slit to release corns" (40). The men "went to the left, toward the plant. This time it was metal they picked, not cotton" (40). Reeling from the memory of the lash, northern migrants found themselves to be wage-slave laborers in another capacity.

Still trapped in her domestic cell, Sunshine watches the street at night, longing to be a part of the "black velvet star-studded night that ran along John R where the beautiful people lived and played" (36). She desires to be enveloped in Blackness, to walk down John R. Street in total harmony with the rhythm of the street, the flashing lights, and the hustlers. Captivated by the sounds of John R. Street's more colorful inhabitants, she trains herself on urban gender expression by watching the hustlers on the strip. The lives of the street workers and hustlers coexist with those of the performers and queers. The nocturnal street life seduces Sunshine into a distinctly queer realm. In preparation for her public life, she ventures into the alternative spaces of bars, where the red-light district and the residential areas collide. She watches the prostitutes, hustlers, and pimps on John R. Street, taking in the details of their clothing and mesmerized by the rhythm of their gender expression as well as their language.

> Sometimes, after Brother fell asleep and the baby was between pulls at her breast, she rose and looked out the window into the night. The black velvet star-studded night that ran along John R where the beautiful people lived and played. Lavish women in rhinestone face, queen lace stockings, and satin dresses that hugged wonderful asses, were all dressed up with everywhere to go! Some with smooth-talking pimps checking their early evening traps, their bodies silk-suited, hiding jewel-encrusted dicks. (36)

As Sunshine watches, it becomes clearer that in order to be a part of the life of the street, she must also become part of the gender play that she sees. Sunshine wants at once to be one of the "lavish women" and to be a "smooth-talking pimp." Her desire to join the displays of urban sexuality that she witnesses from the safety of her home demonstrates how the "ghetto" can be at once a place of violence and exploitation and one of play and pleasure.[42] Muhanji's Detroit is split between the "respectable" working-class domestic sphere and the public "ghetto" street life. The banality of industrial toil in the motor plants and the drudgery of housekeeping and motherhood are set against the ostensibly shiny and exciting life "in the streets." The fact that much of the activity at night on John R. Street takes place in the seedy underbelly of the city also makes it removed from sexual and gendered restraints.

Her anticipates transgender identity and drag stage performance as a primary site for theorizing gender, underscoring the illusion of "real" gender in brief depictions of male-to-female performers at a gay night club, a drag king competition, and a night at Wintergreen's featuring Black queer female attendees. The gay bar is Sunshine's first stop on her search for a gender identity other than what is available to her in the domestic realm. She uses the male-to-female performers as a model to understand femininity. When she does venture out into the nightlife, she goes to Chesterfield's, the neighborhood gay bar, wearing the same clothes as the performers in the bar, looking like "a satin doll with a wonderful ass" (38). When she tries to befriend the performers, they look at her with jealousy because their bodies could never be as "real" as hers. But what is an authentic woman's body, and how do you know it when you see it?

The physical differences between "real men" and "real women" become blurred, and therefore lines are drawn based on gendered practices of looking. What makes the patrons "men" is that they are entitled to penetrate scopically the transfeminine performers. Distinctions between the women that "real men . . . fucked and re-fucked before coming out for the evening" and the (trans)women in the "sculptured asses with the G-strings"(39) they see at the bar melt away as the patrons sexually desire the performers. In Chesterfield's, straight manhood is an iterative and scopic practice manifested by male patrons looking at the femininity that is produced for their pleasure. Kali's "wonderful ass" calls attention to the levels of performance and illusion in the seamless and nonqueer heterosexuality performed by the female impersonators and the male bar patrons, and thus the women performers reject her. Sunshine's time with the male-to-female performers at Chesterfield's precedes her transition to Kali, so she does not yet have the vernacular syntax to produce the gender expression necessary to become part of the life on John R. Street. Thus, the newly formed Kali (Sunshine's childhood alter ego) enlists the help of local blues artist Ricky Wintergreen.

Wintergreen becomes Kali's second mother. She is much more loving and caring than Sunshine's birth mother, Viola, a light-skinned "Georgia peach" who resented living in the "housing project on the near east side of Detroit" (17). Viola is particularly vigilant of the way Sunshine speaks, berating her daughter for any signs of Black vernacular expression. She screams at Sunshine that "only niggers use *be* for everything. I *be* this and I *be* that. You will not!" (16). By prohibiting Sunshine's Black cultural expression, Viola forces Sunshine to push her Black consciousness into herself. All the conditions are ripe for a "tragic" tale of mulatta displacement, but instead the story takes an unexpected turn into queer revision.

In her loneliness and pain, the child Sunshine looks into her mirror to find her anger incarnated as Kali, who "spoke from the mirror with a vengeance" (16). In the mirror Sunshine sees an ideal self that is culturally proficient in Black vernacular. Kali ignores Viola's dictates against Black English and uses it to defend Sunshine and carve a place of belonging in his/her Black community. Without Kali's ability to manipulate Black vernacular culture, the other children consider Sunshine a "freak" among them. Sunshine's performance of Kali provides her with the linguistic dexterity to play the "dozens" with her classmates; an act of signifying that eventually leads her to her Black alter ego and to taking on a queer identity. Sunshine's "mirror stage" of development results in a splitting of her being, and she turns *toward* working-class Blackness, which she accesses through queerness.

This desire for Blackness is a considerable departure from the assumption that whiteness is the preferred identification for everyone, especially light-skinned Black women. The embrace of Blackness by a light-skinned literary protagonist inverts the representation of light-skinned Black women as self-hating embodiments of successful white identification.[43] Making Sunshine's ideal image a Black one resists the interpellative process that requires that Black women displace their anger about the hatred they encounter in the world by incorporating it within themselves "like daily bread" and onto each other.[44] According to Lorde, Black women absorb the loathing that comes from external sources. In order to neutralize it within themselves, they enact a "catabolic process . . . that [leads Black women to] shed each other's psychic blood so easily."[45] Sunshine's ability to look within and love the Black self that she sees in the mirror is an important developmental shift that keeps her from destroying herself through a hatred of Blackness.

Sunshine escapes tragedy in two ways: by conjuring an alter ego who is deft at negotiating and navigating Black cultural language, and by finding an alternative light-skinned queer Black "blues" mother who nurtures her Black cultural dexterity and identification. In the novel, gender play is an effective way for light-skinned women to participate in Black vernacular culture. Sunshine's search for a place in Black culture becomes synonymous with ambiguous gender identity. She finds sympathy and understanding from an older, light-skinned blues singer, Wintergreen, who remakes Sunshine into her own image, building her into a "boy" and providing her/him with the language of fashion to express her queer gender. By helping to transform Sunshine into Kali, Wintergreen is also resurrecting a lost part of herself, for she too crosses gender and sexual lines.[46] For a second time the protagonist faces herself/himself directly in the mirror: "Kali turned slowly and said, 'I look like a boy.'" Wintergreen responds, "No, you look like me in Paris in '24" (92). This comparison suggests that masculine gender genealogies do not necessarily flow from a male "original," but that gender is always already a copy of a copy, reiterated through various forms of embodiment.[47] Kali is both girl and boy. His/her masculine expression in white satin trousers and matching shirt is a reference to how the masculine is often touched by the feminine but is still legible as masculine, or what I call feminine masculinities.[48] The pronouncement that Kali is "like" a boy suggests that this is not a complete transition from female to male but part of a nomadic expedition that does not have a definite ending. Kali's transformation into a "boy" is possible through the blues because it provides the cultural code for that gendered possibility, and Wintergreen is the conduit. She supplants the formerly cold and uninviting reception Sunshine had from Black people as a child with the promise of a warm reception of "family"—a term used to signify queer life. Just as Sunshine's identity is in transition, so are African American culture, community, and family formations.

Wintergreen inaugurates Kali "into the life" (an African American term for street life in general and lesbian and gay culture in particular). "Into the life," in this novel, specifically means into a blues ancestral line. Wintergreen's reconstruction of Kali into her own gender and the ambiguous blues performance style of "Paris '24" exemplify how the novel maintains the blues as the ancestral house of African American queer iconography. Even though the late 1950s and early 1960s inaugurated the rise of the Motown sound in Detroit, the novel's only musical references are to female blues singers like Big Mama Thorton, Ma Rainey, and Big Maybelle. Wintergreen's status as a former internationally known blues singer who now lives in obscurity is a reference to the archive. Her "lost" career parallels historical renderings of Black bisexual, lesbian, and gender-transgressive life that exist primarily in recollections of blues singers like Ma Rainey and Gladys Bentley, yet these recollections virtually disappear in discussions of Black life after the 1940s.[49] Therefore, the blues of the 1920s–1940s are the principal mechanisms by which Black gender-variant and female sexually transgressive cultures still exist, but as a singular phenomenon. Thus, as an eruption of queerness, the blues becomes an important iconic reference for Black lesbian, bisexual, and gender-variant culture and communities throughout the diaspora.[50]

Not only is Kali's gender a nomadic expedition into an indeterminate ending, but so is her/his sexuality. Kali's transformation "into the life" is temporarily rewarded with desire from Monkey Dee in the scene that I quote at the beginning of the chapter. Although Monkey Dee's desires include unwillingly incorporating Kali into his stable of prostitutes, their connection leads us to consider female masculine identities that are not associated with woman-to-woman sexuality. Monkey Dee's attraction to Kali gestures toward how gender variance is also a potential challenge to homonormative expectations. Kali and Monkey Dee are a brief but important historiographical commentary on female masculine genealogies that are assumed to be lesbian but that actually elide the cross-queer desires between transmasculine people and gay men.[51]

Sunshine/Kali is a vexing figure of gender variance. Having firmly established herself into Blackness, this mulatta figure journeys into a space where racial identification is not the only quandary; gender is another point of border crossing and boundary remaking. *Her* deploys the mulatta figure in order to enact a radical Black renaming at the point of regendering. Sunshine refuses the patronymic, becoming instead that creative figure of self-invention who writes a "radically different text" for Black empowerment with her own imagination.[52]

Bitches Bite Back: Blues Spaces and Performing Black Memory

Black queer signification converges in the queer ritual of gender performance in a distinctly working-class African American setting epitomized in the novel's "Bitches Bite" drag performance. Here, the participants comment on and play with the signs of race and gender that delimit and define them. The performers and audience alike—a gathering of femmes, bulldaggers, lesbians, and "passing" women—consciously build epistemological practice based on collective solidarity, mutual recognition, public commentary, and creative remembering. The Black queer signifying in the text does double duty: it is in conversation with queer theory that would suggest that gender is signified through repetition, and it shows that race (and racial belonging) can also be resignified through gender.[53] Kali's search for Black belonging takes her to the queer bars, but Wintergreen, a light-skinned person herself, recognizes Kali's attempt to disrupt racial categories through gender. Wintergreen successfully removes herself from the "wasted venom" of dark-skinned women who sneer at the lighter-skinned patrons of her nightclub through her gender-bending blues performance (82). Wintergreen performs as a dandy in masculine clothes with feminine accents:

> Some nights she wore a shirt and tie—hair slicked back, cigar lit. Pulling the sleeves of her jacket up, she'd play a Fats Waller piano like nobody's business. Or she'd sing the Blues, and the diamond cuff links, odd-shaped buttons emphasizing long, slender fingers, dazzled the eyes and picked up the glint from bridgework behind the blue smoke. (82)

Her extraordinariness leaves other Black women feeling lacking but protects her from their jealous pain and anger. Reminiscent of what Sunshine lived through on the playground, the dark-skinned adult women who frequent Wintergreen's Club and watch her performance with envy "whisper among themselves, turn[ing] their collective bitchery outward, saying things like *She thinks she cute* or *Half-white heifer!*" to the light-skinned patrons (82). They do not dare say this to Wintergreen herself, finding safer, less popular targets and thus "echoing once again the division between Negro women" (82).

Wintergreen's masculinity acts as a protective shield, allowing her to "feel sorry for the hi-yellahs and light browns," who were "slap[ped] across the face" by color-instigated insults, but she remains separate, convincing herself that "this was not her battle and she would have no part of it" (82).

Wintergreen navigates this morass of color difference through her own queer performance and by facilitating Black queer community formation through female-to-male drag performance. Once a year Wintergreen's Club is transformed into "Girl's Night In" where Black women in the neighborhood can perform and critique racial masculinities in the "Bitches Bite" drag king competition. The drag stage performance becomes a primary site for theorizing gender, underscoring the illusion of any so-called real classification. The contestants arrive in the personas of dictators, performers, and male jazz and rhythm-and-blues stars: "Women would line up outside to watch as Julius Caesar, Bo Jangles, Billy Eckstein, Houdini, or Satchmo emerged from sleek cars. The Kodaks went wild" (127). Figures of Caesar and Houdini mock white male power and privilege. The United States is recast as the Roman Empire, and its authority is parodied in the form of Caesar himself, who represents the raw force of American racial dictatorship. The practice of parody also recognizes the limits of white male power. The crux of the competition relies on the performer's ability to remind the audience of the trope and then to critically comment on it in the performance.

In this way, "Bitches Bite" is a hyperbolic display of masculinity and power that serves to temporarily contain patriarchal domination.

While some consideration is given to the performers' enactment of race and gender, the bulk of the description is focused on the actions of the *audience*. It is the speaker or actor himself/herself and his/her ability to manipulate the play of differences between cultural texts that is prioritized. It is this "willful play" that fascinates the audience.[54] As African American musical scholar Samuel Floyd points out, "the *how* of a performance is more important than the *what*."[55] The subversive power of the performance is rooted not so much in what happens onstage as the momentary affinity of the shared experience of the performers and audience, but in the communal agreement that they can all be any gender they want anytime during the evening. The climax of the scene occurs when an impromptu blues performance erupts, indicating that Black gender expression functions improvisationally.

The porous boundary between the audience and the performers creates communal bonds and memories beyond the yearly event. In the world of the novel, blues spaces are the center for Black queer transformation from the South to the North. Because of the isolation and the limited opportunities for queer community, Wintergreen's Club functions as a "safe space" for a variety of queer folk to live and be remembered in ways that they never could in the rural communities described earlier.[56]

> Each fall, Wintergreen's was the place to be. A place for women who were unable to tell the lyin' mothafuckahs they lived with—or the women they didn't—that being who they couldn't be most of the time felt good . . . Then, too, there was the nightly collection of "blues" women, like Lucille, who didn't *have* nobody, didn't *want* nobody . . . There was Joey, her bluesy self dressed in three-piece-wool-worsted suits, who placed her pinstriped trousered leg and short leather boots between the unsteady legs and high heels of young girls, turning them on and out. (128)

Wintergreen's Club is described not by the details of the décor but by recollections of the repeat customers in a litany of personal information. As opposed to the detached voice of history, intimacy is the narrative frame for memory. At strategic points in the novel, such as this one, "woman" is replaced with "blues woman," summoning multiple racialized queer meanings along with the definition of "woman." The blues is epitomized in the gender transgression and queer desire of the bar's patrons. Joey's three-piece suit is an expression of her "bluesy self" that only has support and dignified meaning inside Wintergreen's. Muhanji's use of the term "blues woman" inserts gender as part of the legacy of the blues as an embodied epistemological practice. In the safe space of Wintergreen's, the blues women seek solace and confirmation away from the gendered, sexual, and racial ideologies that degrade, belittle, deny, and reject who they are. In contrast to the biological determinism and desolation that the sisters find on the family farm, the women of Wintergreen's Club find comfort with each other in a space that they control, even if momentarily. In this way the club is a counterpublic space that "contests the dominant public sphere" and creates another liminal public space where inhabitants can be remembered on their own terms.[57]

The final performance of the night involves the incorporation of Laphonya, one of the sisters from the rural farm, in a rousing and raunchy impromptu duet with Wintergreen. The "Bitches Bite" chapter actually begins with Laphonya sneaking out of her sister Charlotte's house to go to the club.

> Laphonya was moving down the stairs as quietly as she could, but the stairs . . . signaled Miss Charlotte from her parlor. The light came on so suddenly that Laphonya jumped. "Ya on yo' way out?" [asked Charlotte] . . . Laphonya's short hair was brushed back and the overhead hallway caught its hint of red color. Annoyed, she asked, "Come again?" She wore a shirt and necktie, a jacket with a vest underneath, and a chain going in and out of the vest pockets on either side, and a long skirt and high boots. (129)

Dressed in classic butch lesbian attire, Laphonya's move from Charlotte's home (a symbol of middle-class domestic propriety) across the street to Wintergreen's Club (symbolizing Black queer cultural expression and gendered possibility) signals the potential for self-creation that exists in the city. This type of movement, while only across the distance of a city street, recalls the large-scale movement of a mostly rural population to an urban center.

Play and pleasure are incorporated into Laphonya's life via gender transformation. Wintergreen adds vocals to Laphonya's music in a dialectical interplay between the two women.

> Wintergreen [appeared] upstage in a purple strapless, standing by the piano, smiling . . . Laphonya . . . grabbed the mike. "Now that's hot!" The crowd whistled and stomped. Then Laphonya, thumping the guitar and keeping time with her right foot, began to sing—making it up as she went along. "Now ain't that a pussy? Da, da, da, da, da. Now ain't that a pussy? Da, da, da, da, da." Wintergreen got in the mood of the thing and seated herself at the piano. Reaching to the side, she picked up the sax

and began trading eights and singing in response: "Now this is a pus-say? Da, da, da, da, da." (132)

From the moment Wintergreen steps onto the stage in her "purple strapless" dress, the audience, "whistl[es] and stomp[s]," expressing their approval of her physical presentation as well as their anticipation of the woman-to-woman sexual tension between her and Laphonya.

The cultural memory of racialized gender signification is produced through the body, created and witnessed in this novel through the blues moan, the grunt, and the swerve of the hip. In this scene Muhanji demonstrates how the blues is "queered" not only by the lyrics, "ain't that a pussy," exchanged by two women, but by the interaction between performers and audience. Call-and-response operates both from within the music itself in the form of exchange between performers and between the performers and the audience. The lyrics "ain't that a pussy" repeated over and over take the term "pussy" away from its sexist evocation as a marker of female inferiority (especially as an insult to men) to connote female-to-female sexual agency and power. The two terms "pussy" and "pus-say" add another layer of singularly Black queer signification, playing with words and rhythms. Laphonya's participation in the duet is also significant, as she represents how communal practices of the blues can resignify the body. Over the course of the novel, Laphonya has gone from a woman whose only function is to grimly reproduce agricultural laborers to a vivacious butch. In the context of the variety of gender expressions portrayed in the club, from the masculine "blues women" to Wintergreen's performance of queer femininity, the lyrics "ain't that a pussy" also highlight the limitation of biology to define gender. The "pussy," although a physical attribute of both the masculine "blues women" of Wintergreen's Club and Wintergreen herself, does not determine their gender identities. Together the sound, music, lyrics, costuming, and performer–audience interaction create an "intracultural, interdisciplinary aesthetic communication."[58] This exchange between a performer and audience members contributes to Black queer aesthetics that become part of communal memory.

By the end of the novel, however, this different deterritorialization of the Black body is set aside as the protagonist is hailed back to gender coherence and stability. Once Kali turns to the collective Black body for support after she has been raped, the only way for the members of the community to recognize each other in a collective form is to return to gender conformity. Kali is forced to strip in front of a room full of Black women to prove that she is "like them." This turn in the narrative symbolizes the transition from

African American Jazz Age expressive insight on race relations to the burgeoning civil rights political terrain dominated by a discourse of rights that are dependent on normative genders and sexuality.[59]

Gender/Sexuality Masking for Political Expediency

The divisions between Black women dominate the novel's denouement, but the solution undermines the expansive politics and aesthetics of the rest of the novel. In the novel's closing pages, the multiple routes of Black sexual and gender identity are shut down or obscured to accommodate a more coherent and accessible narrative of true Black womanhood. In the final scenes of *Her,* the book resurrects a bio-logic of sex and gender that the rest of the novel had destabilized in order to establish the basis for collective action against Monkey Dee. Collective action is initiated through a ceremonial gathering of all the biological female residents of John R. Street. The gender play, ambiguity, and complexity evidenced in the other parts of the novel are suspended, suggesting that it is necessary to subsume difference under racial and gender coherence in order to promote action. This return to standard narratives is also a representation of how the archive closes, filtering out difference in the name of political expediency.

This traditional womanhood emerges in a meeting of the reputable female small-business owners of John R. Street who gather to help Kali. After consenting to be Monkey Dee's new "boy," Kali is raped and brutalized as a final act of "breaking" her into his stable of male and female prostitutes. The final scenes find Wintergreen and Charlotte organizing the neighborhood's women against Monkey Dee on behalf of Kali. Most of the women in attendance are characters new to the novel. Wintergreen personally invites these lower-middle-class pillars of the community to the exclusion of all the others. Gone are the "blues women" from the "Girls Night In" and the female impersonators from Chesterfield's who challenged, redefined, and exceeded conventional definitions of Black womanhood. In what is a return to a standard narrative, for the first time in the novel, Black women are described in terms of the accepted version of African American migration that the book had previously avoided:

> Most of the women here had been part of the first wave leaving the South. They had entered Detroit as young girls, and it disrobed them with cold hands. But they had beat this city at its own game. They owned businesses, some were their own bosses and, each in her own way, took no shit from anybody. (164)

Each lived the American dream, but had "paid the price" (164) through a disavowal of their sexuality. The description of their sexual denial is less than flattering. The narrator describes their sexual isolation and backwardness, chastising them for "languishing" in their respectability and for refusing their own "ripened sexuality buried beneath the eaves of the wall-to-wall urban living" (164). These new characters represent the accepted version of the African American working-class woman's success story. Within the confines of the story, these women are not asked to awaken their "curled up," "closed," and "decaying" (164) sexuality to embrace the gender-variant characters. Instead, Kali returns and must convince them of her/his worthiness.

Charlotte rationalizes the sudden discontinuation of a politics of inclusion and the reassertion of conventional divisions. Her moment of reflection on the need for a conservative approach surfaces when a few young college students arrive at the meeting; they are immediately rejected.

> Miss Charlotte watched the young women's faces as their minds moved toward dismissing the other women in the room. She realized that it would take many more meetings with these students to get them to understand the real history of Negro people. The playin' the dumb niggah, or the crazy one, or the lazy one, wasn't always so easy, but each role played bought time for the next generation, hopefully, to move easier in the world. Now here was the next generation with their accusing eyes, asking, "Why didn't more of you stand up to white folks?" And she had asked the same question of the generations before her. She now knew, unlike these young women, that there were no easy answers. (168)

Charlotte's inner monologue refers to the practice that Houston Baker has termed the "mastery of form," a rhetorical and embodied strategy of masking, deployed to promote a palatable face of Blackness to whites. It is a tactic of negotiation for the purposes of survival.[60] Charlotte employs what I call "gender mastery," a survival strategy that demands, even at the expense of one's dignity and identity, the erosion of previous commitments to multiplicity and gender variance. Charlotte and Wintergreen find themselves in a "tight place" between gender expectations and the desire to organize politically. They attempt to gain the acceptance and commitment of the other women in the room through a process of gender mastery wherein all gender and sexual differences are masked and subordinated to race. They try what Baker calls "strategies of attraction" to keep the audience "attracted" to Kali's story by referring to issues they are familiar with and to help them identify with Kali's plight.[61] Wintergreen tries to gain empathy for Kali by evoking her/his identity as a mother. However, this only reminds the women that Kali "fell from sugar to shit" (169) through prostitution, further distancing them from her/him. The other women reject Kali and refuse to act on her/his behalf against Monkey Dee.

The women's rejection indicates the limitations of the "safe space," which turns out to be only conditionally "safe." Although previously an enthusiastic cross-dressing participant in the "Girl's Night In," Laphonya is the first one to use Kali's gender against him/her. She accuses Wintergreen of fashioning Kali in her own gender-variant image. She says "Ya turned her out, Wintergreen . . . We all know that Kali was in Chesterfield made up to look like ya. Wearin' yo' clothes" (169). Her words imply that Kali's male identity outside the confines of "Girl's Night In" is an act of public gender trespass that deserves the rest of the community's consternation. In the final instance, the women's "safe space" is not safe for everyone but merely a method of containment and control of variant identities.

To the women at the meeting, Kali's "boy" identity and relationship with Monkey Dee means that "she was asking fo' it" (169). The other women do not see the story of Kali's abuse as a catalyst for activism. The women use accusations concerning Kali's fitness as a mother and her respectability as justifications for continued animosity between them and inaction against misogynist violence. The women are satisfied only when Kali reveals the "authentic" womanhood beneath her clothes that her bruised flesh evidences:

> She ripped the loose-fitting gown over her head and stood there naked, slowly turning her body around so they could see the black and blue marks that lined her back and buttocks. Then she changed her stance—bending, she stuck her buttocks out at them and rotated her body so they could see the unmistakable initials, M.D., branded on the side of her buttocks. (170)

At this point in the story, Kali epitomizes the vulnerable and violated female. Kali's gesture triggers another woman, named Mildred, to "remove her own clothes" revealing "small cuts made with curlicues at the ends—healed now into older scars. The letters M.D. were branded in several places down her sides and into her buttocks" (171). Kali and Mildred are branded as Monkey Dee's property, reminiscent of slavery and evocative of the plantation themes of Lizzie and Laphonya's farm. If the Black female body was decoupled from biological destiny in the earlier parts of the book, allowing for a new geography of gender and sexuality to emerge from the devastation of northern relocation, then it is returned to the biological yet again in the last pages of the novel. The ritual of exposure reduces the Black body to its biological function and returns gender to its biological destiny; Kali is female because she is raped.

With gender ambiguity carefully contained and Kali appropriately remorseful for her transgression, the women engage in a ritual of female bonding. Wintergreen and Charlotte's personal reconnection is the catalyst for the group of identified and identifiable women to collectively stand against Monkey Dee's attack on Kali. But more than an isolated revenge, their meeting is a precursor to feminist organizing and a testament to a new political subjectivity that integrates both gender and race into the goals of political action. The racial and gendered subjectivity inaugurated in their planning meeting requires that parameters for inclusion as a "woman" are firmly set and that the meeting participants are willing to identify with Kali to the extent that they see her as one of them and worthy of communal energy. A series of omissions, exclusions, and reductions are produced in the formation of their group identity and healing.

Triggered by the sight of both Mildred and Kali, the women in the room resolve to collective action based on gender solidarity. They initiate a symbolic ritual of Black womanhood that ushers in their cultural and feminist consciousness. The women evoke the sounds of the calabash, the drum, the "deep hum" and rocking motion necessary to commence their healing. In a highly stylized moment in the text, the Yoruba Orisha (deity) Oshun appears to the women in "a large looking glass [that] appeared in their midst. And, as they gazed into it, they could see a woman wearing yellow with a river threading through her hips" (171). Oshun's presence is understood because of the yellow in her clothing and the existence of the river—both symbolic of the Orisha.[62] The deity helps the women recognize how their color prejudice has made them untrue to their own African past, as Oshun is depicted as a light-skinned Orisha. The women reevaluate Kali's body and notice kinship and similarity where they had previously only recognized difference. "All looked long and hard at her pink nipples and understood that those nipples had sucked a black boy, just like theirs had" (172). The women's gathering births a collective subjectivity that is simultaneously rooted in African cultural formations and in feminist principles.

The end of the novel follows a pattern of strategic forgetting and reduction that parallels the formation of historical versions of the African American past. Squeezed into the tight space between possibility and traditional politics, gender play and sexual ambiguity are replaced by a more traditional rendering of the Black migrant experience framed by a restrictive, exclusive, and legible Black womanhood. Charlotte laments that the "real history of Negro people" relies on a system of tactical camouflage wherein African Americans have to hide behind certain prescribed roles of the "dumb niggah, or the crazy one, or the lazy one" (168). She contends that "each role played bought time for the next generation, hopefully, to move easier in the world" (168). In the meeting, they too have to master the form of female gender in order to construct alliances with each other. The meeting's dynamics reveal the narrow story of African American history. First we see the exclusion of people who may disrupt the category of woman on which the meeting is based, and then the tendency to adjust the narrative to accommodate an intelligible representation of Black embodiment and identity, excluding all those who do not fit that criterion.

Imagining Possibilities

Muhanji's creative re-envisioning of the migration novel references the known archive of the blues as a queer art form and places blues women and blues spaces at the center of the migrant Black community. The novel's blues spaces are locations for male-to-female performers and female drag kings to creatively express gender through performance. As an everyday practice of gender nonconformity and resistance to gender norms, the blues and the spaces in which it is played create a queer Black urban community in the novel. However, the work closes with the requirement that Kali reveal her anatomy to prove she is a woman. This return to biology signals the point at which gender fluidity and openness of the blues space shuts down in order to accommodate a rights-based understanding of what is political.

Her presents nonheterosexual and queerly gendered subjects who confound dominant notions of social identity circulated in African American and U.S. cultural formations. The text does so by employing vernacular rhetorical strategies that present possibilities beyond territorialized patriarchal imperatives that map migration as a process of maintaining assumed heteronormative genders and sexualities across space. The novel utilizes the blues as an epistemological practice that offers alternatives to the normative constructions of gender and heterosexuality—the supposedly established truths of African American history and culture. Performance and its spaces support the reconstitution of Black community based on non-normative sexualities and genders, thus facilitating a collective memory of Black queer culture.

The task of making it up or self-invention requires a reimagining of core Black communities. The work of Sharon Bridgforth takes us back to the rural U.S. South, this time with a cast of characters that remake the idealized southern Black community as a queer space. She also turns to the knowledge created through embodied performance to resignify the Black body along irresolute terms.

CHAPTER 3

"Mens Womens Some that is Both Some That is Neither"

Spiritual Epistemology and Queering the Black Rural South in the Work of Sharon Bridgforth

> deep woods crossroads/the dead   living
> it's a party.
> the dice is tossed . . .
> again
> drumming
> again
> drumming
> again!
>
> —Sharon Bridgforth, *love conjure/blues* 1–2

The opening lines of Sharon Bridgforth's 1999 performance novel *love conjure/blues* begins with an invitation to re-remember African American southern ancestors from the early twentieth century.[1] In Bridgforth's work, the South is a locus of Black queer life and the birthplace of Black queer identities and desires. The opening pages of *love conjure/blues* are emblematic of Bridgforth's ability to straddle poetry, drama, and prose simultaneously as a method for bringing the text to the crossroads of ancestral memory and spiritual practices. The space between the words "dead" and "living" suggests the break between dimensions or states of consciousness. In Bridgforth's work, the meanings of "dead" that I have been working with in this volume—in terms of physical and social death—come together as the characters represent the spirits of the past and remember the disremembered. As Jacqui Alexander suggests, the crossroads is "that imaginary from which we dream the craft of a new compass."[2] Trauma, ritual, and celebration are what bring the dead and the divine together at the opening of the novel. The phrase "it's a party in the deep woods" indicates that the setting for the action in the text will be a juke joint, a small, out-of-the-way club usually built by hand or barely kept from falling apart with love and prayers. Juke joints were constructed as a resistance to external impositions from racial and sexual regimes that regulated and attempted to delimit Black families, communities, bodies, and desires according to outside gendered and sexual norms.

Bridgforth has published two books of fiction written in verse and several plays, all of which are tributes to remembering the disremembered Black queer ancestors of the rural South. Her published work includes a collection of short fiction titled *the bull-jean stories* (1996) and the previously mentioned performance novel, *love conjure/blues* (1999). Bridgforth often directs (or "conducts," in her terms) her plays and performances, including her 2009 play *delta dandi*.[3] As an artist dedicated to dialogue between various forms, Bridgforth actually performs her books before they are published.[4] Trained as a filmmaker, Bridgforth was the founder, writer, and Artistic Director of the root wy'mn Theatre Company from 1993 to 1998. She is a cofounder of the writing and performance collective known as The Austin Project, started in 2002 in Austin, Texas.[5]

Bridgforth's commitment to the principle of body-centered knowledge in her work gives us an opportunity to see the fruits of her dialogue between embodied performance and textuality. Building on Diana Taylor's work on embodied performance as a repertoire—or the living, ephemeral document of the lives of those who do not have access to written strategies or formal archives—it is important to remember that textuality can also be an embodied practice and can work in conjunction with, not against, live performance.[6] There is no contradiction between the archive and the repertoire in Bridgforth's work, as she uses embodied knowledge to construct the written text and creates a performative text. As Meta DuEwa Jones suggests, there is a significant and overlooked oral, visual, and graphic component to jazz-influenced written poetry that could be considered part of a variation in performance style in itself.[7] I analyze the play *delta dandi,* alongside the texts of *love conjure/blues* and *the bull-jean stories,* to highlight how these forms connect as an archive of Black queer Southern ancestral memory.

Each of her texts depicts early twentieth-century rural life at the crossroads, blending poetry, theater, and fiction to imagine Black communities in the interstices of gender and sexual norms. The books and plays are epic stories of Black ancestral memory brought to life in tales of rural queer communities. Karla F. C. Holloway states that the presence of ancestors in African American women's literature is a "cultural (re)membrance of a dimension of West African spirituality."[8] Ancestral memory is literalized in Bridgforth's work as the characters, who themselves inhabit the world of the early twentieth-century U.S. South, are in direct contact with slaves, precolonial and preslave ancestors on the African continent, and recently deceased ancestors. The characters communicate with the physically dead through women who have knowledge of ancient African and native American medicines and through the blues space of the juke joint.

This chapter migrates back to the rural U.S. South in order to reconsider its potential as a queer space. In the previous chapters that examine neo-slave narratives and Cherry Muhanji's migration narrative, the rural South is a space that has limited representational possibility for Black desire of any kind. Both in Muhanji's novel and in the neo-slave narratives, Black desire (especially for other Black people) is circumscribed by the plantation economy, which has a destructive reach well into the twentieth century. Muhanji's novel suggests that not only does the early twentieth-century South signify the specter of racial violence, but it also is burdened with an invisible history of Black female sexual obligation that forecloses the development of desire between Black women. For Muhanji, the blues, and its concomitant expansion of genders, can take hold only in the generative setting of the North. Bridgforth joins Muhanji in reclaiming the blues as a gender- and sexually variant practice, but she extends its relationship to Black queer memory by situating the blues as a southern Black queer phenomenon as well as an urban one. This remaking of the South into a queer space is accomplished not only through the blues but also by creating a link to vernacular spiritual practices. Spiritual epistemology, as it emerges in Bridgforth's work, is centered on the communal practices of ceremony that are found in formalized, ritual spaces, but more often in the quotidian activities of the juke joint. The juke joint becomes an interstitial space where the physical and spiritual worlds meet, which encourages the elevation of the consciousness of individuals and the community through extended contact with the divine. The community in Bridgforth's writing extends beyond the material reality of the seen world into the realm of the spirit.

Bridgforth's work allows us to consider gender variance as part of the interstices of Black existence—the interior of what Fred Moten calls "the break" into the realm of spirit epistemology, or conscious contact with ancestral memory.[9] We will see in the next chapter that Jackie Kay examines the space between memory and death to sustain the trans narrative in *Trumpet*. Bridgforth relies on a situated spirit consciousness developed at the crossroads between the material world and the spirit world to sustain a both/and approach to Black genders without compromise. The recasting of Black genders is important given that conforming to gender norms is a crucial way that Black people mitigate "the permanent obliquity" of Blackness, or the open question of Black humanity.[10] As Sylvia Wynter has noted, Western epistemes are split between clerical/lay and body/spirit in order to maximize hierarchies.[11] Bridgforth rejects the separation of spirit and flesh as distinct and disparate sources of knowledge. Her work unites the ancestral knowledge of the divine with the flesh that was torn and ripped in the brutality of the Middle Passage and the plantation. The flesh, lacerated by the whip, provides crucial knowledge about Black "ungender[ing]"[12] which is the basis for what I contend is Black gender irresolvability under Western epistemologies of the human. However, according to West African cosmologies, the flesh, no matter how degraded by human brutality, is the conduit for divine manifestation in the material world.[13] Bridgforth's fiction and drama situate gender diversity at the core of Black vernacular practices through their diasporic connection to West African spiritual epistemology.

The Crossroads

In West African–based practices as they have reemerged in the Americas, on the other side of the Middle Passage, the best-known Orisha (or Lwa of Vodou) are often referred to as the seven African powers, which include both male and female spirits: Eleggua, Oshun, Ogun, Yemanya, Oya, Shango, and Obatala.[14] Each deity has dominion over a specific natural force (e.g., rivers, wind, lightning, the ocean) and also is generally represented on their altar by particular objects that reflect their powers and characters (e.g., peacock feathers, honey, watermelon, cigars). In Yoruba practice, and also Vodou, Santería, and Candomblé, the relationship between the human and the divine is directly negotiated through embodiment. The initiate or devotee is "mounted" or possessed by the Orisha. The human and the spirit are one. The Orisha speaks through their possessed host in a communal ceremonial context. According to these traditions, Eleggua is the deity that stands at the crossroads and facilitates communication between the human and spirit realms. According to Yoruba priestess/scholar Luisah Teish, "All ceremonies begin and end with Him; and no one can speak to any of the other powers without first consulting Eleggua. He translates the language of humans into that of the Gods."[15] Though Eleggua is traditionally associated with maleness and the penis, women including Audre Lorde have been known to be children or priestesses of Eleggua.[16] I read Eleggua in Bridgforth as a force of gender and sexual irresolution, opening up the crossroads for a queer path to the divine and broader possibilities for the interpretation of the Black body and desire. Henry Louis Gates Jr. identifies Eleggua as the figure of African American rhetorical trickstering in the form of the Signifyin(g) Monkey.[17] Lamonda Stallings uncovers an "underengaged phenomenon of trickster-troping in Black female culture that seeks to articulate various sexual desires."[18] In this body of work, the Eleggua figure emerges in order to open a corridor to the divine that unhinges gender and sexuality from the responsibility to adhere to dichotomous structures throughout the community; in Muhanji's work, the proliferation of Black queer genders eventually gives way to the bifurcated split between "women" and "men" at the end of the novel. Bridgforth's use of spiritual epistemology restructures Black gender roles and leaves gender categories open. Black masculinities are expanded to include mothering as well as collective caretaking. The feminine is especially associated with divinity, as feminine characters throughout Bridgforth's oeuvre are the ones who open direct communication with the spirit realm as well as function as symbols of West African deities themselves. In addition, several characters are both male and female, or masculine and feminine, calling attention to a bigendered segment of Black communities and complicating the boundaries between queerness and heterosexuality.

The following analysis moves between gender identities and gender presentations of the characters in all three works. Feminine characters in Bridgforth are often guardians of divine space; they are key figures that bring communities together with the divine throughout Bridgforth's work. The masculine characters are not as much conduits for divine communication as they are representations of the beauty and pitfalls of masculine identification. Some of the masculine characters, like Bull-Jean, exude emotional and sensual authenticity, while others are caught in a gender equation that associates masculinity with violence and abuse. All three pieces feature iconic feminine characters who are not only beautiful, but also powerful leaders in the community. The feminine main characters run the communal gathering places, which are blues spaces and also ceremonial centers.[19] Unlike early scholarship on the blues that claims it is a secular expression of spirituals, Bridgforth's work represents the blues as a diasporic, spiritual practice.[20] Her texts bring the blues, conjuration, and West African religion together in these visions of the South.[21] Bridgforth depicts the blues as part of a West African–based reverence for the ancestors that includes a pantheon of powerful deities.[22] This combination of blues and spiritual epistemologies allows the characters to defy the gender binary and express themselves in both masculine and feminine registers and/or to identify as both male and female simultaneously without retreating to the biological determinism that occurs in the final pages of *Her*.[23] By discussing the texts' various representations of gender embodiment, we see the power of Bridgforth's work to create a reimagined vision of the African American southern past as full of endless possibilities. Once ancestral memory is freed from the bondage of normativity, we are gifted with a queer vision of Black embodiment.

"Long Nail Girls": The Feminine Divine

In *love conjure/blues* Big Mama Sway is the headlining blues singer at Bettye's juke joint. Similar to the urban blues club in *Her*, Bettye's is a space for queer community creation and healing ritual. Big Mama Sway is the representation of the Orisha Eleggua in Yoruba in the text. Bridgforth's inclusion of a feminine representation of Eleggua as the crossroads figure, Big Mama Sway, suggests a queer understanding of divine energy, disaggregating male or masculine energy from exclusively male anatomy. This insistence on simultaneity is epitomized in Lorde's "biomythography," *Zami*, in which she expresses the desire to "be both man and woman, to incorporate the strongest and richest parts of my mother and father within/into me."[24] That Big Mama Sway is the Eleggua figure of the text is a departure from the way in which Henry Louis Gates Jr. situates Eleggua's command over "indeterminacy"[25] in his ability to connect the "sacred with the profane" and "text with interpretation" with his "enormous penis" and powers of copulation.[26] Big Mama Sway's movement from side to side opens the path to ceremony and emotion for the text's audience members. Consistent with Eleggua's power of *nommo*, or the word, the sound of her voice awakens the community to ritual, releases the pain of trauma, and connects them to the divine:[27]

> it was the sound of heat/perfectly pitched.
> heat so clear you could see yourself/past
> the seem-to-be laughter the thickened memories . . .
> packed tight woman carried you in her voice
> so deep between her notes till
> wasn't nothing left to do but stretch out in her sound
> and cry
> about everything there ever was
> cry (22)

Big Mama Sway's voice "unrumble[s] the earth" (22), creating an opening between the community, the divine, and the ancestral spirits. All pretenses of happiness and masking fall away, and all those who covered their sorrow with "seem-to-be-laughter" are released. The community is carried to trance by the swaying of bodies, the beat of the instruments, and the open invitation in Big Mama Sway's voice. In these moments she is the holy priestess or mambo of the community, bringing them into the arms of a spirit where they are safe enough to "stretch out in her sound and cry." In this moment of ritual, Bridgforth's juke joint has a lot in common with a *peristil,* a Vodou dance space that also helps facilitate community survival. Marie Lily Cerat remembers the *peristil* as a welcoming environment:

> The building seemed always to have the space to accommodate the passing traveler, the pregnant teenager just thrown out of her house, or the unemployed laborer who could not afford sleeping quarters. Anyone in need, including those with what was called in whispers the "unmanly" or "unnatural" disease, found a home in the *peristil.* It belonged to the community; the door was always open.[28]

Like the *peristil,* the juke joint becomes an interstitial space where those castaways from society can find solace and where the physical and spiritual worlds meet through the music. With the proper guidance of a skilled priestess, the space itself is meant to encourage the elevation of the consciousness of individuals and the community through extended contact with the divine.

As a representative of Eleggua in the text, Big Mama Sway is a link to the spirits. She is at the crossroads between the living world, the spirits of the ancestors, and the unborn. During the day, she is a conjure woman or healer who cultivates a garden of flowers and healing herbs while she speaks to "the babies to come" (57), the unborn children who are on the way. She and the narrator are given the gift of third sight to be able to "see" and speak to future generations, to help prepare them for the journey ahead. They are the ones who will be willing and able to listen to the ancestors as they impart their stories and knowledge, even after death.

This lineage of conjure women begins with Isadora Africa, the "first/ African conjuration woman" (56). According to the legend, which is featured prominently in the novel as well as in the *love conjure/blues Text Installation* performance, Isadora Africa leads an insurrection on the slave plantation that existed in the fictional community of the novel, using only prayer, ritual, and herbs to stop the white owner and overseers in their tracks. The slave community drummer was so feared that the slave owner cut off all of his fingers in an effort to stop the power of the drum. However, through creative resistance, "with him mouth / make sound / gagaga gagaga ga / low to the ground legs bend feet ba ba ba," he makes rhythm with his mouth and feet (51). This is enough to help Isadora Africa call the force of the spirits, which ushers in a wind that "lift[s] ole marsa up high in the air drop him down flat on the floor" (52). Isadora Africa's magic is a primary example of the conjuration that the text represents as one of a constellation of West African–derived practices that exist alongside Yoruba and Vodou. She uses her access to the kitchen and knowledge of medicinal plants to poison the master's and overseer's food with the very fingers he took. By the end of the night, all the slaves leave the plantation and "ain't no plantation no more never since that time /not / on these grounds" (53). The story is passed down through generations, and each time a conjure woman of strength is born, she is given her name. Big Mama Sway's birth name is Isadora Africa Jr., but "nobody dare speak she birth name / call all them generations of power down" (56).

One deity does respond to their musical supplication for divine manifestation. Change, a "cookie brown woman with tight light brown curls rumbling all the way down / to the bounce on her behind" appears in the juke joint, "swirling a little dust before her" (63–64). When she sang, "the sound that came out shook the entire room"; the power of her voice caused the earth to rumble and the walls to shake (20). From the force with which she swoops in and captures everyone's attention to the multicolored swirl of her dress, Change is a description of the West African Orisha Oya. In the Yoruba pantheon, Oya is a "patron of feminine leadership"[29] and "the Queen of the Winds of Change. . . . She brings about sudden structural change in people and things," and as a "mistress of disguises" she can appear anywhere without warning.[30] She walks in and heads straight for Bettye's hard-drinking, masculine ex-lover, Lushy. Change's targeting of Lushy with her charms brings about a shift in Bettye and Lushy's relationship, initiating their reconciliation. This moment is also an opportunity for masculine redemption, as Lushy goes from being a "drunk" (9) to making amends with Bettye for her irresponsible and selfish actions.

The benefit of fiction is its potential to expand representation and challenge cultural assumptions. In a predominantly butch/femme working-class African American queer cultural context, femme–femme desire is incongruous. However, the opening pages of *love conjure/blues* dispel the common misperception that feminine desire is inevitably directed toward masculinity. The novel's plot begins with Nigga Red's violent relationship with Peachy Soonyay, where she was "whooped on chased down and squished" regularly (3). Peachy finds the courage to leave Red through her affair with Bitty Fon. The narrator describes both Bitty and Peachy as feminine women:

see/bitty and peachy what you call long nail girls.
each one primp and fuss over they hair outfits and

lipstick nails and shoes shape and such and all and
well/we thinking them two fluffing up for a trouser
wo'mn or a man or
both/but nobody figure they been giving   attention
to one the other. (3)

Consistent with stereotypical representations that associate femininity with
superficiality, Bitty and Peachy are seen as impossible lovers because, as the
narrator explains, "how / on earth / could two primpers / work out all
the mirror timing to start the day" (3). The idea that two feminine Black
women (femmes) would find the mirror image of themselves desirable is at
first a joke, inconceivable in a binary gender system that exists even in queer
culture. Bridgforth thus circumvents this limitation by representing Black
femininity as the spiritual center of the community in both *love conjure/
blues* and *delta dandi*.[31]

In *love conjure/blues* Bitty Fon is the embodiment of the mixture of African and native American bloodlines and resistance practices. In addition to
getting her first name because she can "pack more into a teenincy piece of
cloth then a fool filling up in a jook jernt" (4), her last name comes from
the Fon people of West Africa. She is described as carrying "all of Africa on
she lips / in her hips / she Indian earth tones smooth with the Black of her
skin / the rise of she cheek bones / bitty fon be more beauty then beauty can
take" (29). Through Bitty's observance of ritual, the text entreats us to "dance
pray smudge / remember" Houma, Tunica, Choctaw, Chickasaw, Fon, Ibo,
Yoruba, and Wolof, the names of nations captured and/or invaded by European settlers and slavers (26). We are called to remember and imagine these
diverse groups meeting in the swamp woods of the rural South and moving
with a common reverence for the drum and the earth to resist domination
and to free slaves. The memory of their cooperation and common cause is
passed down through the generations as "they childrens they childrens they
/ children carry they story / in cloth / in feet / with hair / when laugh / with
drum / Praise memory" (27–28). Bitty is a living connection to that legacy.
She "sits with the dead," which situates her in communication with the
spirit realm, especially with the ghosts of those who while alive were most
disrespected, disaffected, and disempowered, but who find power after death
through their continued presence in the memory of the living (29). Even
while in prison for shooting Red, Bitty remembers that she "always must
love" and continue the rituals of the warriors from the past that have been
passed down "child to child to child . . . smudge sing pray dance drum cry
praise laugh" (29). There are many different paths to the divine in the novel.
The metaphor of the crossroads aptly describes the position of the narrator

as a witness at the center of intersecting spiritual practices. Bitty Fon takes her ritual practice from an amalgamation of African and native American traditions, while another character, Big Bill, draws on her forefather's use of the drum and eventually the guitar to call the spirits. Big Mama Sway combines these paths, making her the spiritual center of the novel.

Big Mama Sway is the predecessor to Honeypot, a character in Bridgforth's subsequent work, *delta dandi*. Honeypot is a woman who has a divinely inspired facility with music, a queenly control over women and men, and a goddess's ability to seduce both. Honeypot's segments are more in line with the narrative voice of *the bull-jean stories* and *love conjure/blues* in that they come from outside the perspective of the character to interject the only third-person point of view in *delta dandi*. The Honeypot monologues are also consistent with the juke-joint context of Bridgforth's published work. Honey is a crucial element in any altar to the Orisha of love, desire, and femininity; Oshun and Honeypot are depicted in accordance with that tradition. In the monologue, Honeypot is described as "tiny as a bee" but powerful enough to "bloody many a big man and woman" (17). She also possesses the wiles to "steal your gurlfriend" and intoxicate "her right out her natural mind" as her boyfriend helplessly watches (35). Honeypot earns her reputation for "fairness of opportunity / for ass whoppings" in defense of the integrity of her music (17). A consummate pianist, Honeypot controls the other musicians, showing up "in a gown and pearls" and chastising anyone who is not as focused as she is (18). As a powerful figure of the feminine divine, Honeypot is also called to regulate wayward masculinity. Her band mate, the womanizer Delroy, is "so busy sending mental messages to the womens" that he fails to pay proper respect to the music and to Honeypot. She remedies his inattention:

> without missing a beat
> honeypot drain she drink/spiral that shot glass in the air
> cold cock delroy smack middle of the head.
> straighten him out in time to catch the next note
> swing the band round the room/so long and so hard till
> everybody in the joint spin on out they minds.
> baseboards tore to shreads
> all the put together that was
> now just drip pure nasty. (18–19)

Honeypot and Big Mama Sway are female authority figures who displace the male houngan or babalao in traditional Vodou and Locumi practices, respectively.[32] They anchor the text in feminine energy and power and are flawed and quick to get angry. Honeypot's ability to take everyone around her "to the next world" signifies her direct connection to the divine and her place as priestess in the community.

"Trouser Women": Representing Masculinities

Written as a collection of short stories, Bridgforth's first book, *the bull-jean stories,* is the text with the most idealized representation of Black masculinity. The protagonist is Bull-Jean, a butch lesbian who is deeply invested in finding and maintaining romantic love. Her focus on love and relationship represents masculinity in search of long-term connection. As a result, Bull-Jean is consistently and publicly searching for a sustaining relationship. A narrator witnesses Bull-Jean's search for love and provides a community perspective on the various romantic interludes in Bull-Jean's life, but without judgment. In contrast to the expectation that the African American southern community will reject or disapprove of a character like Bull-Jean, the narrator is protective of Bull-Jean and bolstered by her exploits.

Even when Bull-Jean engages in unethical behavior, she is not rejected for her indiscretions. For example, one of the first stories of the collection, titled "bull-jean slipn in," features the observations of the narrator as Bull-Jean has a rendezvous with a married woman. The narrator explains that "every day / 5 am / deacon willie / clara's man / slip out / bull-jean / slip in" (9).[33] Clara and Deacon Willie are a married couple who are both engaged in what the narrator calls "nappy love" (9), or complicated extramarital affairs. The narrator watches each day while the three parties are involved in the same duplicitous ballet. Bull-Jean "slips in" for only thirty minutes a day with Clara. When the narrator confronts Bull-Jean on the impossibility of a relationship with Clara, she replies with a tenderness and vulnerability that distinguishes her masculinity as gentle and romantic. Bull-Jean describes herself as having given her heart away "piece by piece" (11) to women until she does not have anything left to give.

> it's almost gonn/my Heart
> all i really want
> is a kind word
> and a smile
>
> and that wo'mn is kind
> and she Lovves me   and
> it don't' matter if it's thirty minutes a day

or ONCE in the next Life
i'll go git her/smile
whenever she'll let me
have it! (12)

Bull-Jean's declaration that all she wants in this life is a "kind word and smile" goes against the expectation of masculine philandering. Her involvement in an extramarital affair is not a way of establishing a masculine reputation in the community, but a desperate plea for connection. Bull-Jean's declaration of a desire for love is juxtaposed with a description of her as smooth in a moment of crisis. The narrator witnesses Bull-Jean doing her usual 5 A.M. saunter into Clara's house only to see Deacon Willie walk back inside five minutes later. In a gesture that challenges the typical historical memory of southern communities' unreceptive attitude to queerness, the narrator goes to get her gun in order to protect Bull-Jean, as opposed to protecting the sanctity of the married couple. In idealized masculine fashion, Bull-Jean gets the upper hand on Deacon Willie, leaving him sitting outside of his own house waiting for his wife and Bull-Jean to finish their tryst. Bull-Jean's openness about her heartbreak followed by her successful confrontation of Deacon Willie shows the potential for an idealized Black masculine representation to be both forceful and vulnerable. The inclusion of the voices of both the narrator and Bull-Jean allows for alternative perspectives on the Black southern response to queer gender and sexuality.

Furthermore, the text challenges what few representations there are of Black masculine gender transgression in the rural United States, which depict masculine gender-variant people as having no community. For example, in the film version of *Lackawana Blues* (2005), written by Ruben Santiago-Hudson, the character of Ricky (portrayed by Adina Porter) is the lone butch lesbian in the community of Lackawana, New York. Her character does not experience conflict with the presumably heterosexual and gender-normative townspeople because her inclusion is never tested by a public romantic relationship or by the presence of other queer people. Ricky, although recognized by the narrator as "the closest thing I had to a father," is isolated in the community.[34] Similarly, in *Getting Mother's Body* (2003), a novel set in rural 1960s Texas, the character Dill Smiles is a transmasculine rarity in the otherwise gender-conforming southern town.[35] The town sometimes tolerates Dill's identity as a man, although this identity is often challenged by references to his birth sex. In contrast, Bull-Jean is not isolated and is joined by a collection of other queer people.

The *bull-jean stories* and Bridgforth's work as a whole challenge the primacy of heterosexuality as a coherent organizing structure for Black southern relationships and families. For example, Deacon Willie's "nappy love" or extramarital affair happens to be with a local feminine gay man named Frosty Jackson. The narrator explains that Deacon Willie "also been squeezing frosty jackson's onion / and frosty got mo sugga in him shorts / than the sto got sacks to hold it in" (13). The incident with Clara is not the only time when Bull-Jean interrupts the community's heterosexual façade. During a wedding ceremony, which is described as the "biggest / two-preacha-four-choir-twelve-deacon / high rolling broom-jump of all time" (44), Bull-Jean objects to the marriage as a "lie-befo-God" (48). Her lover, Safirra, arranges a marriage of convenience with a man in order to gain financial stability and to make her father happy. Bull-Jean formally objects to her wedding, standing before the community in defiance and stating that, "i / the one put on this earth / to walk wid that wo'mn and / I / the one oughta be up there wid her na" (48). She exposes the hypocrisy of their marriage as sanctified and as "god's choosing." This, of course, resists the current political rhetoric of the sanctity of heterosexual unions in the public debates about gay marriage. In Bridgforth's version of the rural African American past, marriage is less about an exclusive holy bond than it is an incomplete picture of the members of Black communities' desires and sexual practices.

In addition to complicating heterosexuality, Bridgforth represents homophobia as an external violence that interrupts the kinship networks organically established in the community. Bull-Jean is a dutiful caretaker and niece to her aunts, including her aunt Till, who is her great aunt's lifelong partner. Outside forces interfere in the intricate kinship network and remove Bull-Jean's son from his home. The last chapter of the novel is his homecoming. He explains the back-story of his removal: "they called you unholy / a sinner gonn burn in hell said you was unnatural" (103). He describes his long bitter journey after he was taken from his home and then comes full circle back to it, where he exclaims, "I have missed you mamma. / but I'm back home na / and ain't nobody gonn come take us apart again / not in this Life!" (107). Even though the son's story emerges at the end of the novel, it gives us a glimpse into another form of Black maternal representation: the butch mother. In a way that adds dimension to her masculinity, Bull-Jean's familial relationships bring out her nurturing side. Her son states, "[R]eally in them first twelve years of my life / you taught me how to be a man" (105). He credits her with giving him the best instruction on manhood that he received, even though he was in the army and had male influences in his life. Bull-Jean, along with the other masculine characters in Bridgforth's work, provides an important and reharmonized contribution to the archive of Black masculine representation, in this case, the masculine maternal. The masculine is reimagined as a nurturing energy in contrast to the persistent representation of Black masculinity as brutal and violent. Bridgforth's revisioning of gender presents an opportunity to consider the possibilities for Black masculine community and healing.

Even though Bridgforth's work is about the possibilities for queer Black embodiment, she does not portray a utopic southern community, nor does she shy away from issues of violence that afflict women's lives. The narrator in *love conjure/blues*, who we later learn is an older woman named Cat, observes that as a people, African Americans are "borned to violence. not our making and not our choosing. fighting like animals leashed in a pen. maimed if we don't win. killed if we don't fight" (2). The fight for survival in an anti-Black context turns into a struggle against each other and explodes in intracommunal violence. In the opening pages we learn that Nigga Red has been beating her girlfriend, Peachy Soonyay, for several years. Unbeknownst to Red and the rest of the community, Peachy has found true love in the arms of another feminine woman, Bitty Fon. In a moment of anger and in defense of Peachy, Bitty shoots Red in front of a café full of witnesses. Several of the characters then take this incident as an opportunity to heal from the detrimental definitions of masculinity. Similarly to the novels *Her* and *Trumpet* (which I analyze in the following chapter), here Bridgforth explores the possibilities of resituating Black masculine identity through female-bodied protagonists. Although all of Bridgforth's characters discussed here are born with female anatomy, they embrace masculine identification in different ways, and all contribute to the crossroads of uncertainty and possibility that Bridgforth creates in her portrayals.

The masculine center of *love conjure/blues* is Big Bill, who represents the Orisha Shango. A force of masculine prowess and passion,[36] Shango speaks with authority and is known for drum, dance, and making "bad situations better."[37] As a representation of Shango, Big Bill is a commanding presence in the community both as a compelling sexual figure and as a leader. She is a locus of attention, wearing a "suit black / hat low / glasses dark / and shoes so shining make your head hurt" (9). Much like the relationship between the dancer and the drummer,[38] it is the combination of Big Bill's piano or guitar playing and Big Mama Sway's voice that opens a portal to divine magic and ancestral forces. Big Bill entices the patrons at the juke joint as she "walk / pants pull here here here / material ripple across she crotch which appear packing a large and heavy surprise" (9) while she nonetheless plays the piano with an authoritative vigor. She is the novel's representation of responsible masculinity, that is, a character who uses her masculine presence and privilege in a way that is respectful of femininity, not abusive, and willing to create a masculine community based on these same principles. Part of Big

Bill's role is also to be a mentor and leader for other masculine-identified people in the community.

Through the process of multivocal storytelling, we hear from various masculine-identified characters who together construct a reconstructed representation of Black masculinity. In a late-night gathering, five "brothers," Lil' Tiny, Big Bill, Mannish Mary, Lushy, and Guitar Sam, get together to talk about women and masculine responsibility because the youngest one, Lil' Tiny, has been irresponsible and unprincipled in her relationship. The group gathers around Big Bill as she counsels Tiny, "but the main thing is just / don't let the wy'mns know you a fool. / and keep your composition at all times" (35). Big Bill's wisdom is not absolute; it is contested among the group. Each member interjects some point or some wisdom into the conversation, admitting that "ain't none of us really got it all figured out" (36). Then

> guitar sam speak up/he say
> lil tiny
> i'm thinking
> you must like feeling alone and hurt . . .
> and that's alright/if that is what you like.
> but know this   as long
> as you keep on courting pain and misery
> thats what you gone find yourself living with. (37)

With Guitar Sam's closing words, Lil' Tiny "just drop she head to the table / and cry" (37). Bridgforth offers an alternative version of Black masculine camaraderie that is based on emotional connection. Their collective humility and care for the feminine women in their lives is the basis for their brotherhood. It is also significant that it is Guitar Sam who gives the most poignant words of the gathering. He is the only one in the group whom the novel identifies with male pronouns. His presence with the others, who are butch lesbians, epitomizes how the novel works along the lines of gender expression and identity as opposed to biological categories. It is unclear whether Guitar Sam was born female or not, and the novel suggests that the answer is irrelevant. It is more imperative that the group is present to support each other and keep each other accountable in a context of masculine privilege.

Similar to the protagonist in the novel *Her,* Big Bill's story is another example of how the blues is a practice of queer gender. In a poignant moment of unrequited love for the juke-joint operator, Bettye, Big Bill gives her the gift of intimacy, explaining how she is the recipient of a legacy of Black masculine traditions passed down from father to son. Big Bill's father, Henry B. Stonwell, imparts to her the elements of Black manhood as he understood it. She is a "guitar man" (23) by birthright from her father:

> far back as i can remember daddy had me at his side while
> he picked that guitar.
> once i got old enough/he took me   walk them roads to play.
> i believe he wanted to show me how to make my life work.
> daddy say too many a good song done died in the heart of a
> fool. don't drink. don't waste your money gambling. groom
> hard. remember your manners and always/take care of your
> guitar. that guitar is grandchile of the instrument that our
> African/pappy passed down to us. it got the power to reach
> Jesus. (18)

In order to introduce her as his successor, he takes her "on the road" to the "little jook jernts and backyard shacks" (18) where he plays. Even though she has seven brothers (17), Big Bill is her father's blues apprentice who also instructs her on how to make her "life work," or how to successfully negotiate what her father sees as the pitfalls of masculinity—alcohol and gambling. As Henry B. Stonwell's cultural beneficiary, Big Bill is also the heir to an African musical legacy that he designates as male. For Big Bill's father, the guitar is the instrument of a symbolic African father that evokes the divine. Therefore the responsibility of a "guitar man" is that of a ceremonial accompanist: to help call forth the spirits into a space.

Big Bill's role as a ceremonial musician is punctuated by the voices of the ancestors, which precede her story:

> i am he that was king/captured sold and shipped for selling i am she whose
>   tongue
> they took so as not to tell i am he made to walk chained next to a wagon . . .
> we been learned to dream cause in wake we had to
> be dead.
> you is free cause we was captive
> you are the one we been waiting for
> gaga gaga gaga/ga   gaga gaga gaga/ga   gaga gaga gaga/ga
> aaawwwhhh   aaawwwhhhaaawwwhhh (15)

Each line of text is printed in a unique font, indicating a change in voices. Multiple ancestors speak across time to encourage the generation of free

Black people to continue to remember the atrocities and the strength of those who came before. They remind us that our ability to choose the course of our own lives comes at the heavy price of their captivity. One voice says, "I am the one that holds your prayers," indicating the presence of the ancestral spirit in the most private expression of desire (15). They are all listening and they sing to the beat of the drum, which is represented by the onomatopoeia of the drum beat (gagaga). Following this, we learn of Big Bill's inherited command of the guitar as a ceremonial instrument.

Revisioning the Ancestors

Bridgforth's play *delta dandi* carries on *love conjure/blues*'s theme of ancestral voices telling their stories. It represents multiple first-hand accounts from the past lives of one soul, The Gurl, speaking from across centuries of silence with the help of her ancestral spirits and the power of the divine entities. The Gurl speaks the play's first words, saying, "i remember jooking with the moon / i remember jumping in the water i remember hiding in the / trees i remember hanging in the sun i remember gold and / chattel i remember glitter and smoke i remember i i i" (5). The last set of "i i i" is a practice of repetition that serves as a vibrational echo, a ceremonial technique used to usher the main character into memory, calling her back to relive the trauma, in this case, of slavery. The characters are not merely recollecting but reliving the events of her soul across time. Much of the text is from the perspective of characters who do not want to remember but are compelled to do so by forces beyond their control. *delta dandi* portrays a spirit's journey to bring what would otherwise be repressed into what I call spirit consciousness—one that is held not by an individual but by the collective and mediated by the divine so that it does not overwhelm the mortal body.

The Gurl is overwhelmed by her tragic life circumstances. When she is a child, she sees her mother raped and killed by white men, and when she is only five or six, her remaining family trades her to an abusive woman. She laments that "in my dreams / when i wake / all i do is remember" (5). When she does remember, she is afraid that it will be too painful to bear. She runs from the pain of it, saying, "i don't know how to die so i just go along. carry all these things. all these things. till once in the black/blue of day i jump. i jump where the waters meet. i jump. cold cold cut me. i jump. pray / carry me to the ocean. please. maybe i find my mama there" (9). The Gurl prays for death and release from suffering, wanting only to forget the past and to embrace oblivion, anything that will shut down her consciousness from the assault of reliving the past.

Along the way, The Elder Spirit/Returning and the Seer assist The Gurl in her journey to remember and survive her memories. She is almost successful in her suicide attempt but is interrupted by a vision of a woman. "can't move. can't turn head. can't close eyes. no look away. the woman tall tall naked and shining in the water stand . . . stare. stare telling me something / i don't know what" (10). The naked woman is a figure of desire for The Gurl. She is "shining" and literally takes her breath away. The Gurl's desire mixed with awe stops her from committing suicide and brings her to the place of remembering the night she watched as her mother was raped and murdered.

The naked woman in The Gurl's vision is written in the voice of The Elder Spirit/Returning and is also a version of the Orisha Yemanya. In an interview, Bridgforth discussed how she studied Yoruba spiritual practices while she was writing *delta dandi*.[39] As mentioned above, elements of West African cultural/spiritual practices are evident in all of Bridgforth's previous work, including ancestral reverence, the collapsing of space–time, and even the emergence of figurative female deities/healers in each text. However, in *delta dandi,* the Orisha emerge as much more distinctive figures in the story.

We know that it is Yemanya speaking through The Elder Spirit/Returning because of The Gurl's description of her and the way she speaks through the symbols that are associated with her:

> silver pearls and turquoise, yams and seaweed. blue skirts 7 layers. peacocks and fish/watermelons and grapes. monday. shifts. north star half moon rivers and pound cake/strength. (10)

Several of the items in her monologue (e.g., silver pearls, turquoise, watermelon) are actually things that one would place on an altar in reverence of Yemanya. Some parts of the text, such as the numeral 7 and the color blue, are connected to Yemanya, and others are associated with other deities. For example, Monday is usually connected to Eleggua, and peacocks with Oshun. Although this section in the play is connected predominantly to reverence for Yemanya, other deities are also included, which increases the sense of the symbolic divine support for The Gurl. Yemanya's emergence from the water is consistent with her description from Teish: "Yemaya-Olokun in the Mother of the Sea, the Great Water . . . She is the Mother of Dreams, the Mother of Secrets. . . . She is envisioned as a large and beautiful woman, radiant and dark; nurturing and devouring, crystal clear and mysteriously deep. . . . Watch Her shimmering in the light of the full moon and be renewed."[40] The Gurl goes to the river to cry and to pray to Yemanya for release. Teish warns her not to approach the deity in complete despair, for she "does not wish to see you in misery and may pull you into Her arms with the undertow and restore you to her Belly" (133). The Gurl is initially looking for an embrace into the undertow that would remove her from her dire condition, but the text emphasizes instead Yemanya's role as a nurturer and seductress. The arms of Yemanya that Teish describes are used in this capacity to captivate The Gurl sensually and lead her to retell the story without its ripping her apart. Onstage this scene has resembled male and female cast members encircling The Gurl as deities or ancestral spirits loving her into the next phase of her life.

The initial casting guidelines call for "4 women" to play the lead roles: The Gurl, The Elder Spirit/Returning, Blues, and Seer. However, not all of the play's productions have followed these guidelines. For example, in the production that I was part of at the Fire and Ink Conference, there were five performers total, three of whom were men.[41] The script contains both masculine and feminine voices, and the cast is expected to embody different characters across genders, thereby shifting the anticipation that the feminine voice in the text is connected to a female body. The creative and flexible casting is consistent with the primary commitment to a performance aesthetics that privileges improvisation and demands that the actors bring their "specific and idiosyncratic sel[ves]" to the performance and that "visceral knowledge systems" are the basis of performance.[42]

In addition to leaving space for cross-gender performances, these principles provide an opportunity for gender-nonconforming performers to be present onstage and to disrupt representations of binary genders in a Black performance tradition. If "[m]emory and daily living are lodged in the muscles," as Jones suggests, then stage performance is a practice of jogging the "muscle" of embodied memories.[43] Therefore, when ancestors who did not have a binary gender identity are represented in performance, it is a practice of awakening forgotten parts of our past.

I performed the role of The King, which is the voice of a female African king who is actively profiting from the slave trade. This performance came only two months after my own gender-reassignment surgery, and I stood before the audience in a state of liminal gender presentation. Even though I identify as male, I was asked to embody a physical presence of female masculinity that is cruel, uncaring, and misogynistic. In this way, Bridgforth's work is not just a wholesale celebration of butch and trans masculinities. Part of the brilliance of the work is her critique of sexism and misogyny from any source. The King says,

go.
get me more bodies.

from here and there and there and there
bring them to me. now.
i've riches to make
guns beads brandy. SOLD!
my children glow with laughter and fat bellies
guns beads brandy. SOLD!
my wives dance my name in the moonlight (7)

The King's voice is of royal authority and divine right. She is the ultimate authority in her realm and commands obedience. Her voice is that of greed and self-absorption taken to their extremes. The King character is reminiscent of the description of the traditional African division of biological sex and social roles that Ifi Amadiume discusses in *Male Daughters, Female Husbands*.[44] However, biology does not necessarily determine her social role. She is King and therefore is able to claim that "everyone is my servant my slave my concubine" (7). The King's voice is one of the first monologues, along with The Gurl's opening convocation of remembrance and statement that she is "a fallen star they say / i come here baring everything / all at once. / again / again / again / again / me" (6). Together these two portions foreshadow the journey through intraracial histories and dynamics of grief and pain to transcendence.

We know that The King is a female only because The Gurl recognizes her as part of herself. She says,

i know things i think.
like i remember i was king once. a woman looking how she felt. i see her.
just before i running sometimes she come whisper to me.
she scares me.
i feel she reach for me with the mean of her soul. (20)

The woman King is both an example of female possibility and gender autonomy and a menacing part of The Gurl's self. The King is a part of her, her own past life, reminding us that queer ancestors are not unproblematic or universally celebrated in every instance. The King is a figure of pain and grief and an undeniable part of this soul's journey across time and states of being. Without The King, The Gurl would not be equipped with the strength that she needs to survive the fact that her family sold her "for a few chickens and a barrel of shine" (24) and the incredibly brutal treatment that she endured at the hands of the woman whom they sold her to. Bridgforth's use of The King in The Gurl's past life is reminiscent of the white male ancestor in

Octavia Butler's *Kindred*.[45] In *Kindred*, the main character is transported back in time into slavery and meets her own slave and slave-owning ancestors. She comes to terms with the fact that she would not exist if her female ancestor did not experience repeated sexual violence, and she is even in the position of having to facilitate her ancestor's abuse to ensure her own presence in the future. In the case of *delta dandi*, The Gurl witnesses her past lives, their pleasures and their pain, and it is this process of witnessing and embracing all the parts of herself and her past that gives her hope for living in her present.

As disturbing and problematic as The King is, she also is the ancestral/energetic antecedent for The Gurl's experience of her gender. The Gurl says,

> i free when i run so i running all the time. the dresses
> they make me wear choke my skin and heart so i run till the
> touch of no fit leave my mind. always i wonder why
> they yell these dress on me. why boys look like i feel
> but not how i look. (19)

In this description, external impositions of gender are regarded as violent acts as "they" (presumably adults) "yell" dresses on her, which is a quintessential signifier of femininity. The dresses are a "no fit" for her sense of being and "choke" her skin. The protagonist copes by running away to experience a temporary freedom. The gender violence that occurs when she is forced to wear feminine clothing is represented as part of a larger context of brutality that frames her life experience.

Taken together, the narratives of The King and The Gurl's experiences of forced gender conformity are connected to the web of violence in The Gurl's life and constitute part of the reharmonization that *delta dandi* narratively employs. Reharmonization is a process wherein familiar tunes are reworked to fit the harmonic sensibilities of the artist to the extent that the tune becomes "radically defamiliarized" to the listener.[46] Reharmonization is often used to introduce "new harmonies, new chords, to accompany the melody of a song or the improvisations of a song."[47] In *delta dandi* fundamental aspects of African diasporic memory are reharmonized. The story of the female King interrupts how African genders are usually remembered, challenging the reader/audience members to find scholarly sources and verify the text's version of possible African subjectivities. The text challenges romanticized notions in the diaspora of a male-centered and patriarchal Africa of noble kings and beautiful and dutiful queens. It is also in dialogue with the political discourse in parts of West Africa which applies these romanticizations to legal and public policy to criminalize homosexuality and gender variance and disavow the existence of these populations because of the idea that they defy tradition.[48]

Both and Neither:
Bigendered Characters at the Crossroads

Bridgforth does some of her most dexterous storytelling in her depiction of members of her ancestral world who refuse any predictable or fixed pronoun or gender designation. Interestingly, it is in *love conjure/blues* that these characterizations come across most clearly. The two characters from the novel that defy gender definition are Duckie Smooth and Sweet T. Duckie, a cross-dressing performer who does "female interpretations" (26). His depictions of Black femininity are sensual and engaging in their own way, since Duckie is not conventionally beautiful. Nevertheless, he is desirable across the gender spectrum as "the mens the womens the both and the neither / be batting eyes at himshe" (26). The focus on interpretation signals the complex series of individual interpretations of gender at work throughout the text that are not assigned to any particular anatomy or sexuality. Duckie Smooth is a male feminine figure who is in a heterosexual marriage. His wife Cora supports her husband's performance efforts by collecting tips at each show. Duckie's marriage to Cora does not prevent him from joining the line of feminine trustees of the juke joint in Bettye's absence.

Miss Sunday Morning is another feminine guardian of sacred space. She runs the joint *behind* Bettye's joint. Miss Sunday Morning's place exists at the edges of the community. It is "standing way past good timing" and "just outside of right" (43). There are patrons and workers along "dark corners [in] back rooms [and] against the walls" of the joint (42). Those who engage in explicit sexual performance and transactional sex have a place in Bridgforth's schema of the sacredness of Black community. Illicit scenes like Miss Sunday Morning's are usually represented in terms of shadow and despair; however, Bridgforth lights up the dark corners of the sexual margins with love and healing through her representation of Sweet T.

Neither man nor woman, Sweet T lives in the interstices of gender: "a man last life" and now a "woman / feel like a man" (44). Sweet T's confusion and frustration over not having a body that matches her/his gender identity is compounded by a life of abuse and suffering. She/he was "the one that never harmed nobody / but always got beat" from childhood, leaving her/him with a body marked with scars (44). Sweet T is a symbol of the brutality of the past that lives in the scars on his/her body. Again, queer love shows the collective a way through suffering and embracing all of the marginalized parts of the Black community through his/her journey of connection and self-acceptance. Sweet T lives a life of isolation and despair until he/she meets Miss Sunday Morning. Their lovemaking is a sacred prayer for wholeness, their "bodies wrapped / the make holy / every Sabbath" (47). With the help of Miss Sunday Morning's soothing and reassuring love, Sweet T is able to embrace the "girl in he" (48). Sweet T and Miss Sunday Morning unite to take care of the marginalized and discarded and "holy wholly everyday" (48); together they love each other and the rest of the community. Sweet T's transformation from being alone to his/her newfound joy is a metaphor for what can happen to the Black collective when the discarded parts are enfolded into the whole with love.

In Bridgforth's work, the southern community is the locus of Black queer life. It is also the birthplace of Black queer identities and pleasures—both of which are constructed as resistances to external impositions from society and regulating regimes that attempt to delimit and define Black families, communities, bodies, and desires according to outside norms. Performance becomes a staged enactment of unfinished stories and accompanying movements. Performance brings these individual movements to a shared experience. To move with the intent of integrating "lost" bodies from the collective story is a communal act of healing, which in this case involves coming to terms with irresolution.

Every other text analyzed in *The Queer Limit of Black Memory* relies on the renarrativization process that fiction makes readily available. From themes of slavery to migration to diasporic consciousness, each short story or novel that I have examined and will examine has situated Black queer characters at the center. Retelling history in a way that places Black queer experience at the crux of Black life can challenge the dissociative absence of queers in Black memory. In the retelling, the queer becomes a source of strength and a cause of celebration of resistance.

Bridgforth takes this narrative strategy and goes a step further to incorporate information gathered through embodied performance into her recasting of the rural South. Her approach is in keeping with the preliminary findings of contemporary psychotherapists and researchers, such as Pat Ogden. Following Pierre Janet's assertions on the importance of treating somatic symptoms of dissociative clients, Ogden considers the body as crucial to moving unconscious responses into conscious awareness and thereby healing traumatic experiences. Ogden and her colleagues have concluded, "We have already noted that traditional psychotherapies pay scant attention to the physical experience of the client in treatment, in part because there is little theory or training to assist in the consideration of the embodied experience of trauma."[49] According to this research, movement carries its own potential healing energy as the body completes gestures interrupted during the traumatic event. In the context I am writing about here, performance becomes a staged enactment of unfinished stories and accompanying movements. Performance brings these individual movements to a shared experience. To move with the intent of integrating "lost" bodies from the collective story is a communal act of healing. Including this material in a printed book provides an opportunity for the experience to spread to places that live performance cannot, and/or for live audiences to carry the message with them from the theater to create another experience at home. In this body of work, spiritual epistemologies are performed through the body and shared communally.

If Bridgforth represents blues performance as a process of remembering queer ancestors otherwise "lost" to communal memory, Jackie Kay considers jazz as a metaphor for queering diasporic memory. Like Bridgforth's revision of Black masculinity, the following chapter asks, What would the outcome of remaking Black diasporic masculinity be?

CHAPTER 4

"Make It Up and Trace It Back"

Remembering Black Trans Subjectivity in
Jackie Kay's *Trumpet*

> My father always told me he and I were related the way it
> mattered. . . . He said you make up your own bloodline,
> Colman. Make it up and trace it back. Design your own family
> tree—what's the matter with you? Haven't you got an imagi-
> nation?
>
> —*Trumpet* 58

When Jackie Kay's first novel, *Trumpet* (1998), opens,
Joss Moody—a Black transman born in Scotland of a
white mother and an African father—is already dead.
His story is told through the remembrances of his wife, Millie,
and their adopted son, Colman, as well as others who had contact
with him during and even after his life. Joss was born female but
lived as a man his entire adult life, constructing a career as a jazz
trumpet player in his own band, Moody's Men, and building a
family as a husband and father. He kept the secret of his female
anatomy until his death, revealing himself only to Millie. His son,
Colman, feels betrayed when, through Joss's final medical exam,
he discovers along with the rest of the world that "Britain's legendary trumpet player" was born female (6). The novel is constructed
as a jazz composition in that it is a polyphonic arrangement of
multiple points of view. Each chapter is written from the perspective of people in Joss's life—his wife, son, mother, friends—or

those who knew of his biological gender only after his death: the doctor, the funeral director, and others. Through Joss's death and the subsequent remembering of him, the novel rethinks diaspora, taking Black trans lives into consideration.

The story of Joss Moody was inspired by the life of Billy Tipton, a white transmale jazz musician in the United States. When Tipton died in 1989, the fact of his female anatomy was leaked to the press, causing a firestorm of publicity surrounding his decades of success as a male piano player and bandleader. Tipton's life was chronicled in a biography titled *Suits Me: The Double Life of Billy Tipton* by Diane Middlebrook which includes interviews with his former lovers and band mates.[1] Kay incorporates the constellation of voices captured in Middlebrook's biography and expands them to an ensemble meditation on Black Scottish subjectivity that reclaims jazz as a major form of Black queer expression and an epistemology for queering Black diasporic consciousness and identity. Kay is an internationally acclaimed poet and fiction writer well known for her books of poetry, especially *The Adoption Papers* (1980), and for her biography/personal memoir titled *Bessie Smith* (1997).[2] In *Bessie Smith,* Kay first introduces her extended love song to the blues. In the absence of other Black people in her world, she describes her practice of listening to the blues as a stand-in for Black community and a diasporic epistemology for her own Black Scottish lesbian self-making.

As in previous chapters in which I discuss how Black queer history and memory are embedded in the musical forms of jazz and blues, this chapter continues to examine how jazz aesthetics inform Black queer embodiment. As a form that encourages the transformation of standard melodies into multiple improvised creations, jazz is useful in expanding our conceptualization of the potential for Black people to recreate ourselves and our gender identities in a diasporic practice; in other words, to actively engage in and reformulate Black identities in irresolute ways across the Atlantic.

Kay is not the first British lesbian of African descent to adopt African American history and cultural aesthetics in her strategic representation of British queerness. African American music is prominently featured in Black British articulations of resistance and queer cultural products in particular. For example, Black British filmmaker Inge Blackman's short documentary/narrative film, *B.D. Women,* about Black British lesbians features a narrative portion that reenacts a Harlem speakeasy from the 1920s and 1930s as its reference to the longevity of a Black queer past. The title itself is taken from the blues song "B.D. Women" (short for Bulldagger Women) recorded by Lucille Bogan in 1935. The film also supports the live performance of

Ma Rainey's lesbian classic "Prove It on Me Blues" sung by British singer Adeola Agbagbi. In the film, the blues functions as a trope of Black queer culture, visually aided by an array of actors portraying lesbians, gay men, and bisexual people, and also cross-dressers and male-to-female and female-to-male transgender people who are producing or consuming the blues. In an interview, Blackman states that her deployment of the blues, and Harlem culture in particular, gave the British interviewees a context of longevity, a sense that "we have a past and that we have been around for a long time."[3] In the documentary portion of the film, an interviewee alludes to the Black signifying practice of utilizing Black vernacular culture to establish historical presence. In the film, one of the interviewees states that in the absence of historical evidence, "[S]ometimes you have to make up your own history." The act of making one's own history, as practiced in *B.D. Women* and *Trumpet,* implies that the historical archives are not enough and that Black queers have to cull together bits of memory through vernacular cultural practices in order to assert our prior existence.[4]

Critics of Kay's work have read the jazz theme as a way to resolve Black identity in the alienating landscape of Scotland. As Alan Rice contends, "[J]azz allows the Scottish African musician to resolve the contradictions of his multiple identities."[5] Others, however, have eschewed race as a central thematic in the novel, focusing instead on Joss's position as a transgender subject.[6] My reading of *Trumpet* takes up both positions to consider the novel as representing a part of the African diaspora unimagined in the normative construction of gender, sexuality, and Blackness presented in the permanent exhibit at MoAD.

I begin my analysis of the novel through Millie's and Colman's remembrances, which illustrate how mandated dominant norms of the family and the gendered body have erased Black transpeople from the diaspora and have stifled the transgender potential for remaking Black manhood in the diaspora. I then go on to show how the novel presents queer forms of resistance to state-mandated gender categories—a form of biopower that African diaspora scholarship has not taken into account. Because Joss's gender self-reassignment opposes state apparatuses of control and regulation, his transition resists colonial definitions of the Black body. At the same time, Joss's queering of the Black nuclear family troubles his own son's ideal of patriarchal Black manhood and Colman's fantasies about his own Black diasporic identity. Thus through jazz, as a form of knowledge and as a structural element of the novel, *Trumpet* deconstructs a web of normativity in representations of the Black diaspora and reinserts the Black queer body into the diasporic narrative.

"Ordinary Widow": Letting Go of the Oedipal Family

Like it or not, the Oedipus complex is far from coming to being among Negroes.[7]
—Frantz Fanon, *Black Skin, White Masks*

"His eyes look all loving and hurt. Like a tiny pitiful Oedipus."[8]
—Millie, in Kay, *Trumpet*

The two quotes above—one from Frantz Fanon, the other from the character Millie as she observes her child—contradict each other. Millie, the white mother/wife in the novel, sees her son as a "tiny Oedipus," implicating him and their family in the precarious psychological scaffolding made famous (and infamous) by Freud.[9] Freud used the Greek myth of Oedipus, who killed his father and married his mother, to describe the emotional attachments that children have to their parents and to illustrate what neurosis can develop if the child does not go through certain developmental processes. If all goes well, the child grows up to be a "normal" member of society. One wrong turn, and he or she will be mired in neurosis. Later on in the twentieth century, Fanon makes the astute observation that any Black child in the diaspora "will become abnormal on the slightest contact with the white world."[10] For Fanon, contact with whiteness is ubiquitous, displacing the patriarchal family drama of the Oedipus complex with a racial one. In this racial drama, the family patriarch is reduced to his genitals, a state usually reserved for women. If we continue Fanon's theorization to assess the gender/sexual implications of his pronouncement, it is clear that one of the consequences of capture and colonialism is that the Black family is forever touched by the queer. As Hortense Spillers has noted, "[I]n the historic outline of dominance, the respective subject positions of 'female' and 'male' adhere to no symbolic integrity."[11] In the novel, the father—Joss—literally disturbs the symbolic integrity of the dominant order by moving from a position of female to male. By doing so, Joss throws the queerness of the Black nuclear family into stark relief.

Millie's memories are the melodic thread that all the other series of memories riff on, and they are mostly associated with domesticity and the normative patriarchal family. As other people's memories, or riffs, accumulate, Millie's fantasy unravels, revealing the queerness of her normal life. Millie's desire to be "normal" symbolizes the Black diasporic attachment to dominant definitions of the normative family and the dissociative disavowal of the queer. To Millie, her life with Joss had achieved the epitome of the oedipal family unit. One morning after scolding her son Colman, Millie looks at him and notices that "[h]is eyes look all loving and hurt. Like a tiny pitiful Oedipus" (200). After Joss dies and the press bombards her, eager to exploit her grief, she says, "I tell myself I had a life, a family, family holidays. I tell myself to hold on to it. Not to let anybody make me let it go. Not even my son" (99). She repeats to herself that she is "an ordinary widow" (24) and that she is "not alone" (205) in her position as a wife who has lost her husband. In fact, her role as "wife" so defines her that she has trouble redefining herself after Joss's death. She says, "Once I was a fearless girl . . . Now what am I?" (8).

Millie is very protective of the domestic bliss she conjures in her mind of when Joss was alive. Her description of their home life relies on the ideal of the patriarchal nuclear family. She describes their Sundays like a fairy tale, "perfect, ordinary Sundays" (200), when Joss made brunch complete with "perfectly scrambled eggs" and traditional British "black pudding" made with sheep's blood (198). But if Colman expresses even minor discomfort about or objection to Millie's idea of a quaint domestic setting, she becomes infuriated. While "Joss [is] completely unbothered by Colman's bad humour," Millie fumes with a "terrible rage inside" at Colman. When the nine- or ten-year-old Colman refuses to eat scrambled eggs, Millie yanks him from the table, pulls him into his room, and says "stay there until you do like scrambled eggs" (199).

Her desire to hang onto her fantasy of the perfect family is disrupted by realizations that memories of even the most idyllic moments of familial bliss were filled with complicated interrelations between the family members. The juxtaposition of their domestic life with jazz powerfully evokes a dissonance between Millie's fantasy of their "average," "ordinary," and "typical" relationship and the improvisation of life. Joss "scats" at Sunday brunch—"Making it all up," as he "sings to us as he puts each plate down on the table with a flourish. Da da da dah da da da dee da didi bum bum bum brup brup brup baaaaade dup dup. Scatting" (198). Colman's reaction to the Sunday brunch scatting is to tell his father "Stop it, Daddy" or latterly "Shut up" (198). Jazz is a constant reminder to Colman that he belongs to an "untraditional house" (46). Colman's shame and hostility are coupled with Millie's frantic attempts to maintain a façade of perfection. She seethes with anger at Colman, insisting that he "be nice" (199) and not spoil her fantasy. She admits, "I have never felt angry towards anyone in my whole life like the anger I can feel towards my son. It scares me" (199). Millie is surprised about and afraid of the lengths to which she goes to preserve her hold on the "normal."

The interaction between Millie and Colman at the breakfast table is indicative of their warring personalities throughout the novel. Colman's desire to reject difference continuously challenges Millie's desire not to even acknowledge that the difference exists. Toward the end of the novel she begins to come to terms with the fact that her life is not as "ordinary" as she wants it to be. She says, "I am lying to myself. I am always lying to myself and I really must stop it" (205). This is Millie's first step to accepting her own difference. Her insistence that "[m]y husband died. I am now a widow" (205) both validates her claims to self-naming and complicates the categories of "husband" and "widow."

Joss's transgendered body throws Millie's sexual identity into limbo. She claims heterosexuality as both a mechanism of denial of difference and a strategy of resistance that would otherwise erase Joss's and Millie's own senses of self. Millie's assertion of the ordinariness of her family is also a refusal to let others decide her identity. "I can't see him as anything other than him, my Joss, my husband. It has always been that way since the first day he told me. I can't remember what I thought the day he first told me . . . But I don't think I ever thought he was wrong. I don't think so" (35). She uses the term "wrong" to indicate their innocence and basic goodness and also to counter the accusation that both she and Joss are freaks. In Millie's memory, Joss is also what he wanted to be: a father, a husband, and a musician. She refuses to remember him as dishonest, wicked, unethical, or erroneous in his understanding of himself and their family. But why does it have to be a standard nuclear family to not be "wrong"? Is that the only "right" way to be a family? Or to be a couple?

She repeats the plain truth of her situation, which she knows that a public ravenous for scandalous stories will especially deny her. The statement "my husband died and now I am a widow" (205) secures the gender relation that Millie and Joss had arranged. They organized their lives according to strict codes of male/female heterosexual roles: she was the stay-at-home wife/mother, and he was the breadwinning father/husband. They moved to London because it was practical for his career. But the sheer fact of his genitalia disarticulates this arrangement as "natural" to biology. One of the only reminders of the uncommonness of their relationship is Millie's security that he would never disclose his female body parts to another sexual partner. Twice she laughs at the thought that Joss would cheat on her with another woman. She treats the idea as an impossible scenario, as if there would never be another woman who could treat Joss like a man without making his female birth known to the public.

Millie's worst fear is of losing her status as a heterosexual woman. This fear of the lesbian has two implications: accepting a lesbian identity would invalidate her own sense of self and Joss's as well. For many real-life female partners of transmen, there is a great deal of anxiety about being misnamed and misidentified. How their own identities are perceived is often dependent on how their partners are "read" or interpreted by other people. Lesbians who have transmale partners are often disturbed if they are misperceived as straight women. For some straight women, when people learn of their partner's trans embodiment, they suddenly become "lesbians."[12] The trans body creates "vertigo" in the bifurcated system of sex, gender, and sexual classifications. The binary of heterosexual and homosexual are placed into crisis by the lack of clear lines of demarcation between man/woman, male/female. Refusing the mantle of "lesbian" is consistent with Millie's own chosen sexual identity and Joss's identity as heterosexual.

Millie's need for the ordinary contradicts the life she chooses as Joss's wife. Part of the crisis of his death is the public exposure of Millie herself. If Joss is a transgendered man, what does that make Millie? Her claim to normal heterosexuality is complicated by Joss's trans identity.

> My life is a fiction now, an open book. I am trapped inside the pages of it. Anything is possible. My life is up for grabs. No doubt they will call me a lesbian. They will find words to put on to me. Words that don't fit me. They will call him names. Terrible vertigo names. I can see myself holding the book out at arm's length, to see what words they have used, sinking with them. Down to the bottom, below the green film, to where the thick black mud lies. (154–55)

Millie's declaration that her "life is a fiction" speaks both to the disconnection that she feels with the identity of lesbian that others have assumed for her and to the "fiction" of misnaming all female-born people women. In the hands of the unscrupulous reporter, Sophie Stones, and in the minds of her former neighbors and friends, Millie's life turns into a sensationalist story that has little resemblance to what she remembers or experienced. She feels trapped "inside the pages" of the delimiting narrative of gender and sexuality imposed on all of us; she is trapped in a constantly flowing machine of normality that cannot attend to difference or deviation. Under this sex/gender system, Joss's female birth constricts him to an assigned femaleness, regardless of his own interpretation of his life. There is no room for ambiguity; Millie's relationship with a female-born person decides her sexual identity. As his wife, Millie becomes a woman who loves another woman, which is always marked as lesbian.

There is a split between private and public knowledge. Public knowledge of their private world is dangerous, putting her, and her life with Joss, "up for grabs" to be misnamed. Although not stated, "lesbian" seems to be the "terrible vertigo" name that will emerge from public scrutiny. She fears seeing the word in print and figuratively being dragged through the "thick black mud," and then pulled under and suffocated. For Millie, the label "lesbian" is more than untrue; it conjures up an image of Blackness that signifies dirt, deviance, aberration, and abnormality. For most of the novel she makes very few references to race, preferring to discuss how "ordinary"— read raceless—their lives were. Submerged beneath the surface of her desire for conformity is the messiness of her relationship with Joss and her family. Joss's body is thick with ambiguity; he is both male and female, Black and white, throwing all reference points that others use to define her into a bog of race traitors and dykes.

Millie's need to be considered "an ordinary widow" (24) is predicated on her melancholic attachment to normative structures of family and gender. Millie learns from her mother that a woman's identity depends on the strength of her husband. Millie's father is "weak and placid" (86), which Millie attributes to why her mother slowly declines in her marriage. She becomes frumpy and dull without patriarchal power to bring out the "gleaming underneath all the tweed" (86). After she gets used to having a Black man for a son-in-law, Millie's mother warms to Joss. In the presence of Joss's masculine energy, Millie's mother becomes an "entertaining," "fascinating," and "interesting" (86) person who dances and stays up late reminiscing about the loss of her strong, jealous husband. Faced with a withering patriarch, the mother develops alopecia, or hair loss, which uncovers her "flat, white" and "vulnerable" (85) femininity. Early in life Millie resolved to find a man that is "big and strong" and who will fill her life with a "fast ferocious love." She finally reached that goal once she met Joss, the "ferocious" Black man of her African fantasies (10). Millie clings to this ideal until the very end of the novel, never reevaluating the nuclear (oedipal) family as the perfect model for her life. She muses, "There must be a mistake we made. A big mistake; hiding somewhere that I somehow missed" (10). Millie's "mistake" is her reliance on the heteropatriarchal nuclear family as her ultimate shield against difference and as her standard of value. Millie's coveted position of "wife" is dependent on maintaining control over Joss's body by protecting his categorization as a "man."

Biopower: Losing the Body

Millie's life starts becoming chaotic when she first comes into contact with the force the state uses to control its subjects. This particular form of biopower,[13] the regulation of gender identity and documented gender markers of those under the state's purview, can give us more information about the state's mark on the body in an African diaspora context.[14] For the transperson, to deny one's gender identity is comparable to suspending life: one is alive but not living. When taken within the context of how Black identity is manipulated, controlled, and partly erased by the process of domination and dispersal, for Black people to engage in acts of self-determination is an incredible form of resistance. In *Trumpet,* Kay pays special attention to the role of state archives as structures of domination and arbiters of memory. The novel reveals that quotidian moments of filing and filling out paperwork—death certificates, funerary documents, adoption papers—are part of the state's regulation of the body. Millie and Joss manage to subvert the state's regulating structures, especially the medical establishment, until he dies.

From the moment that Joss's body is examined by Doctor Krishnamurty, who grants the death certificate, and the registrar, Sharif Nassar Sharif, both the definition of Joss's body and the way his body is regarded and understood by others are out of Millie's hands. The doctor and the registrar attest to how state policies and practices define our very physical beings through the minutiae of everyday bureaucratic procedures. The chapters in the novel written from the perspectives of the doctor and the registrar deliberately reveal every detail of their thoughts during the brief moment of deciding how to catalogue Joss's body. Joss represents chaos and disarray in the British colonial nation-state, a "proliferating difference that evades that eye, escapes [the] surveillance"[15] of state apparatuses of sex regulation, until death makes him vulnerable to the gaze of state power.

The first stop, according to British law, on the road to state-sanctioned gender reassignment is the medical profession.[16] The doctor who is sent to declare Joss dead redefines him. As she examines his body, she is baffled and "struck" (44) by the fact that Joss's male body has breasts and a vagina.

> Doctor Krishnamurty got out her medical certificate and started filling in the obvious, prior to her own examination. Time of death: 1.12. Date: 21 July 1997. Sex: Male . . . She undid the pyjamas to examine the body. There were many bandages wrapped around the chest of the deceased which she had to undo . . . Doctor Krishnamurty felt as if she was removing skin, each wrapping of bandage that she peeled felt unmistakably like a layer of skin. . . . When she first saw the breasts (and she thought of them again driving home, how strange they looked, how preserved they looked) she thought they weren't real breasts at all. At least not women's breasts. . . . They hadn't aged. It took her pulling down the pyjama bottoms for her to be quite certain. (43–44)

The mundane act of cataloguing the "obvious" exposes how the categories of "male" and "female" are more nuanced and complicated than medical definitions allow. Doctor Krishnamurty at first sees Joss as he saw himself: a man. However, the medical eye is caught off guard by what it considers a contradiction, and the doctor is not really able to process what she is looking at. She creates various scenarios of explanation of why a man would have breasts. She is taken aback by Joss's "proliferating difference," and she is rendered unable to categorize the body. Her initial report of "male" is challenged by a set of "strange" and "preserved" breasts. Actual binding makes breasts flat and saggy; however, in Kay's fictional realm, Joss's breasts are perfectly preserved, symbolizing that although still physically attached to his body, they are from another part of his life.[17] The bandages are "unmistakably like a layer of skin" (43); they have become part of his body as opposed to an artificial covering that hides his "true" biological sex. In her mind's eye, his body morphs from male to some uncertain category of female. The doctor is overcome with a dissonance that makes her check his genitals to be "quite certain" of his sex.

Shortly after *Trumpet* was published, the British state issued a report on the legal status of transsexuals in England, Northern Ireland, Wales, and Scotland. According to the April 2000 British Home Office's "Report of the Interdepartmental Working Group on Transsexual People," the state is particularly invested in identifying and keeping track of individual transsexual people.[18] The focus of the report is to legitimize transsexual individuals through the process of surgical reassignment. It states that "what can be achieved through the transsexual person's own efforts and with counseling, drugs and surgery is social," not a "real" biological change. According to the report, "the biological sex of an individual is determined by their chromosomes, which cannot be changed."[19] In other words, the social reassignment of gender roles must accompany multiple and permanent changes to the body. This transformation is possible and legitimate only if sanctioned by a variety of medical authorities, including psychologists, epidemiologists, and surgeons. Thus the state figures prominently in issues of sex definition because individuals have to appeal to power in order to be recognized. Of supreme importance to the recognition of a person as "genuinely" transsexual is evidence from a medical practitioner that the individual lives and functions as a member of the "opposite biological sex."[20]

Birth registration is also heavily policed, and a great deal of effort is made to secure the birth sex as official and immutable. The health service notifies birth registrars of every birth, including the baby's sex.[21] Subsequent changes to birth records are not considered unless medical evidence is provided to show that there was a clerical error in identifying the child's assigned birth sex. However, even with specific regulations as to the immutable character of birth-sex registration, birth certificates contain a warning, indicating that the state recognizes that cracks in the system nullify the efforts to make identity immutable.[22] The coupling of the physician and the registrar is embedded in British gender law and practice. The separation of fact and fiction is not always easy to determine, a concept that is implied in the novel's inclusion of separate chapters dedicated to official pronouncements.

The report by the British Home Office is particularly interested in the areas of "birth registration, marriage, family law, the Criminal Justice System, pensions and benefits, insurance, employment and sport."[23] In Scotland it is possible for a transsexual person to apply to the court to be considered a parent of a child if her or his partner already has a child, "even though according to the birth certificates both persons were of the same sex."[24] As part of what Judith Butler describes as a myth of origins or biological ideal of sex,[25] the state medical guidelines require appellants for official sex reassignment to create a narrative that they feel "trapped" and have the "wrong" bodies that can be corrected only with medical intervention. Despite the Home Office's insistence that surgical and hormonal intervention "make" the transsexual, Joss has accomplished his male identity through his own efforts.

Joss's male identity and body is essentially "lost" to the state when the doctor designates him "female." As a result of her "striking" confrontation with queer embodiment, Doctor Krishnamurty cautiously crosses out "male" and prints "'female' in large childish letters" (44) on his death certificate, thereby setting in motion the official state negation of Joss's life as male. Immediately, Millie fears that she too will be lost in the process of misidentification. She is immediately suspect; the doctor looks at Millie in wonder, giving her a "searching look" (44) in the hope that Millie's face will reveal the "strange" circumstances. She leaves Joss and Millie's home "in her white car at quite a considerable speed" (44), only to be haunted by the image of Joss's young breasts as she drives. The doctor goes through a transformation after confronting Joss's corpse: "The pale, bloodless light dawned on her" (44). The reader is not privy to this epiphany. Maybe she recognizes that her previous reliance on official knowledge regarding identity and embodiment was inadequate. Perhaps the light is a new awareness of the variety of bodily permutations that resist duality, which she cannot flee no matter how fast she drives.

The doctor's disorientation and vertigo are experienced by most of the other characters in the novel, as the revelation of queer embodiment disrupts each character's desire for the normal and ordinary, exposing those constructs as illusion and fantasy. One of these characters is the district registrar who catalogues Joss's death certificate. The medical certificate and the death certificate together are required in order for Millie to bury Joss. They are links in a chain of events that require others to endorse Joss's passing into death. Several chapters in the novel, including this one, portray state regulation and classification as a slippery, porous system, flawed and stymied by difference. The power of state classification is juxtaposed with the disorienting presence of a dissimilar subject. Joss throws the system into a crisis of categories, failing "definitional distinction" showing sex and gender to be a "borderline that becomes permeable, [permitting] . . . border crossings from one (apparently) distinct category to another."[26]

"The registrar had seen everything" (73). The registrar, Sharif Nassar Sharif, is a man enamored with his place in the order of things. He loves the shear simplicity of the organization of the state catalogue, and he is honored to be part of the systems of classification and regulations. "He kept a tidy office. Every person was special to him; the crucial moments, a privilege. There surely can be few moments to compete with the awesome finality of Sharif Nassar Sharif's birth, death and marriage certificates" (75). In the logic of the state, "birth, death and marriage" mark the beginning, middle, and end of an individual life. As an instrument of biopower, registration tracks, traces, and regulates the lives of state subjects.

Both Sharif and Krishnamurty are members of (formerly) colonized peoples who live in the metropole and continue to support the state structures of domination. Sharif brings some humanity to the office, believing that "everyone in his office needed a moment of quiet" (75). His sense of paying special attention reveals his determination to allow people to reflect, to appreciate the power of the process of registration itself, the solemnity of classification, and the magnitude of the official state inventory. He states that "the signature on paper was momentous" (75). He attempts to make the process more civilized, not the "in and out with conveyor belt brutality, cancer, divorce, stillbirth" of the other registrars (75). The certificates themselves are made with his "marble fountain pen" (75). The phallic power of the state is symbolically extended through Sharif's marble pen. Sharif is a kind bureaucrat, a gentle masculine presence who "loathe[s] violence" and makes his secretary handle any physical altercations that take place in the office. The naming ritual arouses special passions as registrants engage in arguments and fights with "slaps and punches" (76). He coolly witnesses these acts of desperation, which demonstrate the frustration that people have with officially registering with the state—in birth or in death. Sharif admires the humbling authority of the archive itself.

Millie enters his office with reverence for the weightiness of attempting to register a person who was "never officially sanctioned anywhere" (80). Joss's records reflect his life:

[A] birth certificate for the deceased bearing the name Josephine Moore. A medical card for the deceased . . . under the name Josephine Moore . . . no pension book . . . a marriage certificate for the deceased bearing the name Joss Moody. It was all fascinating stuff for Nassar Sharif. (78)

Sharif is awed by the dizzying set of inconsistent documents and resists his desire to ask Millie "how it was done" (79). The novel is very adamant about not focusing on how Joss is able to maneuver without official sanction; rather, it pays attention to how his life challenges official structures of power and arrangements of affinity.

Sharif is impressed with Joss's achievement and Millie's pride in her husband and marriage, enough to compromise on the death certificate and write "Joss Moody" in his perfect, "elegiac" handwriting. This scene is a testimony to the strength of small, intimate moments to undermine the authority of the state. In the Home Office Report the phrase "opposite biological sex" is crucial to the state's definition of a transsexual as one who is "really" one sex but has a medical condition that drives him/her to live like another. People who identify as both male and female, or neither, or who do not change themselves through hormones or surgery, are not recognized by the state at all.

Sharif is shocked that Joss was "never officially sanctioned anywhere," which is anathema to state power. As Homi Bhabha argues, "It is not that the voice of authority is at a loss for words. It is, rather, that the colonial discourse has reached that point when, faced with the hybridity of its objects, the presence of power is revealed as something other than what its rules of recognition assert."[27] Difference can throw the colonizing state into a crisis of categorization, which leads to the recognition of its own lack of absolute power. Kay's use of individuals to represent state power is in keeping with Foucault's assertion that power does not flow top-down through a centralized, nameless, faceless form of the state, but flows more insidiously through individuals multidirectionally.[28] It is the prerogative of the biopolitical state to make policy and law and to use internal and external forms of coercion to enforce that law.[29] In this case, the policies and laws of sex reassignment are enforced by a denial of access to state recognition and participation in state-regulated functions. The human component to state power is the secret to its weaknesses. The state's assertion (and lack) of power through categorical order is witnessed by the inability of its agents to accommodate every case of identification, undermining the bureaucratic authority of Doctor Krishnamurty and the registrar, Sharif Nassar Sharif. The state has a stake in maintaining order and imposing racial and gender hierarchies through identifying the "norm and the deviant."[30] However, when the distinction between normal and deviant clashes in a cloud of uncertainty, the individuals who represent state power mourn the loss of their ultimate authority through a presentation of disorientation.

Sharif matches his ardor for names and registration with his passion for the instrument of marking itself. He considers the red pen to be a "brash, loudmouthed, insensitive cousin who ought not to have received *anything* in the family fortune" (77). Sharif's "family" of official instruments is nothing without the "fine" white paper that is used for the certificates, or the "family fortune" (77). The pens and the paper are symbolic of the archive of the (post)colonial state, representative of the lost grandeur of the empire. As phallic emblems of the "lost" empire's power to create and destroy with one stroke, Sharif's pens are imbued with a familial lineage and ranked in terms of worth and inheritance of their privilege to mark the paper. Sharif's Bangladeshi childhood prepares him to grace the page with "elegiac" homage to the state catalogue (75). He is upset by the doctor's red markings, having "never in his life seen a medical certificate where male was crossed out and female entered in red. On the grounds of pure aesthetics, Sharif found the last minute change hurtful" (77). He conceives of the state registry archive as an aesthetic object, a masterpiece of order to be admired and respected. The disruption by Dr. Krishnamurty's red "female" is an assault on those aesthetics. Red is a color reserved primarily for the purposes of correction (especially associated with students). "The red biro," he says "should never have been born. It was a cheap impostor, an embarrassment to the fine quality [white] paper used on such certificates" (77). The perfect symbiosis between the white paper and the Black pen stroke is ruined by the evidence of the registry's vulnerability to error.

The funeral director, Albert Holding, is one of the most virulent agents of the state concerned with preserving official "genital classification."[31] As opposed to the final "dawning" (44) of insight that appears to Dr. Krishnamurty and the empathetic, "elegiac" (75) compromise of Sharif, Holding relishes the idea of "correcting" anything "untoward in the death certificate" (112). The red pen again becomes the instrument of correction that will rectify Joss's breach of the sex/gender system.

Holding considers it his "duty" to "brutally and violently obliterat[e] 'male' and insert female in bold, unequivocal red" (112–13). However, he is robbed of the "satisfaction" (112) of obliterating Joss's life and identity with the stroke of his pen, a phallic image suggesting a "brutal" and "violent" reclaiming of phallic power from Joss's usurpation. Holding is frustrated that he does not have "something [official] to do" (113) in order to correct Joss's convincing masculine presentation, even in death. As a way to quell his "terrible [castration] anxiety," Holding again imagines what he expects to see. Unable to reconcile the "disturbing incongruity"[32] between his anticipation that Joss's genital anatomy must follow his masculine gender, Holding transforms Joss into a "woman" in his mind. Suddenly "the face . . . transform[s]" (110), metamorphosing from the "man" he first encountered into the "round, more womanly" face (110) he needs it to be. The "threat of a gender-ambiguous world"[33] haunts Holding, creating a memory that he finds himself "compelled to return to again and again" (111).

Joss's vagina severely disturbs Holding's security about his own manhood. When he undressed the body he

> noticed that he had rather a lot of pubic hair. A bush. The absence of the penis did not strike him straight away. Perhaps because he was expecting it, he imagined it for a while. When he did notice after a few moments that there was no visible penis, he actually found himself rummaging in the pubic hair just to check that there wasn't a very, very small one hiding somewhere. The whole absence made Albert Holding feel terribly anxious, as if he had done something wrong. As if he was not doing his job properly. (109)

Holding's inability to find a penis on Joss's corpse causes an anxiety attack. He rummages for Joss's "lost" penis with a concern for his own performance as if he is "not doing his job properly." He quickly compensates for his anxiety with his desire to violently destroy the evidence of his own impotence. Holding's main regret is the "horrifying" (113) realization that he does not have anything "official" to do "in such an unusual business" (113). This cold fact disturbs his unfaltering belief that what made "a man a man and a woman a woman was the differing sexual organs" (115). He worries that his unconscious will never be the same, that the terrifying image "where she appeared to him as a woman and nights where he appeared to him as a man" (113) will haunt his sleep. He is left to ruminate on the fact that a "horrifying" ambiguity exists, "hiding somewhere" (109), perhaps deep inside of himself, and there is no thorough, effective, or official way to obliterate its presence.

Colman, too, is haunted by the overwhelming feeling that he has "lost" his Black manhood once he knows his father's secret. His sense of loss of self is facilitated by his relationship with Sophie Stones, an ambitious reporter. Stones is a symbol of the vulgar way that mass culture transforms sexual and gender difference into freakery and perversity. At first Stones convinces Colman to divulge the details of his childhood in a tell-all book that she will write about Joss's life. She anticipates "Big Money" from the book (125).

Determined to unveil the details of what happened in the "curtained secrecy of his bedroom" (126), Sophie narrates Joss's life in terms that distort and destroy what he had attempted to build.

Her character represents the fragility of (Black) celebrity and its vulnerability to the caprices of cultural regulation. Joss easily slips from being "Britain's legendary trumpet player" (6) to "the Transvestite Trumpet Player" (125). She says,

> The word transvestite has got more in it than the word cross-dresser. What is a cross-dresser anyway when he or she is at home? . . . *Transvestite* has a nice pervy ring to it. When we have finished the Book, Joss Moody's records will be selling better than they ever did. We're doing her a favour. We're making her immortal. (126)

Stones's insistence on referring to Joss with female pronouns and terms that she considers more "pervy" or perverse is part of the way she degrades his life and memory. Popular cultural memory is easily manipulated for the purpose of maintaining categories of normalization. She is, in Foucauldian terms, part of the regulatory matrix of society that keeps categories from slipping into ambiguity. If "Britain's legendary trumpeter" (6) can be both Black and Scottish, male and female, heterosexual and transsexual, then the categories by which society is arranged would begin to unravel. In *Freaks Talk Back,* Joshua Gamson argues that when disruptions confuse the strict binary order of sexual and gendered identity arrangements, it is the role of the mass media to "stitch things back together, to hide the seams and make sure the either–or categories are still intact."[34] When the nation cannot fold individuals into its plot, it must displace them in order to recover its rigidity. The (British) nation needs exemplary Blacks in order to maintain its façade of multiculturalism. When Joss ("the good Black") turns "bad," the nation recovers itself, through the media, with claims of being duped. As a "pervy transvestite," Joss is unthreatening and made palpable to a public culture anxious about its own hybridity and ambiguity. As the token Black Scottish person, Joss is the example of the nation's tolerance of difference. In addition, Scottish manhood is on the line, and a premium is placed on not acknowledging gender and sexual uncertainty and unfixity. For example, Joss's friend and band mate, Big Red McCall, admits to Sophie Stones that he "beat up anybody who said [that Moody had a baby face]" (148). To let the comment stand would open up Big Red's own ambiguous desires to public scrutiny.

For a nation that has difficulty admitting that there is a history of Blacks in Scotland, Joss is the ultimate "unadmittable" figure because he is Black *and* gender nonconforming.[35] Public acknowledgment of Joss would release the openly suppressed secret that gender and sex are not immutable; that patriarchal manhood in particular is vulnerable to "trespass" by female-bodied persons; and that gender transgression happens often *undetected* by both the state and its subjects. Stones places her career on the line by pursuing the book because she counts on the public's ambivalence toward those it considers "abnormal." She laments that "the public may hate perverts, but they love reading about them" (264). By placing difference outside of itself, the dominant culture can deny that "every person goes about their life with a bit of perversion that is unadmittable, secretive, loathed" (264).

Joss Moody's fictional existence as Black, Scottish, and queer is in direct confrontation with the national understanding of Scottish identity. In one of the few critical pieces devoted to the novel, Monterrey states that Kay does not revise Scotland's "long (social and political) history or [emphasize] well-known cultural differences."[36] *Trumpet* also recalls and rewrites Scottish history as a mixed Afro-European lineage, asserting syncretic relationships between desire and race, and national and gender identity. Through the deployment of a mixed-race transgendered character, Joss Moody, Kay redefines Scottish manhood in terms of its lingering African impressions and multivoiced resonances. Kay uses the aesthetics of jazz, namely, polycentricism, to provide a picture of Scottish manhood as richly layered and inexorably linked to the movement and condition of peoples of African heritage.

"My father didn't have a dick": Giving Up the Diaspora Patriarch

Once Joss dies, the pretended stability of the "normal" crumbles, revealing a crisis of Black masculine identity for Colman. His revelation that "[m]y father didn't have a dick. . . . My father had a pussy" (61) is more than a recitation of body parts; it is also a terrified recognition of the fragility and structural femininity of Black manhood relative to white heteropatriarchal masculinity. Once Stones suspects that Colman will no longer cooperate, she writes in Colman's voice: "On the person who I thought was my father, breasts and the pubic hair looked disgusting. Freakish. . . . His pubic hair and breasts looked grotesque, monstrous" (265). Stones's appropriation of Colman's anger and shock turns into an opportunity to produce Joss as "monstrous" and "disgusting."

Stones's words are reminiscent of Colman's first memory of hearing a Black man being called an "ape" (54) on a public bus in Glasgow. Colman remembers not being able to stop looking at the Black man who "was just sitting with his eyes low, looking at the bus floor" (54). Colman realized he was another example of Black monstrosity for the "nasty man" (54) and the other whites on the bus. Colman becomes conscious of his race at the moment the adult Black male is animalized by the whites on the bus, which provokes him to look at the color of his skin. The Black man is symbolically "castrated"; that is, he is stripped of the patriarchal manhood displayed by the white racist men who have the power to force him to bow his head in shame.

Colman repeats this memory when Stone asks him for the earliest memory of his father. He remembers the castration of the man on the bus in connection with his anger about discovering his father's "castration," thereby linking Colman's mourning of his father with the larger mourning of Black manhood. Colman's rage and pain regarding the loss of the Black male phallus are not unique to his character but speak directly to the ongoing condition of Black men's melancholic desire for their fathers, melancholia being the inability to cease the mourning process and replace the lost object. The "lost" Black father stems not only from the absence of Black men from individual households but also from the male child's witnessing Black male devaluation.

Colman's memory of the Black man on the bus is consistent with David Marriott's concept that the initiating crisis of Black manhood arises with the Black male child witnessing his father's debasement. This lynching can be real or part of the cultural imaginary of Black men as "phobic object— beaten, disfigured, lynched," which circulates through the unconscious of the Black child as much as it does anywhere else in society.[37] The male child's exposure to white racist "hatred predicated on . . . the sadistic desire to witness the spectacle"[38] of Black (male) death exists as a "reminder of how fragile his possession of himself, his 'manhood' can be."[39] Realizing the "real difference between black and white men" creates the condition in which the Black male experiences himself as castrated.[40] Colman is haunted by the Black *imago* of the white fantasy of the Black male "mugger."[41] He observes that "[m]en who look exactly like Colman are always on the news" identified as "more likely to be muggers" to the racist eye of the police (224). He recognizes himself as the epitome of criminality in the white mind, at risk of racial brutality, often symbolized by the specter of the lynched Black man.[42]

Colman "worship[ped]" (49) his father and felt inadequate in every way—he could not match his father's talent, wealth, celebrity, or style. Joss manages to have the patriarchal dream of a wife, a son, and a successful career.[43] No matter how much Colman appreciates the life that his father has given him, he still says, "No man wants a lesbian for a father. Maybe for his mother. But for his father!" (66). The conversion of Joss from (trans) man to "lesbian" reveals Colman's own fears that he has suddenly "lost" his Black father figure, leaving him vulnerable to never being recognized as a "man" himself. His father's absent penis leaves him with a need to reassure his own manhood and convince himself that his "cock is bigger and harder now that his father was dead" (140). With the desire to have a "hard" and "big" cock comes the desire to use his phallus as a tool of domination and revenge. He fantasizes about sodomizing Sophie Stones: "He imagines lifting Sophie Stones onto the desk in the office he has not seen. He pulls down the zip of his jeans. He gets it out. He runs his finger up the crack of her arse. This is what she'll like. . . . Fucks full of cruelty and sleaze" (140).

As a white woman, Stones is what Frantz Fanon called the Black man's "revenge." The white woman's body is the instrument of a lost humanity and manhood, whereas Black women's are not because of their alleged "worthlessness."[44] By "fucking" Sophie Stones, Colman wants to unleash his own rage at being "fucked" by her and everyone else (including his parents). The white female is a constant reminder that he is Black and therefore never man enough, always in a subordinate—and therefore "feminized"—position to dominant white patriarchy. Caught in the "nonmen–nonwomen" ambiguous gender category, Joss enters into the realm of other Black men as a reminder that Black men in general are a hybrid type.[45] Black men *and* Black women are seen as nonhuman absence, and as Lewis Gordon argues, white men are pure presence, "manliness *in toto,*"[46] while Black men are "penises that are holes."[47]

In an anti-Black, misogynist schema, white men can deny that they have any holes at all. White masculinity "attempts to close all its holes," denying the anus, and "when he kisses, nothing enters his mouth—he enters" and penetrates only.[48] Black men are reduced to and "fixated at the genital," disallowed access to the realm of dominance in the (white patriarchal) social realm.[49] Colman must come to terms with the fact that his father did not have a penis and that he too will have to live in that hybrid gendered space of Blackness. Reminders of Black male proximity to the feminine become the source of incredible anxiety for Black men and manifest in an internalized misogynistic need to distance themselves from Black femininity.

Josephine is a phobic presence for Joss. He tells Millie to "leave her alone" (93), but at the same time it's Josephine/Joss who sends his mother, Edith Moore, letters and checks. He is still Josephine in Greencock, Scotland. She (Josephine) is the absent presence of Black female experience in the diaspora, the denied past that sustains the present and the future. Without her, there can be no Joss. He is his own mother, so to speak. However, in order to be a (Black) "man," he has to deny his own reproduction. That is, his biological mother and his figurative "mother" in Josephine constitute the feminine that must be displaced from desire in order to fulfill the oedipal contract. To be a proper oedipalized male requires the phobic denial of identification with the (castrated) mother in favor of becoming the father.[50]

As Fanon has said, Black men do not "have" the phallus; instead, the Black man "*is* a penis."[51] That slippage between penis and phallus is vital to unpacking Joss's relationship to the oedipal family and to understanding how Joss's presence complicates the Black masculine melancholic relationship to oedipal masculinity. For Fanon, Black men are constructed through the white imaginary as sexual "beasts,"[52] an extremely frightening or "phobogenic" object of sexual revulsion.[53] White patriarchy becomes the universal "father" in the form of the master, the colonizer, and even the welfare state.[54] This displacement of Black patriarchy makes Black men even more attached to the Black paternal, turning Black responsible manhood into a melancholic object for Black men (and women).

In *Trumpet,* both Joss and Colman prioritize the relationship with the father to the exclusion of the mother. In chapter 1, I discussed the tendency in three Black lesbian neo-slave narratives to replace the white mistress for the "lost" Black maternal figure. However, in *Trumpet,* the father entirely displaces the mother as the first primary love object with whom the son experiences the feeling of wholeness and perfection. As discussed in chapter 1, according to Lacan, this feeling of wholeness is always an illusion,[55] yet for Black men the "father" himself is an elusive and illusory figure. As David Marriott has stated, Black fathers are "murdered, usurped and withheld, by a culture, and a nation" intent on representing Black fathers as "inadequate," "weak," "brutal," and (irresponsibly) absent.[56] If the son rejects identification with the white "father," then he is left to a disappointing eternal search for the Black father and Other, the Black phallic father who will lead him into the Symbolic.

Black male mourning and longing for "daddy" and anxiety about legitimate paternity are predicated on a phobia of Black female uncontrolled sexuality. The presumed Black female sexual uncontrollability propels Black families into a "tangle of pathology."[57] (This nightmare of uncertain paternity and usurped masculinity has double meaning for Colman, who thinks that he was gifted with the perfect Black father, only to be faced with the ultimate oedipal nightmare of the father with female biology.) The oedipal drive is in crisis as a result of slavery, and colonial domination propels Marriott to reposition the need for the Black father to reassure the son, to provide him with a model of manhood that foments and nurtures his manhood, and to be the primary attachment for him.[58] In psychoanalytic terms of development, this Black father–son bond is the main interaction at the crucial stage before language and before the recognition of difference, usually associated with the pure bliss of being one with the mother. Instead, the Black male is connected to the father, and all subsequent relations are about yearning to experience pure father-love.

This primary father–son bond is demonstrated in the novel in the scenes where Colman remembers his childhood:

> I goes in my father's bedroom. I am six years old. I opens their wardrobe. My daddy keeps his trumpet in here. I opens the big silver box, and there it is, all shiny inside. I touched it. I did touch it. Then I strokes it like I've seen my father do and it purrs. I runs my finger over the keys then along the fur, the purple fur in the box. My fingers are burning hot . . . Then my mum finded me . . . She says, Colman, what are you doing? Get out of your father's trumpet. (49)

The trumpet is an obvious phallic symbol; however, like a dildo, it is detached from Joss's body, able to be taken with him or left behind. Colman experiences reassurance in Joss's absence and pleasure in being close to his father's phallus. He "strokes" it, imagining that it purrs under his fingers. Joss's instrument of Black manhood is hybrid. Like Gordon's description of the male penis as an "ambiguous organ,"[59] Joss's trumpet has a hole (at both ends). Tomás Monterrey has also suggested that the trumpet is an "ambivalent" instrument; however, he suggests that Joss chooses it in an attempt to compensate for the organ he lacks.[60] Colman's fascination with the instrument speaks to an ambivalent structural positioning that is broader than Joss's but that Joss's anatomy makes salient for Colman. He claims to Sophie Stones that he is "one hundred percent heterosexual" (57); however, masculinity can never be completely sealed off from the feminine, and its claims of purity are a "chosen falsehood, a form of denial."[61] In this way, Joss is like any other Black man, ambiguously gendered and caught in tangles of denial of his own femininity in order to claim manhood.

The mother is an interruption in the bonding between Black fathers and sons. Millie disturbs Colman's fondling of his father's phallus, which is tucked away inside a "fur" case lining, creating the image of pubic hair surrounding a vagina. Both the case or "box" and the trumpet are soothing to young Colman, who enjoys touching them both without anxiety or ambivalence. Colman has urges as a child to see his father's penis. His friend Sammy compares his father's penis to his own, only to be disappointed in his own lack. Colman too is afraid that he won't "measure up" to his father's manhood and therefore fights his temptation to peek into the bedroom door (55). He satisfies his need for reassurance and curiosity with the trumpet as a stand-in. However, when adult Colman finds out about Joss's female past, he is repulsed that he could have been confronted with Joss's "big frigging mound of venus" (55). The feminine is tolerable only in displaced subordinate association with masculinity. The fur lining is there to protect the trumpet, not to usurp its place as the primary object. Joss's "mound of venus," however, strikes fear into the hearts of both Colman and the funeral director; it stalks their manhood, threatening to render it obsolete.

If Black masculinity is not in the penis, then what is left for Colman? He declares that his "father didn't have a dick" (61), but Colman modeled his own Black masculinity on Joss's. Colman lives his life in his father's shadow as his "father's disciple" (62), desiring his approval of him "as a man, as a black man" (49) and finally admitting, "I fucking worshipped him" (49). He studied his father's look, his way of walking and talking in the world, with awe and admiration.

The desire for legible manhood demands a heterosexual and patriarchal nuclear family for its coherence, and Joss, Millie, and Colman are no exception. As a result of the demand that manhood makes on family structures and gendered relations, Joss, in the last instance, is the "diaspora patriarch" so woefully desired and mourned. Kay attempts to intervene in this project by making Joss a gentle figure of a man who loves his family; however, the novel remains in the patrilineal register. Marriott describes the Black father as existing in a tradition of "theft and distortion" that haunts the experiences of contemporary Black men and can be resolved only through telling the Black father's story.[62]

Joss's father, John Moore, is resurrected at the end in order to finally give Colman the "father story" of origins that he craves.[63] At first Joss scolds Colman, saying that he lacks the imagination to "pick" from the richness of the African diaspora in order to make up his family's story, as we read in the quote at the beginning of this chapter. However, by the end of the novel, Joss writes to Colman, revealing that Moore was a child in some unremembered African country and was sent by his father to Scotland for education and opportunity. Joss finally clarifies the Moore/Moody patrilineage, relieving some the "cultural unconscious fantasies of black men" to "lay claim to particular accounts" of the diaspora.[64] John Moore traveled across the Atlantic from Africa to Europe, bringing with him very little cultural knowledge and leaving his then-daughter Josephine in the predicament of loss, displacement, alienation, and a vague memory of music. Josephine uses this memory to construct herself as Joss.

Colonialism causes rupture, such that John Moore's African past is lost in the move. Joss says, "[M]y father felt as if he too was disembodied. His own body became broken up in the fog" (273). John Moore's body is dismembered and disremembered in the violence of the break from his African childhood. Although his birth country is "drowned" (273) in a sea of forgetting, he is haunted by the ghostly "wailing" of an Africa mourning his absence (273). What Joss hears is the wailing of the disremembered on both sides of the Atlantic, moaning/mourning their lost ones. In *Trumpet* it is the Black father-love loss that fills Joss's letter to Colman, giving him the opportunity to then write his own "father story." Joss says, "I am leaving myself to you . . . I will be your son in a strange way. You will be my father telling or not telling my story" (277). This reversal of father and son presents a possible way to feed the Black father-hunger that starves Black men's ability to reinvent themselves, to create a "loving epitaph" through which to "play out [the] wishes and dreams" of Black men in order to facilitate a new beginning.

Joss emphasizes his dedication to displacing a story of paternal origins in favor of diasporic creative imagining. He implores Colman to "make it up" (58) and create his own story instead of relying on an external "truth" to solidify his identity. "Joss had built up such a strong imaginary landscape within himself that he said it would affect his music to go to the real Africa. Every black person has a fantasy Africa, he'd say. Black British people, Black Americans, Black Caribbeans, they all have a fantasy Africa. It is all in the head" (34). The Atlantic triumvirate that Joss identifies—"Black British people, Black Americans, Black Caribbeans"—makes connections throughout the diaspora as a result of the shared music of jazz. Jazz improvisation creates the possibility of self-invention toward the "creat[ive]-imagining" of identity.[65] These points of the diaspora are not the same, but each geographic locale interprets, envelops, reorganizes, and transforms itself. In this way, the memory of shared origins is never completely "lost" but is in a constant state of "becoming." Through a process of constructed "memory, fantasy, narrative and myth," the need for a "law of origin" or consistent and tangible "home" is not dependent on a single physical site that holds the key to authenticity.[66] What is important is that these cultures do not stop at their reformulation in Accra, Kingston, London, Havana, or New York, but continue on, remaking and reconstituting the circuit in a never-ending exchange of repositioning, unfolding "beyond any arbitrary closure it [reformulation] makes."[67] In the novel, jazz is an epistemology that drives the reimagining of components of identity that are generally seen as immutable. In this case, Joss remakes his own gender identity, growing up a girl and then transforming himself into a man as a concrete expression of the improvisational element of jazz. Jazz becomes a practice that allows for the continuous production of the body's meaning. Joss is in a constant state of gendered "becoming," even through death.

"Music":
Authenticating and Dislocating Black Masculine Gender

In the final pages of "Mama's Baby, Papa's Maybe," Hortense Spillers insists that the rupture of African genders through the Middle Passage and the denial of Black gendered being in the New World load Blacks with the burden of decision: to keep chasing the genders of white society that we are excluded from or to embrace other possibilities. Sophie Stones's description of Joss as "monstrous" is in keeping with dominant white images of Black corporeality. However, Spillers suggests that we as Black people should stop trying to be "normal" and embrace the "monstrosity" (of the female with the potential to "name").[68] In other words, embrace the feminine in Black masculinity, and reposition Black women in a place of authority on the level of the symbolic.

Millie observes that it was the "early days for jazz and early days for [Joss], for his new life" (16). Joss creates himself, and Millie watches "Joss walk up the street, hands in his pockets. He has a slow deliberate walk, like he's practiced it" (15). Joss derives his manhood from copying other Black male jazz artists. Colman notes that the Black men who are Joss's professional and political role models are, to Colman's frustration, from the United States. He says, "All jazzmen are fantasies of themselves, reinventing the Counts and Dukes and Armstrongs, imitating them" (190). In fact, Joss is actually a revision of the Black masculinity that African American jazzmen construct for themselves. Instead of being a classic womanizer or abuser, Joss is a responsible family man and faithful husband.[69] Black men become ideals of civic or cultural manhood, just as Joss is "Britain's Legendary Trumpet Player" (6), through the process of copying other (Black) "icons and models"[70] in order to mitigate their "demoniac or bestial typecasting."[71]

As if in answer to his own questions about his father's affinity for African American masculinity, on his way to gather more information for Stones's book about Joss's mother, Colman sees (or dreams) a man on the train who literalizes his idealization of his father. The man walks down the aisle of the train, balancing "two cups of tea. . . . Graceful. He doesn't bang into anyone or trip over any foot. Colman watches him come along the corridor when suddenly he sees that it is his father." Colman pursues the man until he is reassured that the man is not his father. Colman's man on the train is representative of both Joss's delicate balance between his past and present and his balance of African diasporic masculinities. The man does not have an easy walk; he sways "from one side to the other" but balances the cups "with such dignity, such fine balance . . . as if that is all he has been doing his whole life." In this case, Joss is a composite of the best parts of Black masculinity, which require a balance of masculine and feminine attributes.[72]

Joss experiences his African diaspora consciousness partially through mimicking the gender performativity of other Black men, as transatlantic racial connections often take place through the circulation, consumption, internalization, and recirculation of "particular definitions of gender and sexuality."[73] As Marriott argues, the act of imitation may be a situation of relief from white fantasies of Black monstrosity. The resistance to white imagination is also a disclosure that (Black) manhood is not "natural" or "original" but socially constructed and performative (a copy of a copy) and therefore not restricted to the born-male individual.[74] In Joss's world, Black men reinvent themselves outside the *imago* of the "criminal" and the "mugger," though still maintaining a "misogynistically and hyper-heterosexually politicized black manhood."[75]

The performative nature of heterosexual Black masculinity is occluded in the pressure to naturalize it in the face of white patriarchal racial castration.[76] Black manhood is authenticated by the successful reproduction of aesthetic principles. Everyone who meets Joss is impressed with his smooth appearance—his Black masculinity studied, copied, and performed to perfection. Seemingly immutable and stable gender identities become "special symbols" of racial subjectivity.[77] To question naturalized gender norms is to "place oneself outside of the racial kin group."[78] As much as Black music is a location for authenticating Black (masculine) gender, it is also a site of gender ambivalence and dislocation.

Kay says in an interview that she wanted to write *Trumpet* like a jazz composition, and the novel achieves this, both structurally and in its theoretical implications. Instead of using the transmasculine body as a metaphor for some other narrative, it is more productive to look at jazz as an epistemology for Black gendered and sexual improvisation. Joss turns to jazz in order to create his Black masculinity; he practices his trumpet as he practices his walk (and vice versa). Mastery of a jazz instrument gives him access to the closed world of the male jazz ensemble, which allows him to "claim a wider brotherhood."[79] As Joss's band mate Big Red McCall remembers, Joss is well loved by the other members of "Moody's Men" jazz ensemble. This kind of love, Fred Moten argues, is a "love that is never not sexual."[80] Big Red defends Joss against people who question his gender. "One time he caught a guy saying, 'There's something strange about that Moody' . . . He cornered the guy, poked him hard with his fat fingers. Who, jab, are, jab, you, jab, calling, jab, strange?" (144).

Big Red is one of Joss's "disciples"; when faced with various questions about Joss's "squeaky voice" and "baby face," Big Red "rushed to [Joss's] defense" (147). In the "ensemble's internal space,"[81] intimate devotion to ensemble members is permitted. Big Red has a dream in which Joss comes to him and challenges his idea that he did not know of Joss's birth sex until the funeral. Joss says, "Don't be soft, McCall. You knew all along!" (150). Afterwards, Big Red cries (sobs, actually) for the first time in years. Joss's death brings out the softness and vulnerability in his overwhelming, tough masculine façade. The intimacy of the ensemble initiates uncontrollable feelings and deep urges to protect each other, exposing the "effeminate" and "overemotional" side of the jazz collective.[82]

During the first stages of their relationship, Millie accompanies Joss to his performance at a club where she witnesses some of what Moten calls the "(primarily male homo)erotics of ensemble."[83] She says, "When the sax starts Joss closes his eyes and keeps them closed for the longest time" (17). Moten asks, what would a "(homo)sexuality of this music sound like? What would it look like?"[84] Millie experiences the rapture that the erotics of the jazz ensemble produce for itself and the audience. Gradually, the rest of the audience is pulled into the music as well. The audience is "rapt," "euphoric," and "dedicated" to the music (17). In the performance, "heterosexual and homosexual cut and augment one another," creating an environment where "ecstasy is the end of a perverse, interracial consumption."[85] Big Red lets the tears flow for Joss; he gives into his love for him, letting "the snot run down his face till he has to wipe it with the back of his big hand" (151).

Jazz is a re-articulation of Black gendered possibilities; however, at the same time, a melancholic attachment to Black manhood and masculinity erases all other possibilities. If, as Moten, Marriott, and Gordon have argued, Black manhood exists in the "vaginal cut" and is already feminized,[86] then why not "make it up and trace it back" (58) as Joss advises? African musical heritage privileges polycentricism, allowing the music to weave different melodies into one song. Improvisation is a strategy whereby each player creates his/her own take—moving the song forward, signifying on past melodies, changing and commenting on them. Jazz's dual nature of featuring the individual and privileging the collective is a useful vehicle for Black queer signifying on the relationship between the collective identities of Scottishness and Blackness and the individual expression of gender. However, Joss's identity is not constituted through any one category. In jazz, individual expression is supported and framed by the collective structure. Joss's race and gender identities are his alone to define, but he does so surrounded by multiple collectives that give the identities context and help shape their meaning.

Each segment of this chapter, therefore, has been an investigation of the various perspectives on Joss's solo improvisation of race and gender. The solo is at the core of the collective expression; it helps define the music. Black people use jazz and blues in order to make connections between content and time. Music is a tool for diasporic linkages. It establishes a timeline, a temporal link between then and now. It establishes a presence that is not simply contemporary but also has longevity. Thus, Kay's use of jazz is a reference to a cross-Atlantic, African diasporic cultural connection that manifests in the novel as a signifier of Black masculinity and Black queer subjectivity.[87] The African past is revived through the music, and it is in the music that we can see the possibility for a reinvention of a Black diasporic consciousness not predicated on patriarchy and patrilineal ascendancy. Joss's voice comes through unfiltered in two ways: through his letter to Colman about his father, and in the chapter titled "Music," which symbolizes his last moments before death.

This novel is a jazz text, but the structural relationship to jazz does not end with how the novel is composed. Lamia A. Gulcur interprets this chapter and the jazz metaphor in the novel to suggest Joss as a figure of racial and gender "improvisation and reinvention" through two separate and distinct registers (suggesting he has a hybrid racial identity and a hybrid gender identity).[88] I see jazz as providing a guiding metaphor regarding rethinking Blackness, and Black masculinity in particular. There is an aurality to Joss and Colman's disagreements, like two melodies clashing in the same tune. They are like a musical arrangement struggling against its own contradictions. Like the ending of Bridgforth, the end of *Trumpet* suggests a possible "reharmonization," or a harmonic shift through improvisation that recreates the chords of the melody, defamiliarizing it from the original. This transformation differentiates "reharmonizing" from any other term of cultural combination. More than hybridity, synchronization, or Muñoz's disidentification, reharmonizing suggests that legibility has been deprioritized, leaving only traces of the familiar. This is the genius of jazz artist Thelonius Monk, who is very much a "queer" yet indispensable figure in jazz.[89] The queer makes unfamiliar what was once familiar. Kay's text suggests we can become accustomed to new harmonies. They do not have to make us comfortable or relaxed; the song does not have to march toward an inevitable resolution or conform to explicit or implicit goals, which the novel argues is an inexorable part of Black consciousness and culture.

Reharmonizing

Trumpet closes with the reconciliation of Millie and Colman written from Millie's perspective. As Colman walks toward her, she observes that "he [moves] so like his father" (278). At this moment Joss and Colman become one inseparable symbol of Black manhood. Interestingly, it takes Joss's letter to produce a synchronous riff between father and son and to allow Colman to approach his mother, literally and figuratively. In his letter to Colman, Joss describes how he made the decision to leave his mother's love behind and to embrace the phallic position of his father. He writes

> When I was eleven, he died, my father. I remember my mother's pinched face, her terrible hush. I remember the awful quiet in our house without him. The dreadful dream-like quality the whole thing had. . . . I remember the sadness in my mother's baking; once I caught her weeping into the dough. We were both changed for ever by the death of John Moore. There was no one to look at me like he did, with shining, adoring eyes. . . . My mother's love was sensible, but different. Not like him. I missed holding his black hand in the street. Looking at it, comparing it to my own. I was on my own then. Looking at my own hand, trying to remember my father's lines. They were darker than mine, his lifeline, his heart. (276)

As a little girl, Josephine's home falls into a silent void without her father's presence. As an adult, Joss remembers Edith Moore as a sad and vacant figure of sorrow without her husband. Edith's love is inadequate, "sensible, but different" from the "adoring" and validating look that Josephine craves from her father. Young Josephine's comparison of her father's dark hands symbolizes her evaluation of her male future. She follows her father's lifeline in pursuit of the phallic position of Black husband and father. In order to achieve Black manhood, Joss leaves his mother behind. Ironically, Colman's search for his father leads him back to Edith Moore and to Josephine. In the final dream sequence of the novel, Colman sees Edith Moore "in front of him at the seaside, holding the hand of a small girl, his father" (260). Colman follows little Josephine into a house that suddenly starts to fill with water that is "leaking from everywhere" (260). The leaky house represents the edifice of heterosexual, patriarchal, middle-class Black manhood.

When Joss dies, the structure falls apart as dominant regimes of power seep into Millie's and Colman's lives, threatening to destroy Joss's memory. In the dream, Colman is determined to save Josephine, putting her on his back to keep her from drowning. He thinks, "He has a little girl's life on his back. He has to save her. Has to" (260). The need he has at the beginning of the book to prove his manhood through his penis is replaced by a drive to recuperate the female part of his paternal heritage. The dream leads Colman to find his mother in her childhood home in Torr. At the moment that the mother and son meet, a nearby bird soars into the sky, and they hear "it calling and scatting in the wind" (278). The scatting bird resonates with an earlier scene of Joss's scatting at Sunday brunch, making up his own tune.

The ending of the novel has important implications regarding the ability of Black people to reimagine and rename ourselves. Hortense Spillers ends "Mama's Baby, Papa's Maybe" with a radical retheorization of Black male proximity to femininity. Instead of the tragic melancholic longing for "authentic manhood," she proposes that Black men "learn *who* the female is" within themselves.[90] She suggests that we as Black people "make a place for [a] different social subject."[91] Spillers's essay suggests that an alternative Black social subject would revere (Black) femaleness instead of being phobic of associations with, in Moten's terms, the "vaginal." Unlike Sophie Stones's vilification of the "monstrosity" of a Black, differently gendered body, Spillers invites us to "[claim] the monstrosity."[92] From this place of reclaiming and improvisation we have a new way of imagining Black bodies, to "pick" and to "make it up" for ourselves. In this way, the archive becomes an embodied practice that points us to resistance strategies that have been "forgotten" or ignored.

In the following chapter, poet and novelist Dionne Brand's work also provides a model for the process of embracing irresolution, especially from the displacement and feelings of unbelonging that are characteristic of the diasporic condition.

CHAPTER 5

What Grace Was

Erotic Epistemologies and Diasporic Belonging in Dionne Brand's *In Another Place, Not Here*

> If she could not go with this woman, whose speed she loved, who was all liquid, whom she took and agreed was her grace, her way of leaping into another life, then she could not live in any way worthwhile.
>
> —*In Another Place, Not Here* 113

> A small space opened in me. I carried this space with me. Over time it has changed shape and light as the question evoked has changed in appearance and angle. The name of the people we came from has ceased to matter. A name would have comforted a thirteen-year-old. The question however was more complicated, more nuanced. That moment between my grandfather and I several decades ago revealed a tear in the world . . . But the rupture this exchange with my grandfather revealed was greater than the need for familial bonds. It was a rupture in history, a rupture in the quality of being.
>
> —*A Map to the Door of No Return* 4–5

This book began with an examination of pleasure in Black lesbian neo-slave narratives as an imagined strategy of resistance for enslaved women. In order to imagine pleasure in the torment of slavery, the authors created irresolute, "undead" characters to navigate the incongruous terrain of social death, suffering, and momentary satisfaction. *Trumpet* also provided an opportunity to discuss embracing irresolvable genders through the relationship between physical death and Black social death in the context of contemporary Scotland. Questions still remain concerning the representation of erotic love for "the dead," the disremembered and structurally disenfranchised. For example, how do the dead love and what can come from loving the dead? This final chapter turns to the descendants of slaves still trapped in plantation settings in the Caribbean for a discussion of how the erotic functions as an epistemology of revolution and a practice of belonging. As long as part of the condition of the African diaspora is displacement, then finding ways to ameliorate the effects of rupture will require some thinking about self-love in a context of anti-Black violence. Each archival text that I have examined in this volume incorporates some form of erotic love between queers as an essential and complex element to recreating a disremembered Black past. In each instance, Black queer erotics are not to be taken lightly; rather, they are a necessary ingredient to creating sustained and persistent alternatives to displacement and loss.

In *A Map to the Door of No Return,* Dionne Brand contemplates the point of African capture/departure from the continent as a tear in history, a collapse in what she calls "the quality of being" (5) and the psychic rupture that comes from separation from anything that can be called a "beginning" (6). As Brand explains, this rupture of being, of history, and of geography continues to take up tremendous space in the minds of the descendants of captured Africans—so much so that the moment of rupture has created a crisis of what Brand calls "belonging" and "unbelonging" for those of us who are diasporic subjects on the continent and in the dispersal (6). According to Brand, belonging can occur when memory is unbroken. The second quote above is from Brand's description of an ongoing conversation that she has with her grandfather. He cannot remember the African nation that they are descended from, despite the fact that he thinks he once knew. She continues to beg him to remember, but he cannot. Brand connects the terms of unbelonging to the loss of memory.

Brand's discussion in *A Map to the Door of No Return* resonates with what is now a well-worn academic argument: that the mass capture, transport, and subsequent colonial domination of African peoples has caused tremendous disruption, fracturing, and reconfigurations of Black identity and experiences of belonging and unbelonging.[1] One of the many consequences of forced dispersal due to slavery is the disremembering of groups of Black people from the collective based on the modern categories of sexuality, gender identity, and gender expression. These physical and emotional displacements have led to a displacement of Black queer subjects from Black memory, leaving the queer often unrecognizable to the collective and therefore vulnerable to multiple forms of violence from external and internal sources. As Marlon Bailey has argued, it is just as important to pay attention to emotional displacements as geographical ones. Black queer unbelonging happens through the emotional register. Bailey urges us to reconsider diaspora with regard to the affective breaks that take place between members of Black communities and to acknowledge that Black queer people face multiple displacements at once.[2]

In the introduction to this volume, I discussed the Black queer effacement from collective Black memory that occurs in part as a result of the historical displacement from the homeland and the subsequent affective ruptures between Black communities and families. Black queer people contend with both, and the Black lesbian authors I have studied in this book write about creative ways to invoke healing on multiple registers. To repair the affective break and to preserve intraracial connection requires resituating the queer from the outside of Black experience to the intimate inside. Brand deals with the pain of effacement and displacement by situating the literal "Door of No Return" at Elmina slave castle in Ghana as a psychic threshold that, once crossed, cannot be restored. Her disturbing assertion that there are "no beginnings" urges us to consider that perhaps the answer to rupture is not in the reclaiming of where, of place, but in the claiming of the who, the affective bonds between Black people.

Brand contributes to this volume's investigation into the affective bonds between Black people through epistemological practices of Black queer resistance and self-making. In her now-groundbreaking essay, "Uses of the Erotic: The Erotic as Power," Audre Lorde claims the erotic to be an internal epistemological source. It is epistemological because, as Lorde describes, it is a resource for information concerning the resistance to oppression. Specifically, she says, "[E]very oppression must corrupt or distort those various sources of power within the culture of the oppressed that can provide energy for change."[3] According to Lorde, once touched, the erotic is a tremendous source of knowledge. It is where political consciousness takes root to become action.

Brand's first novel, *In Another Place, Not Here,* imagines the erotic epistemology as a practice of diasporic belonging from the perspective of two Black Caribbean women, one a sugar-cane worker named Elizete, and the other an activist named Verlia, living on an unnamed island that is suggestive of Grenada. The novel portrays a multitude of racial and gendered violence, displacement, and disconnection as the female protagonists travel to and from the Caribbean and Canada feeling unrest and dissatisfaction at each location. Their unrest signals that the definition of "home" is independent of where they are on any geographical map. Instead, the novel steers us in a direction that highlights the potential of intimate emotional bonds between the women as the most powerful strategy in which to mitigate affective rupture. These strategic practices of love and caring take place in the context of a burgeoning revolutionary movement on the island. Elizete and Verlia's love exists in contradistinction both to the sexist hypocrisy of the revolution and to the misogynist violence in the Caribbean and in Canada. Even though the end of the novel is tragic, their relationship shows us a reconfiguration of diasporic belonging.

In Another Place, Not Here begins in the Caribbean in a context that speaks to the last days of the New Jewel Party in Grenada and ends with a fictionalized account of the U.S. assassination of the party leader, Maurice Bishop, his supporters, and civilians on October 25, 1983.[4] Like *Trumpet*, discussed in the previous chapter, this is the story of two women who use their bodies and minds for actions unimaginable in the dominant mode of endless exploitation extended from slavery. When the two women meet, Elizete is living in brutal circumstances with an abusive husband she does not love, and she is enduring daily, backbreaking toil in the cane fields. Verlia is originally from the island but was brought up in Canada. She returns to the island as a revolutionary bent on changing the oppressive conditions of the working class. When the revolution falls apart, Verlia commits suicide by throwing herself off a cliff.

The novel offers a queer commentary on a politically redolent moment in twentieth-century Caribbean history, namely, the revolutionary movement in Grenada and the U.S. invasion of the island. Elizete and Verlia meet and form a sexual relationship just as the socialist movement on the island is disintegrating and American troops are descending on the leftist insurgents, including Verlia. The text places Black women-loving-women squarely in the center of the Black struggle for political autonomy and social recreation.[5] This centering of an intimate relationship between Black women in a Caribbean political context in and of itself is a radical intervention into how Caribbean history is imagined and, on a broader diasporic scale, how struggles of resistance and revolutionary actors are remembered. Furthermore, the novel interrupts conventional conceptualizations of Black political subjectivity by representing Elizete as a political subject in her own right. Both Elizete and Verlia comment on and respond to the violence of structural inequality and actively resist these conditions.

Although it is partially a love story, the novel does not let us rest safely in the romance plot (any more than it allows us to romanticize the revolution); rather, it highlights the ways in which class differences come between the two women. As diasporic subjects, they are constantly negotiating structural oppression in neo-colonial or colonial contexts that generate a sense of unbelonging and alienation, even when at "home" in the Caribbean. Elizete's and Verlia's stories are laced with accounts of loss and forgetting that fuel their loneliness and alienation. This lost memory refers to the African diasporic condition of separation, and it is a metaphor for their symbolic position as "lost" subjects in Black memory. Their relationship and its overt political context call attention to how Black queer people often seek to ameliorate multiple forms of displacement through becoming active participants in Black anti-oppression movements, only to be forgotten by the movement itself. Although Verlia is the self-proclaimed activist, she is the one who does not have the emotional tools necessary to survive the pain of political loss. She cannot find her grace.

For both women, detachment, alienation, and displacement keep them from being able to love and sustain each other over the course of time. However, when they do come together, for brief moments, the novel shows us the grace of belonging that can be found in the arms of a loved one. Though not idealized, the ability to love and be loved, for Elizete at least, soothes the pain of unbelonging. In this way, the novel gives us a glimpse at the difference queerness makes to diasporic reimagining. Ultimately, the novel suggests that since we cannot return to an idyllic African "home," and no diasporic site is without exploitation and alienation, the love and care that we show for each other is the closest we have to a return home.

"Home" is an unstable and volatile category for both main characters. According to Homi K. Bhabha, "The unhomely moment relates the traumatic ambivalences of a personal, psychic history to the wider disjunctions of political existence."[6] Verlia and Elizete experience the moment of "unhomeliness" from different places of trauma. Elizete has lived with abuse and alienation since her early childhood. Elizete's ancestors' story is told along with hers, positioning her personal sorrow in a broader context of collective displacement and despair. As Mbembe states, the biopolitical manipulation of slaves includes the refusal of "home."[7] The end of slavery does not cure this condition but propagates a continuation of "unhomeliness," which is consistent with Elizete's immediate surroundings growing up. In Verlia's case, she does not feel a sense of belonging in her aunt and uncle's home in Toronto, and she is unable to connect that lack to a greater longing for redress until she becomes part of the political anticolonial movement. Building on Omise'eke Natasha Tinsley's work on companionship in the Middle Passage, in this chapter I suggest that Black queers have come to embody "home" in each other, in our lovers' arms, and in the way we recreate gender and the Black body. This is how we find grace through multiple displacements and disremembrances.[8]

Adela's Flight

Elizete's presence in the novel pushes up against the institutionalized silencing of the voices of those whose labor maintains the ongoing plantation structure that is hidden from view. The novel successfully places women cane workers and non-normative families at the center of the story of Grenada during the last days before U.S. invasion forces dismantled the revolution. The lives of the women who inhabit the lowest point of society's socioeconomic structure are often forgotten and therefore not prioritized even in sympathetic versions of the history of the leftist movement.[9] By focusing on their stories, the novel foregrounds the ways that racism, capitalism, and patriarchy work together to exploit Black women's bodies. Elizete's memories of childhood and her marriage to her abusive husband, Isaiah, reminds readers that slavery and wage slavery are designed to instill a sense of hopelessness and resignation in its victims and that these structures are connected to struggles in the domestic sphere. Regimes of capitalist exploitation, racism, and misogyny encourage exploited and abused people to withdraw from connections in order to survive these traumas, even though isolation and disremembrance foster despair.

Elizete's memories of her childhood are a string of bleak episodes of abandonment and abuse. From a very young age, Elizete has lived in a condition of displacement resulting from generations of desertion and isolation. Little is known about Elizete's blood relations except that they left her at the doorstep of a single woman in the community who is relatively financially stable. Her foster-child situation is a reminder that kinship is created in various ways, not just through bloodlines. Similar to the irresolute complications and contradictions of queer kinship evidenced in the previous discussions of the neo-slave narratives, Bridgforth's communities in the South, *Her,* and *Trumpet,* this kinship arrangement is not a redemptive alternative family but is fraught with resentment and violence, a stark reminder that nonbiological or queer kinship models are not free from brutality. The surrounding community forces Elizete's foster mother into childrearing because it sees her as the logical choice to take on an orphaned child. Elizete's early home environment addresses two crucial points in the novel. First, even a home of only women can be an "unhomely" space and not necessarily a refuge. Second, blood ties are not the only means of transmission of ancestral coping strategies for "unhomeliness," but they incorporate a variety of kinship relationships, even when strained or reluctant.

Elizete's estrangement and alienation from her foster mother are symbolized in the fact that her foster mother's name is not even mentioned in the text. She is simply "the woman they'd given her to" (28) or "the woman" (32). The woman resentfully takes care of Elizete, mumbling bitterly, "[I]f I wanted child I woulda make child. . . . I look like I want any child?" (28–29). She resists the expectation that Black women have to be caregivers by using traditional folk methods to "[tie] up her womb in brackish water" (31). She does not want the additional labor of caring added onto her already overburdened life as a cane worker. As another queer character in the text, the woman wants to navigate her life outside the normative expectations of heterosexual relationships and childbearing, but the community denies her that right. The woman is the "logical choice" to be Elizete's foster mother because she is not married and does not have any other children. Elizete surmises that the woman "had been left by everyone" (33). The woman's isolation suggests that one of the effects of defying normative gender roles for women is often community rejection and isolation. Consequently, she takes her frustration out on Elizete, abusing and neglecting the child, explicitly refusing to show her anything that could be confused with love. The woman is especially concerned that her need to express her anger through language would be considered affection. Therefore, she makes Elizete face the wall in silence while she complains about her life circumstances. The woman does this so that Elizete will not feel as though she was being engaged in a conversation or so that the child would not "imagine loving" (32). The novel rejects the expectation that an all-female environment is a space for nurturing. The female-centered home is not inherently oppositional to the patriarchal abuse that Elizete will encounter with her husband later on in life. It takes Elizete's finding of Verlia to create a counterspace of erotic pleasure and love that (painfully) cracks open possibilities for an existence beyond suffering for Elizete.

However, Elizete does connect to love in her childhood through an ancestor. During her tirades, the woman often speaks of her slave ancestor, Adela. Elizete develops a strong tie to Adela that is based not on blood but on a kinship strengthened by the oral retelling of history. Throughout childhood, she waits, staring at the wall, for the woman who takes care of her to tell Adela's story. She savors whatever bits of memory the woman shouts to her. "Turned to the wall she could feel the story crawl over her shoulders and up her neck, she could feel it like something brown and sweet making the hair at her neck tremble" (33). Imagining Adela is the only sweetness in her life. The story itself is like a caress and a kiss on her skin. The kiss of memory that Elizete experiences in the Adela stories is the first hint in the novel of the power of the erotic to demonstrate how the dead love each other. The novel shows us that even when extreme measures are taken to prevent love from entering into the imagination, it still creeps in, for Elizete, up her neck and over her shoulders. The story of the dead is her first brush with erotic possibility and heralds her tremendous capacity to embrace the dead as a way to resist suffering.

The act of remembering further instantiates the queerness of the house, creating a lineage and a connection to ancestors outside of a nuclear family setting. Elizete soaks up Adela's story, including the names of the line of ancestors from Adela to the woman to herself. Their lineage is afflicted with sorrow, rage, and forgetting. A powerful woman, Adela was able to focus her energy and make things happen. She kills the slave master by focusing all of his evil into a circle for three years until "he could not resist himself" (18), and he physically dies on the very spot she has cursed. Her curse follows his entire lineage into perpetuity, such that none of his line are ever happy, despite their wealth (19). Adela's sorrow at not being able to remember her African homeland and being forced to exist in a foreign and unwanted territory turns into a melancholic longing for her homeland. "Adela call this place Nowhere and with that none of the things she look at she note of or remember to pass on. She insists so much is nowhere she gone blind with not seeing" (19). Remembering Adela and her struggles is what links the generations and creates a bond for Elizete that she otherwise would not have had. It also opens Elizete to Adela's profound grief and displacement. Adela is so filled with mourning and rage that she goes blind from her refusal to notice or remember where she is. Adela resists her circumstances by not remembering or acknowledging anything, including her original name or language. She refuses to name or mother her eight children. She could not love, could not see where she was; but more importantly, she could not see her own importance to those who came after her, her own place as a revered ancestor. What she does pass down through her lineage is the inability to love and the memory of her abandonment.

For Adela, love has been warped by the violence of displacement. She does not allow herself to feel anything, nor can she recognize the impact of the retraction of her emotions on generations to come. She does not let in any emotions or sensory information. Her only coping strategy is to close out the world in order to protect herself from the tremendous pain of having what she loved ripped away from her—a strategy that has appeared in slave narratives and neo-slave narratives alike. For example, real-life runaway slave Harriet Jacobs asks, "Why does the slave ever love?"[10] Adela copes in a similar way, shutting herself off from emotion and memory: "Her heart just shut. It shut for rain, it shut for light, it shut for water and it shut for the rest of we what follow. Adela feel something harder than stone and more evil than sense. Here" (22). The word "Here" is left dangling by itself as its own statement. The "here" of the island will later be juxtaposed with the "here" of Toronto. Both are brutal and difficult places to live in—hard like the experience of capture that Elizete imagines for Adela. Eventually, Adela walks away from the plantation, "naked as she born" (23) and into the darkness. Finally, Adela disappears. One explanation that the novel offers is that she committed suicide, and another is that she joins her ancestors by flying "all the way back to Africa," like the legendary Igbo, leaving her progeny behind (23).[11]

Elizete feels Adela's abandonment for "all we that follow" as if she were someone she knew in the flesh. The loss of Adela's love is so close to Elizete because she took her memories when she left—her memories of her African language and culture, of the plants and their medicinal purposes. At first, Elizete learns to shut down in the face of suffering, a strategy she picked up from Adela. Even though Elizete envies Adela for being able to "put [her] foot in the darkness when the time come" (23), she realizes that Adela's strategies are too limited. She says, "I used to make my mind as empty as Adela's but I never like it because it make me feel lonely and blind an sorrowful and take me away from myself and then I know is so Adela fell when she come here" (20). Elizete's love for and identification with Adela almost leads her to follow Elizete into physical death. Already in a context of despair, Elizete recognizes that adding to her situation with more loneliness, sorrow, and blindness is not a path to relief. She instead begins to deepen her relationship with Adela by speaking to Adela in ways that make it possible for her to find beauty. As a child she converses with the spirit of Adela, thinking,

> how the names of things would make this place beautiful. I dreaming up names all the time for Adela's things. I dream Adela's shape. . . . Tear up cloth flowers, stinking fruit tree, draw blood bush, monkey face flowers, hardback swamp fish. I determine to please she and recall. . . . I say to myself that if I say these names for Adela it might bring back she memory of herself and she true name. And perhaps I also would not feel lonely for something I don't remember. (23–24)

Elizete's naming is an embodied practice of remembering and a practice of erotic connection to the land and to Adela. She moves through her world imaginatively recreating what has been disremembered through the lyricism of her voice. Unlike most of the other texts I have analyzed, *In Another Place, Not Here* does not rely as heavily on traditional musical forms to structure its vernacular epistemologies. In this way, it is similar to the neo-slave narratives. There is no music represented on the island except in Elizete's own thoughts and their lyricism and in the spoken language of the novel. In her idioms, heterosexist and patriarchal regimes unravel. The novel prioritizes the lyricism of Anglophone Caribbean speech, positing the body as an epistemological vessel. Elizete's words are a love song of remembrance for Adela. She names the plants and birds in her world: "busy wing, better walking, come by chance, wait and see" (24). The words are light and seductive to the tongue. The erotic is Elizete's resource for creating beauty in her life, a tool Adela refused to use. The act of remembering/singing offers a chance to introduce more than sorrow and toil in her life; it is an act that contradicts the purpose of the laboring body, which is exactly what Adela could not do. As Paul Huebner points out, Brand highlights the "relationships to both human and nonhuman elements" in order to "remind us of the transformative power of relationships."[12] In this case, Elizete's relationship to her surroundings is the beginning link to the erotic.

The lesson of Adela is that a heart shut to love can be open only to temporary resistance strategies. Both Adela and Verlia take flight from the "fleshy" (247) dimension of existence fueled by racist misogyny, abandoning possibilities for some form of healing through their connections with other Black people. Elizete connects Adela's shutting down to Verlia's suicide: "I know Adela set her mind to stopping her breath after that. Verlia leave me like nothing too" (22–23). Elizete places Adela's giving in to death and Verlia's suicide in the same register of abandonment.

Elizete's Relief

The opening pages of the novel come from Elizete's perspective, thereby foregrounding Black working-class women's viewpoint and voice. Elizete is raised to consider herself lucky to have a domestic arrangement with her husband, Isaiah. She describes an exhausting, plantation-driven life for which she is expected to be grateful: "I born to clean Isaiah's house and work cane since I was a child and say what you want Isaiah feed me and all I have to do is lay down under him in the night and work the cane in the day. It have plenty women waiting their whole blessed life for that and what make me turn woman and leave it I don't know, but it come" (4). Elizete distinguishes her choice to "turn woman and leave" from the limited options offered to the women around her. She is aware that many women want to fit into the dominant framework as a resolution to emotional and economic uncertainty. She is conscious of the relationship between the cane plantation and the patriarchal home, seeing them as cooperating extensions of power over her life and body.

Under a capitalist and patriarchal regime, Elizete is expected to endure backbreaking labor in the fields, create a home for her husband, and stay sexually available in order to reproduce plantation labor. The scars on her legs left from her husband's brutal beatings and from the slices of the cutlass as she worked in the field symbolize the cooperation of capitalism and patriarchy. She remembers the beatings she endured from Isaiah:

> "All over from one thing and another, one time or another, is how Isaiah whip them for running, is how he wanted to break me from bad habit. Whip. 'Don't move.' Whip. 'Don't move.' Whip. 'Run you want to run! Don't move.' Is how the cane cut them from working. Same rhythm." (55)

Her scars show where both Isaiah and the cutlass eat away at her mobility. Piece by piece, through the grueling toil of domestic and field labor, not only is she hampered by the physical restriction of her husband and not having the available capital to change her situation; she is also mired psychologically in the resignation and hopelessness that keep her bound to continued exploitation. Slowly she becomes disconnected from any hope of escape. She runs away only to be stopped by Isaiah and his whip at first; then she gives up: "When I see it was his play, I resign" (8). Once she gives up, she begins to forget where and why she ever decided to run. She does this for many years until Verlia appears in the cane field to organize the workers.

Brand shifts the terms of diasporic displacement to consider emotional bonds as the site of beginnings. What we know from the opening page is that Elizete considers it grace, the "free and unmerited favor" of the divine that gifts her Verlia like a "drink of cool water" (3) in her arid existence. She says, "GRACE. IS GRACE, YES. AND I TAKE IT" (3). These are the first words of the novel. Elizete finds a small grace; comfort and belonging come to her not in or from a nation-state but in Verlia's arms. Elizete uses her queer desire to realign the alienation of rupture, shifting belonging and beginnings from a geographical site to an emotional one. Under these circumstances, the novel suggests that perhaps the only reprieve or escape is through grace, or the unexpected circumstance. The only space of comfort that she has is in the arms of Verlia, and that too is temporary.

Loving Verlia is a resistance to the patriarchal and capitalist regimes of exploitation and raw extraction of labor power that situated her as supposedly "lucky" in her brutal existence. By taking Verlia as a lover, she resists structures of patriarchal violence and racist misogyny that offer up her body for her husband to consume. Once another option is presented to her, Elizete "turn[s] woman and leave[s]" her secure yet soul-killing routine. Elizete takes a chance on an improvised future, one that does not have a clear set of expectations or a predetermined outcome. Before Verlia, she had tried to leave Isaiah, to escape to Maracaibo, but could only make it to the junction.

The junction takes on an almost mythical quality throughout the novel. It is metaphorically a crossroads, as seen in the work of Sharon Bridgforth, a place that represents the intersection of the living and the dead. Adela's trip to the junction is the precursor to her journey to be with the ancestors. It is also a literal jumping-off place. It is the cliff where Verlia takes her leap at the end of the novel. One of the outcomes of the regulation of bodies is that people are often brutalized into a tacit disregard for life—their own lives as well the lives of others. This disregard creates a situation in which it seems better to physically die than to exist under conditions of social death and brutality. In effect, as Achille Mbembe argues, biopolitics and necropolitics create the "living dead."[13] In this case, I read Verlia's and Adela's suicides and Elizete's thoughts of suicide as a consequence of biopolitics.[14] When Verlia comes into Elizete's life, she temporarily shifts the endless suffering in Elizete's state of living death to a state of increased sensory and emotional depth. This shift is not painless; it does make her reconsider jumping off at the junction. We can learn from her decision to return.

Verlia provides Elizete an alternative to abandonment and instead embraces longevity. Her longevity comes from developing a muscle of pleasure and caring. She soaks in Adela's story but moves toward another strategy to resist annihilation by her willingness to love and be loved. Through Elizete's character, the novel reminds us that the erotic is an underrecognized source of political consciousness. According to Lorde, once touched, the erotic is a tremendous source of power. It is where political consciousness takes root and becomes action, where "we begin to give up, of necessity, being satisfied with suffering and self-negation, and with the numbness which so often seems like [the] only alternative in our society. Our acts against oppression become integral with self, motivated and empowered from within."[15] Lorde contends that the erotically empowered person rejects "resignation, despair, self-effacement, depression, self-denial."[16] These are the very states-of-being demanded of the dispossessed, displaced, and oppressed according to the representations of Adela and Elizete. Both women suffer tremendously from various forms of sexual violation, physical torture, and extraction of labor that create a deep desire for "home" that they continuously seek; also created is a feeling of "unhomeliness" that they try to resolve by withdrawing from the world to different degrees. For Black women, the compounding of racism and misogyny in a context of ongoing labor exploitation all too often eradicates spaces of refuge in the domestic sphere. This is as true for Adela and Elizete on a diasporic scale as it is for them on the level of personal space. In their daily surroundings they face sexual exploitation and endless physical toil, both of which are indicative of continuous structures of oppression.

For Elizete, the way out of the ordinary drudgery of heteropatriarchal oppression appears in the form of Verlia, whom she describes as a bridge: "A woman can be a bridge, limber and living breathless, because she don't know where the bridge might lead, she don't need no assurance except that it would lead out with certainty, no assurance except the arch and disappearance . . . a way to cross over" (16). Elizete's affirmation of uncertainty is an eloquent articulation of a politics of improvisation. She is willing to see where the bridge might lead her, without being certain of the destination or having a map of the route. She knows that if she follows, she will be able to "cross over" into the grace of unexpected possibility—something that certainty forecloses. In contrast, in *The Wretched of the Earth,* Fanon describes the bridge as a utilitarian object of expressed desires of the "citizens." He says, "If the building of a bridge does not enrich the consciousness of those working on it, then don't build the bridge." Verlia is the bridge that Elizete crosses over to reach a burgeoning erotic consciousness. Fanon goes on to warn that the bridge "should come from the muscles and the brains of the citizens."[17] Far from Fanon's bridge meant for conclusive ends, Elizete imagines Verlia as a bridge to erotic abandon, letting her flesh swallow her, open her, enjoy the "shudder between her legs" and "the swell and bloom of her softness" (5). She lets desire lead her somewhere unpredictable—to something close to escape, to "home."

Fortunately, the novel does not make desire between women an easy ideal, and it acknowledges the "inescapable" (54) and unbreachable distance that class creates between the two lovers. At times Elizete sees the estrangement between them in Verlia. She sees "someone she did not know. . . . [someone] . . . not from here, someone who felt pity for the people less capable" (54). The class divide between the women disrupts the ways that they recognize and acknowledge each other. One moment Verlia is the bridge from a life without meaning to a life worth living; the next moment she is just "someone," an unfamiliar stranger from a different place. Elizete sees the pity on Verlia's face, which she experiences as "coolness like a draft of cold air passing a doorstep" (55).

However, Elizete is not simply oppressed in their relationship. The text honors Elizete as a political subject, not a sociological object. Early in their relationship, Elizete reminds Verlia that she is not just someone to study but is her own person. "I tell she I not no school book with she, I not no report card, I not no exam, I not she big-time people with they damn hypocrisy, she want to dig and probe she could go to hell" (77). Elizete is quite aware of external and academic methods of dehumanizing her as a tragic and pitiable object of study. Verlia is part of a vanguard movement that portends to know what is best for the cane laborers, and as a labor organizer she probes Elizete with questions about her family. For Elizete these questions are an interrogation. She says, "She make things hard, she make me have to say everything, she make me have to tell everything" (76). Elizete concludes, "Love is too simple and smooth and not good enough name for it. It was more rough. Coarse like a bolt of crocus sacking full of its load of coconuts or husks for mattress ticking" (75). The novel does not rest at lesbian love. Elizete says, "All that touching. Nothing simple about it. All that opening like breaking bones" (78); instead, it's where the work begins. The moment that she sees Verlia, she is no longer a body to be used on the plantation and held under her husband's physical and sexual control. Unlike in the work of male anticolonial theorists like Frantz Fanon or Che Guevara, who do not focus on women's experiences but do appear in the novel as Verlia's intellectual mentors, the novel follows Elizete's perspective as she encounters desire for the first time. What unfolds is a decolonization of Elizete's consciousness through an epistemology of the erotic.

Furthermore, Brand's erotics appear not only in the realm of enjoyment but also through pain as well as physical and emotional discomfort. The text describes that the coupling of pleasure and sorrow, sweet sensations of ecstasy along with excruciating agony, is necessary to open up Elizete's consciousness. In the opening pages of the novel Elizete says this mixture is the bridge to consciousness: "I See she. Hot, cool and wet. I sink the machete in my foot, careless, blood blooming in the stalks of cane, a sweet ripe smell wash me faint. With pain. Wash the field, spinning green mile after green mile around she. See she sweat, sweet like sugar" (3–4). In this moment, Elizete takes her own leap, embracing the pleasure and the pain of her new erotic consciousness. When her hand slips and her machete cuts her foot, Elizete's blood washes the fields in a ritual that cleanses her from her past limited familiarity with love. Verlia's presence requires her to be willing to make herself open to a different kind of pain than she is used to. The gash on her foot foreshadows how her relationship with Verlia cuts her open, making a fresh wound and a new map of her body that includes sweetness along with blood. She herself is the sacrifice, but it does not take her life.

Verlia's Sacrifice

While Elizete's story is contextualized through the memory of women's lives in Caribbean agricultural work, Verlia's narrative deals with the disremembered urban revolutionary. Verlia spends her teenage years with her aunt and uncle in their middle-class apartment in Sudbury, Canada. She decides to leave them because she cannot stand how her middle-class family is encouraging her to forget her Blackness. They urge her to "blend in and mix," to forget her skin "so that no one will notice" (142). They primarily want her to live with them so that they can fit in with white heterosexuality. According to Elizete, "they need her for perfection, acceptability" (140). The pair dreams of conformity, "man, woman, husband, wife, couple, parents" (141). Verlia considers their vision of middle-class acceptance a "grave" (149) and heterosexual marriage a "coffin engraved in ice" (149), so she decides that "she does not want to be harmless" and leaves after college to join the Black Power movement in Toronto (150).

She embodies the quintessential revolutionary ideal: a woman who has emptied herself of connections except to the cause and to her love for "the people." By seventeen, Verlia has become disillusioned with her aunt and uncle's middle-class suburban existence and goes in search of engagement and belonging. She leaves her family with a tremendous anticipation for finding the joy that she is lacking in her family's bourgeois environment, which she experiences as complicit with racism. She idealizes the movement, anticipating that she will find all of the answers to her questions.

Verlia becomes a dedicated student of revolution, following the path laid out by Fanon to a new consciousness, only to find duty, sadness, and an emptiness that drains the life from her soul. Verlia's romance with revolution is a seduction of words. From Frantz Fanon and Che Guevara to the Last Poets and Nikki Giovanni, she takes inspiration from various sectors of the diaspora. Frantz Fanon is an icon of revolution in the text, giving Verlia some of her guiding principles for revolutionary change. As Darieck Scott has stated, Fanon was "a kind of Abrahamic father for intellectuals and artists associated with the Black Power Movement in the United States" and for anyone interested in decolonization around the world.[18] Brand gives us a glimpse into the scope of how Fanon's work coupled with Black Power perspectives outside of the United States. The text includes quoted passages from the first chapter of Fanon's *Wretched of the Earth,* "Concerning Violence." In that chapter, Fanon describes the process of the "native intellectual" extricating himself/herself from the limiting linguistic episteme of bourgeois capitalism. In the novel, Verlia adapts Fanon's discussion of the process of decolonization. She quotes him:

> Decolonization is always a violent phenomenon. . . . It is willed, called
> for, demanded . . . in the consciousness and in the lives of the men and
> women who are colonised. . . . This change is equally experienced in the

form of a terrifying future and the consciousness of another "species" of men and women: the colonizers. (157)

Verlia follows Fanon's suggestions and assumes that her transformation into a revolutionary would create a "terrifying future" for the colonizer she imagines in Toronto. According to Fanon, the formerly colonized bourgeois subject will return to "the people" and find a "different vocabulary" that releases him/her from the raw desire of accumulation to the desire for camaraderie in "brother, sister, friend" and from the isolation of individual advancement to the appreciation for collective processes of community in the "people's committees" and "village assemblies."[19] For Fanon, language is the gateway to consciousness. In *Black Skin, White Masks,* he devotes much attention to the effect that absorbing European language has on the Antillean who travels to France and then returns to the Caribbean. It is the doorway into affective erethism or white identification and Black self-annihilation.[20] Productive decolonization slays the colonizer's linguistic hold on the native. Language represents an epistemological shift from bourgeois sources of knowledge to local sources. Fanon contends, "The native intellectual takes part, in a sort of auto-da-fé, in the destruction of all his idols: egoism, recrimination that springs from pride, and the childish stupidity of those who always want to have the last word."[21] The "auto-da-fé" that the native intellectual must take part in suggests both a leap of faith and an internal coup that roots out the bourgeois colonial individualist indoctrination and displaces it with a language of collectivity and camaraderie. At all times this native intellectual is ready for battle, preparing to strike when the opportunity arises. Fanon writes, "This is why the dreams of the native are always of muscular prowess; his dreams are of action and of aggression."[22] Fanon imagines the native potential revolutionary as a male with pent-up aggression and frustration. "He is overpowered but not tamed; he is treated as an inferior but he is not convinced of his inferiority. He is patiently waiting until the settler is off his guard to fly at him. The native's muscles are always tensed."[23]

In her mind, Verlia is ready to take on the white majority. In her imagination she is powerful, causing whites to tremble with fear at the audacity of her stride and the magnitude of her pride in Blackness, symbolized by her Afro, which demands "Black power straight up" (158) to anyone who sees it. She stays up all night "learning this new language" (166) of resistance and dreaming of embodying the "terrifying future" (157) of decolonization in her interpretation of Fanon's *Wretched of the Earth.* Once she finds the movement in Toronto, she feels that "she's come into some real love" (158). Verlia falls in love with the ideal of political activism and the apotheosis of the movement, "the people." When she leaves her family, her intention is "to walk right into the Movement when she arrives" in Toronto and she expects to find "joy, just plain joy" (164).

Verlia tracks the revolution to Toronto, where she imagines that the (lyrical) language of the revolution will engender communion with other like-minded urban rebels, and that in itself will be her shield against the racist onslaught. The poetics of revolution echoes in the musicality of the verses from the Last Poets and Nikki Giovanni that resonate in her daydreams. She hears the Last Poets confront racism head-on in a fusion of jazz and spoken word: "But you see, but you see, me knowing me Black proud and determined to be free could plainly see my enemy" (157). She uses Nikki Giovanni's call for Black women to "stop the pattern" of Black women's tragic and early deaths to "deliberately misunderstand her family saying go make something of yourself" (160). She immediately begins to "read Fanon and Nikki" (160). The twist of this moment of deliberate recalculation of words is also an unfortunate mishearing and misinterpretation of Giovanni. Giovanni's "Poem for Aretha" actually warns against the use and consumption of Black women's talents. Aretha Franklin, the main character of the poem, is a tired and drained musician who is pulled at from many sides but who has to keep going no matter what—a symbol of how Black women are valued for their labor only as long as they are continually in motion and producing. Giovanni says that "the way we're killing her / we eat up artists like there's going to be a famine at the end / of those three minutes" when the song is over and she is begged again, "just sing one song, please!"[24] Giovanni's poem is a warning to "stop the pattern" of Black women sacrificing their lives (160), but Verlia does not understand its warning. Instead, she plunges full on into a movement that demands her obedience to the will of the party and to political doctrine.

In another act of misinterpretation, Verlia sacrifices the women in her life for the movement. Quoting Che Guevara, she selectively memorizes a line of his speech: "At the risk of seeming ridiculous, let me say that the true revolutionary is guided by great feelings of love" (165). She interprets this line as an encouragement for revolutionaries to evacuate the erotic from their lives, giving her an excuse to abandon whatever emotional reservoir she has to the movement. Verlia leaves out key elements of context from Guevara's 1965 "Socialism and Man in Cuba" speech:

> Within the country the leadership has to carry out its vanguard role. And it must be said with all sincerity that in a real revolution, to which one gives his all and from which one expects no material reward, the task of

the vanguard revolutionary is at one and the same time magnificent and agonizing. At the risk of seeming ridiculous, let me say that the true revolutionary is guided by great feelings of love. It is impossible to think of a genuine revolutionary lacking this quality. Perhaps it is one of the great dramas of the leader that he must combine a passionate spirit with a cold intelligence and make painful decisions without flinching. Our vanguard revolutionaries must make an ideal of this love of the people, of the most sacred causes, and make it one and indivisible. They cannot descend, with small doses of daily affection, to the level where ordinary men put their love into practice.[25]

Verlia distorts Guevara's message into a demand for emotional ascetic denial. Her lovers fill a need for contact, for touch, for physical comfort. She stops short of love, emotionally intimacy, caring. Verlia refuses the parts of Guevara's message that would align with the erotic—his call for "passion" and the depth of feeling that creates a "true revolutionary." Similar to her misinterpretation of Giovanni's suggestion to not repeat the past mistakes of other Black women, Verlia misunderstands Guevara's words and proceeds to do just the opposite. His warning not to engage in simple "small doses of daily affection" is not heeded. This is exactly what she does, portioning out her affections in small doses with different women lovers.

For Verlia, the movement comes first, but that too leaves her empty. She does not have anything to give to the women in her life. She gives herself to the work. Her life is filled with a haunting vacancy. Verlia replaces connection with a detached sparseness: "She wants nothing more. Not the bed that comes with it, not the kitchen, not the key to the door. She hates the sticky domesticity lurking behind them. She doesn't want wanting more. Just her sparse room, sparse, sparse and clear, just the empty floor and sometimes a woman with her back to kiss, company to keep all night" (204). This does not turn out to be a viable substitution for real human relationships. She writes in her diary: "I was going to write about the revolution; instead this book is full of loneliness" (220). She says, "As soon as I think I'm all right it falls apart. And nothing I can put my finger on, just some small knowledge that it won't work out or if it does I'll still be unhappy. No one is enough company, no one enough absence" (220). She is the quintessential romanticized Black political subject, focused on "the people," acting on behalf of the liberation of the collective, and propelled by revolution, so much so that her body is taken over by the anxiety of covert operations. Abena, her lover before Elizete, remembers, "She was all adrenalin, so tense after every action that her eyelids jumped uncontrollably," and she was smoking and drinking more often (190). While in Toronto she becomes so estranged from her own pleasure that she cried when she made love with Abena, weeping that she was "too open" (190).

In *Salvation,* bell hooks discusses the crucial importance of love in Black resistance struggles. However, even she separates love from militant Black resistance. hooks posits Martin Luther King's religious love ethic in contra-distinction to the Black Power movement's secularist militancy. In hooks's ideal, Black radicalism's religious roots are necessary in order to maintain a strong connection between love and liberation. She states that "as black radicalism was divorced from its religious roots, becoming more secular, discussions of love were silenced."[26] hooks equates secular militancy with patriarchal domination, citing that the "creation of strong black patriarchs" brought about a message of the "will to power" not the "will to love."[27] In this schema, love and radical militant politics are seen as distinct and dispa-rate strategies of healing and resistance.[28]

Verlia, too, cannot see the connection. Her misinterpretation of Gue-vara leads her to eschew the power of the love that arrives in her life. She dismisses the transformative potential of the loving relationships that circle through her world. Overwhelmed by the tedium of constant struggle in Toronto, where she feels that the movement has become "useless" and inert, Verlia decides to join the fight for socialist revolution in Grenada (190). She returns to Grenada to "move" again (190). There she finds Elizete, and for one moment she allows herself to open up to possibilities, to understand resistance from another frame, and to feel comfort. However, when Elizete's husband finds them together in bed, Verlia resolves to get out of the rela-tionship. She says, "I stayed with her the night in case he would come back and kill her. I didn't know what I thought I'd do. Shit. How many times have I heard that this is what fucks up revolutions? How the fuck am I going get out of it? She didn't talk to me all night, just touched my face" (218). Verlia's preoccupation with protecting herself from emotional ties removes the potential for her to grow as a revolutionary in that moment. She could return the affection and embrace Elizete's love, but instead she sublimates her desire and passion to standing with the militia and absorbing "the love of the people" (218).

The language of revolution fails Verlia. Her comrade in the movement warns her that "if the people go one way and the party another, the party is wrong no matter how correct the political line" (223). All of her train-ing as a "materialist" (219) does not prepare her for the contradictions she encounters between leftist theory and her experiences on the ground. The split is so disturbing to her that it is literalized in the splitting headaches that she endures on the island.

The erotic is a powerful force in the novel. When it is ignored, the consequences are dire. The revolutionary government does not recognize how much the people of the island love their fallen leader, Clive. Thus not only are they vulnerable to outside pressure from the imperialist forces of the United States and Britain, but they also lose the confidence of the island population who back Clive. He is a "romantic" (225); he uses the power of the erotic in his leadership, and the people are willing to follow him whether or not he is guilty of crimes against them. As long as Verlia cannot integrate the erotic in her life, then she will be an ineffective lover and revolutionary, and eventually she will not able to go on living.

True to character, she misreads this affection from "the people" just as she misreads Isaiah's reaction to finding her in bed with Elizete. Verlia believes that the crowd loves the militia, but really it is Clive they love, and they support the militia only to the extent that the militia supports him. Again Verlia distrusts Elizete's interpretation of events. When Isaiah runs off in emotional turmoil from Elizete's infidelity with Verlia, Elizete states that "it's vindication" (219). However, Verlia doesn't trust Elizete's perception of divine vindication, stating that she is "a materialist" (219). For a brief moment, while she is trying to sort out the events of her relationship with Elizete and their discovery by Isaiah, Verlia begins to doubt her purpose on the island and declares that she was afraid that she was "losing parts of [her] memory," but she stops questioning and comes to the conclusion that she's perfectly fine (219). However, she is wrong on both counts. Isaiah never returns; he goes insane and disappears. She doesn't recognize parts of the island after a big rain, and she loses a prized possession, both of which indicate that she is not as in control as she thought. Lorde warns of "the false belief that only by suppression of the erotic within our lives and consciousness can women be truly strong. But that strength is illusory" (53). Verlia's illusion of control and strength in isolation begins to crumble the moment that she realizes that "the people" love Clive and that his success was in being a "romantic" (225). She learns too late that "[p]eople love of flesh and blood. They love who speaks to them" (225). By the time she learns this lesson, the U.S. imperialist forces are already on their way to the island, and all is lost.

Through Verlia's dismissal, the text helps us realize that love is necessary, in a Marxist sense, to reproduce the revolutionary. It could nourish, sustain, and motivate her to continue on even when the revolution falls apart. Her distant love of "the people" proves to be an insufficient epistemology for long-term thriving. It is not enough to love the people and separate oneself from a range of pleasures. Discovering desire is not the same as succumbing to lust. Each woman has only one half of the equation. When joined together, they make a powerful resource for creating a sustainable life. Separate, they fall. When the two women are together, they provide a narrative of an epistemology of resistance through erotics that contributes another dimension to the revolutionary expressions that inspire Verlia at the beginning of her journey.

Verlia's training from Fanon did not prepare her for the ways in which her own body could discover embodied epistemologies through the erotic. Fanon theorizes decolonial consciousness through the figure of a formerly bourgeois-aspiring native (male) intellectual and his reacquaintance with local epistemes as reintroduced through revolutionary language and embodied within a set of tensed, battle-ready muscles. Fanon writes of taut muscles ready for a fight; this act of muscular tension brings the mind into (decolonial) consciousness. For the women in the novel, it is the point of muscular contraction and release in pleasure that brings one into consciousness. Elizete says,

> I sink in Verlia and let she flesh swallow me up. I devour she. She opened me up like any morning. Limp, limp and rain light, soft to the marrow. She make me wet. She tongue scorching like hot sun I love that shudder between her legs, love the plain wash and sea of her, the swell and bloom of her softness. And is all. And it is all I could do on Earth, is all." (5)

In a woman's body, muscular tension (and release) can be initiated by a different set of muscles than Fanon imagined. Elizete uses her muscles as a springboard to other dimensions of decolonial consciousness. Instead of the body being a site of a separate consciousness, it is this embodied act of mutually pleasurable erotic experience that cracks open the boundaries of self-making, as was the case for Joshua Davis and Booka Chang, and for Miss Sunday Morning and Sweet T in *love conjure/blues*. Here as well, for Elizete especially, orgasm makes her aware that her body can be used for other things besides demeaning labor and sexual violation. For the first time, she experiences her body as a vessel for the fulfillment of her own desires and the creation of a mutually satisfying sensation. This point of fulfillment and satisfaction is an epistemological juncture, creating the knowledge of belonging and connection and upending the previous narratives of displacement, alienation, and disappointment that were depicted in the story of Elizete's childhood and past marriage, in Verlia's experience in the movement, and most drastically in Adela's extraction from the world. The couple's lovemaking nurtures their mutually inchoate consciousness.

The text does not sentimentalize the muscular epistemologies unearthed in their sexual relationship but rather introduces us to the profound psychic reorganization such revelations require—a reorganization that Elizete is willing to make, although Verlia is not. Verlia's training did not prepare her for the decolonization of desire, and without it she is at the mercy of a doomed and incomplete revolution. Verlia signs up to cut sugar cane with the seasoned cane workers in order to "come close to the people" (203). But she begins to wilt and blister under the sun and from the backbreaking labor. She takes a moment to "[look] up from her exercise in duty and revolutionary comradeship" to notice the "avenging grace" of the arc of Elizete's arm as it comes down to slice the cane stalks (203). In this moment, she falls in love with the arc of her arm and realizes that she was wrong to think that she could arrive from Toronto and think that she "knew everything" and that she could "change this country woman into a revolutionary like her" (202). Instead she realized that this "country woman" "would know more [and] be more than she" (203). In this moment she "left herself so bare" (203) that in the morning she "reached over and felt for her," letting Elizete soothe her loneliness by "pulling the woman towards her, comforted in the thighs lapping against her" (201–2).

Eventually, Verlia does not allow herself the comfort and the escape provided by Elizete's arms. She returns to a narrative of displacement and reliance on a physical geography to create her belonging. She does not find it. The island is crowded with forgotten meanings and disconnected memories: "The meanings underneath are meanings I don't know even though I was born somewhere here, but I can hear in the way people say them" (211). She is simultaneously from there, but not of there. Not even Elizete's strong and ample arms can hold onto her, and she returns to a state of restless emptiness. She cannot accept her grace. Eventually, her estrangement consumes her. Before Verlia dies, Elizete says that "she bet all of she life on this revolution" (114). When the revolution unravels, there is nothing left of Verlia.

Verlia's suicidal death is a metaphor for the sacrificed queer—one who is dedicated to the struggle yet unseen by history, disremembered by the collective because it is deemed a threat to or a disruption of the collective's progress, however defined. Usually, queer identity and activity are considered to be the cause of nonbelonging. In the novel, Verlia is an unfailing revolutionary in the core of armed struggle and covert resistance, yet this does not calm her inescapable loneliness. Elizete's acceptance of grace is the key to resistance to structural disparity. Only when they take advantage of the grace that brings non-normative, unconventional pleasures and love into their lives do the women rest for a moment, each belonging to herself and to the other and, by extension, remapping diasporic belonging in each other's arms.

Elizete and Verlia's struggle with the work, pain, and pleasures of creating home with each other is an elaboration on the story of Bastua and

Champagne Lady that ended the first chapter. Two Black women from disparate backgrounds look to each other for some resettling of the questions of what happens next. In both stories slavery has separated them by chasms of privilege (to varying degrees of course) and the tragedy of unrecoverable histories. The ones left behind, Abena and Elizete, come together to love the dead by remembering the story. Ultimately, what comes of loving the dead is what Abena and Elizete do—they embark on the task of mutual recognition and a commitment to the bone-cleaving work of sitting, as Lorde suggested, "eye to eye."[29] In the "Champagne Lady" and *In Another Place, Not Here,* we get to witness the dialogue begin before it is interrupted by the end of the narrative or the end of the character herself, just as Verlia has taken the leap and abandoned corporeal form for an existence less "fleshy" (249). Who can blame her? After all, it is the flesh that Hortense Spillers reminds us is "ripped," torn, and enervated with suffering.[30] In all instances, the story is just beginning, just as this book only begins to excavate this archive.

Grieving the Queer

Anti-Black Violence and Black Collective Memory

> When you kill the ancestor you kill yourself.
>
> —"Rootedness: The Ancestor as Foundation" 344[1]

> Not only humans made the Crossing, traveling only in one direction through Ocean given the name Atlantic. Grief traveled as well. The dead do not like to be forgotten . . .
>
> —*Pedagogies of Crossing* 289[2]

I n the opening of this volume I shared my desire for a resonance of queerness in Black memory that I sought on the metaphorical face of Africa as represented on the walls of the Museum of the African Diaspora in San Francisco. This text ends as it began: with the ancestors, through an examination of the registry of the dead. I have been paying homage to the ancestors all along, acknowledging, through fiction, the ingenuity of their epistemological technologies. Each chapter has examined ways in which Black lesbians have commented upon and expanded the available known archives of slavery, migration, diaspora, revolutionary movements, and rural life by offering epistemologies for Black resistance, community building, and self-making.

The alternative fictional archive created by the Black lesbian authors in this book makes interventions into familiar narratives of Black life, asking questions about how the ancestors are remembered. Or, more pointedly, which ancestors do we include in Black collective memory? Throughout this book I have discussed the representation of "the dead," or the disremembered and disenfranchised. At the book's close I acknowledge that "the dead" all too often die premature, state-sanctioned deaths. What happens if Black queers are not remembered by Black people? Can Black queer people be the subject of Black grief? Which deaths ignite Blacks to take to the street in protest and insurrection?[3] Grief often ignites Black political action; it can be a catalyst for forming community, and it can help define Black structural positioning. But when disremembered, Black queers become unrecognizable as part of Blackness and disqualified from collective grieving. To be unrecognizable as Black opens up a process of disrecognition, the transformation of Black queers into not being Black after all.

In 2009, President Obama signed the The Matthew Shepard and James Byrd, Jr., Hate Crimes Prevention Act, which gives federal support to state and local jurisdictions that want to prosecute hate crimes.[4] In the naming and representation of this legislation, anti-Black violence and anti-gay violence are separate. The law itself reinforces the separateness of these two spheres, identifying "offenses involving actual or perceived race, color, religion, or national origin" distinct from "offenses involving actual or perceived religion, national origin, gender, sexual orientation, gender identity, or disability."[5] In the language of the law it is assumed that "certain hate crime acts" are clustered such that race and color are coextensive with religion and national origin in ways that sexual orientation, gender, and gender identity are not. Entire communities are implicated in these processes in that the individual and "the community sharing the traits that caused the victim to be selected" are "savaged" by the hate crime.[6] The law takes for granted that collectives based on race and color may also share religion and national origin, but gender and sexual orientation and gender identity are disassociated from race. In the bill, race itself is defined in relation to the history of slavery and involuntary labor, thereby concretizing the decoupling of Blackness from gender and sexuality, belying the histories of Black queers as integral to Black communities that the Black lesbian fictional archive here asserts.[7]

Matthew Shepard is the symbol of victims of anti-gay violence, and James Byrd is the symbol of anti-Black violence. This split is indicative of how the nation has come to understand these histories as distinct and separate spheres. In 1998 Byrd was dragged behind a car, his body violently mangled on an east-Texas road. Later that same year, Shepard was found beaten, tortured, and bound to a fence where he was left to die. As Eric Stanley states, "[T]he queer inhabits the place of compromised personhood and the zone of death."[8] However, not all queers are the same. The story of Matthew Shepard's murder has become a national symbol of the consequences of homophobia in ways that the murders of Black queers cannot because of the banality of Black death. Part of the shock of Shepard's murder is the spectacular way that he was mutilated and displayed—a fate usually reserved for Black men. James Byrd's horrifying murder is recognizable as part of a history of lynching in the United States that goes back to the nineteenth century.[9]

In 2008, ten years after Byrd's death, Brandon McClelland was murdered under similar circumstances in east Texas. In 2009 the district attorney dropped the murder charges, citing lack of evidence.[10] Brandon's murder shares the context of state-sanctioned anti-Black violence with that of an endless litany of others who were killed by police, a list I merely touch on here. In fact, the list of the murdered is too long for this epilogue and would indeed fill the pages of this book. The following accounting of well-known deaths of Black people at the hands of police actually stands in for a much longer list and symbolizes how Black people across the United States collectively grieve anti-Black violence. My intention here is to do what the language of the Shepard–Byrd Act implicitly denies is possible: to place the relatively unknown deaths and beatings of Black queer people in relation to general trends of anti-Black violence and premature death. The following is a calling of the names of the dead, but it is by no means a comprehensive list. There are just too many names. The sheer number of cases of murder and Black state-sanctioned premature death physically and emotionally overwhelms me, even as I cite cases that made it into local or national mainstream news. And citation is key in the recognition of their deaths. Which ones do I name? Even as I write this epilogue, more Black queer people die transphobic and homophobic deaths, and often at the hands of other Black people. Here I hope to spark a continuation of the dialogue started in this volume through Black lesbian literature. Whom do we remember as part of Black collective memory, and how does disremembering the queer make that person a constitutive outsider to Blackness, and thus someone who can be excised from the world without collective grieving?

Calling of Names

Eleanor Bumpers was a 66-year-old grandmother who was shot twice by the New York City Police Department during her eviction in 1985. Mrs. Bumpers threatened the police with a large kitchen knife, but the first shot by the officer blew off her hand and shattered the knife she was holding. The second shot killed her. The officer was acquitted of all charges.[11] In 1999 Amadou

Diallo was shot 41 times on the steps of his apartment as he reached for his wallet. The officers were acquitted of all charges. Also unarmed, Sean Bell was shot and killed in a hail of 50 bullets by New York City police detectives in 2006 while outside a nightclub. The detectives were acquitted of all charges.[12] On New Year's Day, 2009, police in Oakland, California, shot Oscar Grant in the back while he was handcuffed. Grant's case differs from the others listed in the fact that the police officer that killed him was convicted of involuntary manslaughter in 2010.[13] The list goes on. In each instance, the case has come to national attention. Of course, there are many more anti-Black murders committed in the United States that did not receive national news coverage and others that I do not discuss here. These cases became news events because of a combination of African American organized public protest as well as pressure on local and national print and television news outlets. More importantly, for my purposes, these are the cases that Black people around the country remember as heinous examples of structural racism and collective vulnerability. Often, these deaths are the punctums in Black history that my undergraduate students know by heart, even when they have very little other information about African American pasts.

In general, as we see in the Shepard–Byrd Act, anti-Black violence and anti-queer violence are considered mutually exclusive. As a result of a lack of Black collective attention, the cases of Black queer people who suffer at the hands of the police or other state agencies have not become part of African American collective consciousness. There are many examples of attacks or murders against Black queer people that are less well known, even though they happen under circumstances that are familiar to African Americans as state-sanctioned anti-Black violence. For example, Logan Smith was an intersex person who had surgeries in order to help him live as a man from the time that he was 15 years old. In 1996, when he was 23, Logan and his brother were on their way back from errands when they were stopped for the failure to use a right-turn signal while driving near their home in an affluent suburb of Chicago. After an altercation with the police, Logan was taken into custody, beaten, and subsequently sustained fatal injuries. Logan died of a septic infection from a ruptured bladder. The first reports stated that "Smith died not from trauma, but from complications arising from a sex-change operation."[14] The police involved in the case were not convicted of Logan's murder, but his family did receive compensation from a civil suit.

Tyra Hunter died in 1995 from neglect by medical personnel. She was involved in a car accident that resulted in life-threatening injuries. While the medical emergency response team was working to help her, they discovered that Tyra had male genitalia. The emergency medical team proceeded to back away from Tyra, laughing and joking about her body. Tyra died on arrival at a Washington, DC, hospital.[15]

Duanna Johnson

Duanna Johnson was beaten in police custody while under arrest for prostitution in Memphis, Tennessee, in 2008. Duanna's beating was caught on video by the Memphis Police Department security cameras and was subsequently shown on the local news. The news footage included a brief interview with Duanna, giving us a unique opportunity to hear Duanna talk for herself and analyze the immediate circumstances of her beating. We can use this moment to think about the question of how the recognition of anti-Black violence disappears when it comes to Black queers.

While Duanna was still in booking, one white officer restrained her while another white officer punched her in the face and head with his handcuffs wrapped around his fists. She was pepper sprayed, handcuffed, and left on the floor writhing in pain. Duanna told local TV news reporters that the police officer was angry that she did not submit to his anti-queer slurs. In Althusserian terms, she refused the officer's efforts at interpellation, stating, "That wasn't my name. My mother didn't name me a faggot or a he/she."[16] In 2010, her attacker received a two-year prison sentence, but she did not live to hear of the verdict. Later in 2008, Duanna was shot down on a Memphis street.[17] At the time of writing, there have been no arrests in her murder.

Given this historical and contemporary context, the police attack on Duanna Johnson is not atypical or surprising. What is interesting, though, are the responses from the Black people who witnessed the attack. There are several other Black people in the booking room who watched Duanna's beating and did not intervene or speak up afterwards, including other police officers and a nurse. Duanna was particularly disturbed by the nurse's reaction to her beating. As Duanna lay on the floor, handcuffed and rocking in pain, the nurse walked directly past her to attend to the minor injuries of the officer. Duanna said in her interview, "I didn't feel like I was a human being. Even the nurse came in and she just ignored me and I begged her to help me."[18] Out of the group of people gathered in the booking room, including staff, other people being processed for arrest, and additional police officers (including a Black woman officer), Duanna looked to the Black woman nurse help her, to recognize her humanity.

The Black observers of Duanna's beating did not identify with her. They seemed to be under what Lewis Gordon would call a delusion of non-Blackness, when the observer identifies with those who are non-Black in order to occupy a position of humanity and dignity.[19] In addition to not identifying with her as a Black person, the women in the room did not find common cause with Duanna as another Black woman. As Duanna correctly identified, she was not treated like a human being while in police custody. Using Gordon's schema in Duanna's case, by their nonaction the observers identified with the white people around them and against the person being oppressed. Extending the phenomenological example, which is traditionally theorized with regard to racial allegiance, Duanna's oppression (and desertion by the other Black people in the room) centers on her racialized gender identity. She is a Black transwoman and as such is viewed as one who defies nature and therefore deserves punishment. In this case, to "defy nature" is to be Black and to dare to create a body that corresponds to her gender identity. To stand against those who deserve to be oppressed places one on the level of those who do not deserve to be oppressed.[20]

As I have argued elsewhere, "Black transgression of gender norms can be construed by mainstream Black communities as dangerously close to being complicit with racist discourses. This situation creates a dilemma for differently gendered Black people in the past and in the present."[21] To embrace terms such as "transsexual" or "transgender," claiming identities that are not culturally recognized in African American communities, can mark one as *not* Black. The circumstances of Duanna's case (and others) require an extension of anti-Black sentiment to also include a consideration of anti-queerness and misogyny. Being trans placed Duanna in the position of an unfathomable traitor to Blackness and therefore outside of the realm of affiliation for the Black men and women in the booking room at the Memphis police station. The Black women police officers and the nurse become convinced, through anti-queerness, that Duanna was not a Black woman in distress, but someone who is *not* entirely Black. The observers are under the delusion that the queer person being attacked is not connected to them by race (or gender); that is, the Black person watching the assault regards the Black queer person being beaten (Duanna Johnson) as some lesser form of Black or someone who is not Black, not really Black or female, or not *us* in any event. To be "not us" means that the person has jumped ship, joined with whiteness, and is collaborating with the oppressor. In the United States we saw this with Leroi Jones's work *Home,* wherein he expressed this very fear in the imagined figure of the Black gay man who enjoys being penetrated by white men and is therefore in collaboration with the oppressor.[22]

This consideration of the queer as "not us" is not exclusively a U.S. phenomenon but part of a larger diasporic struggle with colonialism.[23] The Black queer often becomes morphed into an agent of the oppressors, or even one with them. To punish the Black queer is to give the oppressors what they deserve. In a recent case in Malawi, a transwoman and her partner faced up to fourteen years of hard labor for having a "gay wedding."[24] The international press marked the couple as "gay" even though one of the couple clearly identified herself as a woman.[25] They were released after international pressure for human rights. These human rights are claimed in a context of a colonial history. Formerly colonized Black people are put in the impossible position of having the only avenue for human identification in the form of the colonizing power.[26] Even after the formal end of colonialism, the colonizer's reach is still felt in various ways, including in the religious beliefs left in their wake that have become law, such as their admonishments against sodomy.[27] But there is a catch, because the colonizers have changed their minds. In the case of Malawi, many other countries, including the United Kingdom, South Africa, and the United States, took the opportunity to remind Malawi of its political and cultural atavism. The U.S. State Department said that the Malawi sentence was a "step backwards in the protection of human rights."[28] These declarations obscure the anti-queer and other violence that takes place in sites that are recognized for human rights, and they represent the former colony as obsolete and backward.

South Africa is interesting in this regard. It is consistently held up as the exemplary former colony that all other African nations should emulate. The *New York Times* described the case as "not just a matter of the state versus a same-sex couple" but as "a matter of Malawi against the developed world."[29] Again, the former colonizers can chastise their former colonies and suggest that they still need their guidance. Malawi's response was to declare their independence from colonizers and state that they have a right to decide who is part of African society and who is not. The Malawian Minister of Information and Civic Affairs, Leckford Mwanza Thotho, declared the conviction of the couple to be in keeping with Malawian culture and traditions. He further described the case to be a matter of national protection, stating that "if there is something very strange in nature which would have a very negative impact on the country, I think it is the duty of government to uphold the constitution and laws of that country."[30] Black queers are in the middle of this struggle as perpetually *not us* and allied with *them*.

In this case, the "them" in question is the colonizer himself. In the Malawian example, the two defendants, Tiwonge Chimbalanga and Steven Monjeza, were described as belonging to the realm of the un-African; it was specifically suggested that they were outside agitators working on behalf of the colonizers and therefore no longer part of the African "us." Minister Thotho described the case as concerning "immoral acts" that "are not in our culture; they are coming from outside. . . . Otherwise, why is there all this interest from around the world? Why is money being sent?"[31] Through their act of queer union the couple had become part of the West, an entity of oppression and control whereby the perceived encroachment of moral decay leaks into the country and the culture through the body of the queer. These perceptions have implications in other African nations as well. In June 2010, Ghana saw anti-gay protests in the city of Sekondi Takoradi. The protest was organized by Muslim community leaders to address a perceived threat of homosexuality to the youth of Ghana.[32]

Across the Atlantic in Guyana, a similar transformation occurred in some people's minds. In 2010, controversy sprung up over the annual queer film festival sponsored by the Society Against Sexual Orientation Discrimination (SASOD). Bishop Juan Edghill, Public Relations Officer of the Inter Religious Organisation, spoke out against the ongoing Gay and Lesbian film festival, stating, "We cannot allow the western world to come and foist their lifestyles and way of thinking onto us."[33] He claimed that it was just another form of colonialism.

The United States is not exempt from this phenomenon of Black people "becoming" the oppressor/colonizer the moment that queerness is perceived or "discovered." As the U.S. headlines were filled with the news of young gay men committing suicide after being bullied by peers, a case in New York also briefly garnered some attention. In October 2010, a group of young men in the Bronx that called themselves the Latin King Goonies, all of which have family ties in African diasporic countries, discovered that one of their 17-year-old potential members had been in a sexual relationship with a 35-year-old man. The members of the gang proceeded to rape the young man with the handle of a plunger and then raped his lover with a plastic baseball bat, eventually turning on the potential member's brother and beating him as well.

In a series of moves of identification reminiscent of the Duanna Johnson case, the Latin King Goonies stand against the gay initiate, relegating him as "one who defies nature" and establishing themselves as the ones who do not deserve such treatment. Of course, this exemption is an illusion, and their position as men of color made them vulnerable to the exact same treatment once they were booked for rape and assault. It is precisely their own vulnerable positioning in relation to the police that creates a dynamic in which the potential "brother" gang member becomes the "other"; the initiate becomes one with the oppressor, a force of violation and brutality in the gang members' lives. In that way, the gay initiate exists as *not us* and instead is one of *them*. The initiate, his lover, and his brother become instruments of revenge, a way to act out rage and frustration at a brutal system.

On Archives and Memorials

Being Black and queer and living in the world is a dangerous proposition. Each example above is part of the manifest legacy of disremembering Black queers in the history of the African Diaspora. The fiction that I have discussed throughout this book is a memorial for the dead and an archive for the living; it is part of a constellation of Black queer practices of remembering. As I quoted at the beginning of this epilogue (Alexander), the dead do not like to be forgotten; thus we must honor them with our acknowledgment. There is a growing movement of Black queer archiving practices around the diaspora that remember our own living communities so that we can celebrate ourselves while we can still witness the celebration. Various forms of cultural production[34] and digital and institutional archives[35] acknowledge the lives of those who have passed. Activist organizations around the globe[36] collect testimonials from queer people of color who have been assaulted and help report them to policing agencies.[37] Recently several of these organizations were called to speak to the United Nations.[38]

Each of these forms of archiving, activism, and cultural production has an important function as a historiographical tool.[39] The work of these activists, artists, and writers gives us an opportunity to see Black queer people engaged in our own processes of remembering and our own ways of defining Black resistance and Black self-making. Expansive historiographic texts also present a productive tension between the known archives and counter-memory. They depict a form of irresolution that pushes against forgetting by continuing to grieve. Continual grieving, or melancholia, can also be understood as necessary in the struggle against amnesia.[40] Grief can be a practice of celebration. Black lesbian literature and the archives created by Black queer people around the world are symbolic altars to commemorate and celebrate the ancestors and encourage the living. They go beyond the queer limit of the known definition of Blackness, extending beyond a precipice of Black memory into the darkness of queer irresolution and unpredictability.

NOTES

Introduction

1. Brent Hayes Edwards, *The Practices of Diaspora: Literature, Translation, and the Rise of Black Internationalism* (Cambridge, MA: Harvard University Press, 2003); Robin D. G. Kelley and Tiffany Ruby Patterson, "Unfinished Migrations: Reflections on the African Diaspora and the Making of the Modern World," *African Studies* 43, no. 1 (April 2000): 11–45.

2. The photomosaic also exists in an online exhibit at the MoAD website. "Photographs from the African Diaspora," *MoAD* website, accessed October 22, 2009, http://www.moadsf.org/salon/exhibits/photomosaic/index.html.

3. For more on the punctum see Roland Barthes, *Camera Lucida*, trans. Richard Howard (New York: Hill and Wang, 1981).

4. Fred Moten discusses the photograph of Emmett Till as the photograph that screams. "Black Mo'nin' in the Sound of the Photograph," in *In the Break: The Aesthetics of the Black Radical Tradition* (Minneapolis: University of Minnesota Press, 2003): 192–211.

5. Marianne Hirsch and Leo Spitzer, "Testimonial Objects: Memory, Gender and Transmission," *Poetics Today* 27, no. 2 (Summer 2006): 353–83, 358. The term "postmemory" refers to the recollection of experiences and memories associated with the traumas of a previous generation. Also see Marianne Hirsch, "Past Lives: Postmemories in Exile," *Poetics Today* 17, no. 4 (Winter 1996): 659–86.

6. Hirsch and Spitzer, in "Testimonial Objects," define points of memory as "objects and images that have remained from the past, containing 'points' about the work of memory and transmission" (358).

7. For more on the heterosexual matrix, see Judith Butler, *Gender Trouble: Feminism and the Subversion of Identity* (New York: Routledge, 1990); and Judith Halberstam, *In a Queer Time and Place: Transgender Bodies, Subcultural Lives* (New York: New York University Press, 2005). According to Halberstam, queer time is a disruption to the linear, heterosexual expectation of what makes a "normal" life—birth, marriage, children, death.

8. *The Watermelon Woman*, directed by Cheryl Dunye (1996; New York: First Run Features, 2000), DVD.

9. Enoch H. Page and Matt U. Richardson, "On the Fear of Small Numbers: A Twenty-First-Century Prolegomenon of the U.S. Black Transgender Experience," in *Black Sexualities: Probing Powers, Passions, Practices, and Policies*, ed. Juan Battle and Sandra L. Barnes (New Brunswick, NJ: Rutgers University Press, 2009), 57–81.

10. Of course the urtext of African American family pathology in the mid-twentieth century is the Moynihan Report. Daniel Patrick Moynihan, *The Negro Family: The Case for National Action*, prepared for the Office of Planning and Research, United States Department of Labor (Washington, DC: Government Printing Office, 1965). However, this idea haunts Black life across the diaspora where the Black family is also seen as "incomplete, deviant and ruptured." See Paul Gilroy, '*There Ain't No Black in the Union Jack': The Cultural Politics of Race and Nation* (Chicago: University of Chicago Press, 1987), 59.

11. Evelynn M. Hammonds, "Toward a Genealogy of Black Female Sexuality: The Problematic of Silence," in *Feminist Genealogies, Colonial Legacies, Democratic Futures*, ed. M. Jacqui Alexander and Chandra Talpade Mohanty (New York: Routledge, 1997), 170–82.

12. Xavier O'Neal Livermon, "Usable Traditions: Sexual Autonomy and the Black Queer in Post-Apartheid South Africa" (unpublished article).

13. Sylvia Wynter, "Unsettling the Coloniality of Being/Power/Truth/Freedom: Towards the Human, After Man, Its Overrepresentation—An Argument," *CR: The New Centennial Review* 3, no. 3 (2003): 267.

14. Hortense J. Spillers, "Mama's Baby, Papa's Maybe: An American Grammar Book," in *Black, White, and in Color: Essays on American Literature and Culture* (Chicago: University of Chicago Press, 2003), 229.

15. For a discussion of feverish attachment to the archive see Jacques Derrida, *Archive Fever: A Freudian Impression,* trans. Eric Prenowitz (Chicago: University of Chicago Press, 1995).

16. According to the Smithsonian website, the National Museum of African American History and Culture is expected to be finished in 2015. Even though the physical site is not finished, the museum has content online, including its inaugural exhibit of photographs titled "Let Your Motto Be Resistance." Resistance is embodied in each of the African Americans chosen for the exhibit. Although none of the biographies actually mention the gender variance or sexual orientation of the subject, the description of James Baldwin gives some subtle indication of the criteria for embodying resistance. The description juxtaposes Baldwin's femininity with his presence as a writer and spokesperson for Black liberation in a way that suggests the combination is unexpected: "While physically slight and soft-spoken, Baldwin emerged at mid-century as one of the most passionate and eloquent writers about the problem of race in American society." "Let Your Motto Be Resistance: African American Portraits," *National Museum of African American History and Culture* website, accessed January 23, 2012. http://srv00000221.si.edu/section/programs/view/14. For more on Baldwin's gender fluidity see Page and Richardson, "On the Fear of," 57–81.

17. Achille Mbembe, "The Power of the Archive and Its Limits," in *Refiguring the Archive*, ed. Carolyn Hamilton et al. (Cape Town, South Africa: David Philip Publishers, 2002), 19.

18. Mbembe, "The Power of the Archive," 19.

19. Ibid.

20. Ibid., 21.

21. I am using the term "repertoire" in the way that Diana Taylor suggests, which is embodied, "expressive behavior," to suggest the performative quality of these texts. Diana Taylor, *The Archive and the Repertoire: Performing Cultural Memory in the Americas* (Durham: Duke University Press, 2003), xvi.

22. Lisa Merrill, "Performing History: A Politics of Location," in *The Sage Handbook of Performance Studies*, ed. D. Soyini Madison and Judith Hamera (Thousand Oaks, CA: Sage Publications, 2006), 65–71, 67–68.

23. Taylor, *The Archive and the Repertoire,* 20–21; José Esteban Muñoz, *Cruising Utopia: The Then and There of Queer Futurity* (New York: New York University Press, 2009).

24. Roderick A. Ferguson, *Aberrations in Black: Toward a Queer of Color Critique* (Minneapolis: University of Minnesota Press, 2004). Ferguson discusses the Moynihan Report as a document which suggests that African Americans are pathological because of our seeming inability to adhere to heteronormative standards of family formation and sex roles as a collective.

25. Homonormativity is the embrace of heteronormative values. See Lisa Duggan, *The Twilight of Equality? Neoliberalism, Cultural Politics, and the Attack on Democracy* (Boston: Beacon Press, 2003). Also see Susan Stryker, "Transgender History, Homonormativity, and Disciplinarity," *Radical History Review* 100 (2008): 145–57. Transnormative describes a transsexual or transperson who, once transition has occurred, is just like any cisgendered, or "biologically matched," person, except for a small accident of birth.

26. Ferguson, *Aberrations in Black;* E. Patrick Johnson, *Sweet Tea: Black Gay Men of the South* (Chapel Hill: University of North Carolina Press, 2008); Mark Anthony Neal, *New Black Man* (New York: Routledge, 2005); Darieck Scott, *Extravagant Abjection: Blackness, Power, and Sexuality in the African American Literary Imagination* (New York: New York University Press, 2010); Phillip Brian Harper, *Are We Not Men? Masculine Anxiety and the Problem of African-American Identity* (Oxford: Oxford University Press, 1996); and Jafari Sinclaire Allen, "Means of Desire's Production: Male Sex Labor in Cuba," *Identities: Global Studies in Culture and Power* 14, no. 1–2 (2007): 183–202; Rinaldo Walcott, "The Struggle for Happiness: Commodified Black Masculinities, Vernacular Culture, and Homoerotic Desires," in *Pedagogies of Difference: Rethinking Education for Social Justice*, ed. Peter Pericles Trifonas (New York: Routledge, 2002).

27. Henry Louis Gates Jr., *The Signifying Monkey: A Theory of African American Literary Criticism* (Oxford: Oxford University Press, 1988), 131.

28. My conception of "vernacular epistemologies" is an expansion on Clyde Woods's theorization of the epistemological potential of the blues to comment on and resist racial violence. I go further to recognize how the vernacular also enables queer gender and sexual identities. See Clyde Adrian Woods, *Development Arrested: The Blues and Plantation Power in the Mississippi Delta* (London: Verso, 1998).

29. Wynter, "Unsettling the Coloniality of Being/Power/Truth/Freedom," 266.

30. Sander L. Gilman, "Black Bodies, White Bodies: Toward an Iconography of Female Sexuality in Late Nineteenth-Century Art, Medicine, and Literature," in *"Race,"*

Writing, and Difference, ed. Henry Louis Gates Jr. (Chicago: University of Chicago Press, 1985).

31. Hazel V. Carby, *Reconstructing Womanhood: The Emergence of the Afro-American Woman Novelist* (New York: Oxford University Press, 1987). Carby argues that Black women remodeled the category "woman" to fit their condition as women for whom the "cult of true womanhood" was denied.

32. Evelyn Brooks Higginbotham, "African American Women's History and the Metalanguage of Race," *Signs* 17, no. 2 (1992): 257.

33. Siobhan B. Somerville, *Queering the Color Line: Race and the Invention of Homosexuality in American Culture* (Durham: Duke University Press, 2000), 26.

34. Kali N. Gross, *Colored Amazons: Crime, Violence and Black Women in the City of Brotherly Love, 1880–1910* (Durham: Duke University Press, 2006), 134.

35. Sharon Patricia Holland, *Raising the Dead: Readings of Death and (Black) Subjectivity* (Durham: Duke University Press, 2000), 145.

36. See Paisley Currah, "Stepping Back, Looking Outward: Situating Transgender Activism and Transgender Studies—Kris Hayashi, Matt Richardson, and Susan Stryker Frame the Movement," *Sexuality Research and Social Policy: Journal of the NSRC* Special Issue 5(1), (2008): 93–105, 99; and Page and Richardson, "On the Fear of Small Numbers" 63.

37. From Janice Raymond's anti-trans book, *The Transsexual Empire: The Making of the She-Male* (New York: Teachers College Press, 1994), to the discussions by genderqueer and transgender authors Judith Halberstam, *Female Masculinity* (Durham: Duke University Press, 1998) and Patrick Califia, *Sex Changes: The Politics of Transgenderism,* 2nd ed. (San Francisco: Cleis Press, 2003), a tremendous amount has been written on butch and trans border wars and on uneasy tensions between trans and lesbian communities. This is in line with the fact that lesbian communities in general have been continuously involved in open debates about transsexual inclusion of FTM and MTF participants.

38. Cathy Cohen describes Black queerness in terms of being "outside of the dominant constructed norm of state-sanctioned white middle- and upper-class heterosexuality." I would also add outside of gender norms. Cathy J. Cohen, "Punks, Bulldaggers and Welfare Queens: The Radical Potential of Queer Politics?" in *Black Queer Studies: A Critical Anthology,* ed. E. Patrick Johnson and Mae G. Henderson (Durham: Duke University Press, 2005), 25.

39. Ferguson, *Aberrations in Black,* 115.

40. Ibid.

41. C. Riley Snorton, "Transfiguring Masculinities in Black Women's Studies," *The Feminist Wire,* May 18, 2011, http://thefeministwire.com/2011/05/transfiguring-masculinities-in-black-women%E2%80%99s-studies/.

42. Rinaldo Walcott, "Reconstructing Manhood; or, the Drag of Black Masculinity," *Small Axe* 13, no. 1 (2009): 75–89, 76.

43. I use the term "transmasculine" to describe someone who was labeled as female at birth and who is a masculine person (who may or may not identify as a man). A "transfeminine" person is labeled male at birth and is feminine (and may or may not identify as a woman). I deploy these terms in order to describe the complexities of gender nonconformity that cannot be understood through the term "transgender." An example of a feminine transmasculine character is Sunshine/Kali from Cherry Muhanji's novel *Her,* analyzed in chapter 2 of this book. Sunshine/Kali cross-dresses in men's clothes and has a mixture of masculine and feminine attributes. Cherry Muhanji, *Her: A Novel* (San Francisco: Aunt Lute Books, 1990).

44. Toni Morrison, *Beloved* (1987; New York: Vintage Books, 2004), 323.

45. Holland, *Raising the Dead*, 15.

46. Ibid., 6.

47. Abdul R. JanMohamed, "Negating the Negation as a Form of Affirmation in Minority Discourse: The Construction of Richard Wright as Subject," *Cultural Critique* 7 (1987): 245–66.

48. J. Douglas Bremner, *Trauma, Memory, and Dissociation* (Arlington, VA: American Psychiatric Publishing, Inc., 2002), 11.

49. Darlene Clark Hine, "Rape and the Inner Lives of Black Women in the Middle West: Preliminary Thoughts on the Culture of Dissemblance," *Signs* 14, no. 4 (1989): 912–20.

50. Frantz Fanon, *Black Skin, White Masks*, trans. Charles Lam Markmann (New York: Grove Press, 1967).

51. Saidiya Hartman, "Venus in Two Acts," *Small Axe* 12, no. 2 (June 2008): 5, 2.

52. Ibid., 2

53. Judith Butler, *Undoing Gender* (New York: Routledge, 2004), 18.

54. Dunye, *The Watermelon Woman*.

55. Mattie Richardson, "No More Secrets, No More Lies: African American Women and Compulsory Heterosexuality," *Journal of Women's History* 15, no. 3 (2003): 63–76.

56. Hartman, "Venus in Two Acts," 2.

57. Ibid., 2-3.

58. Toni Morrison, "Unspeakable Things Unspoken: The Afro-American Presence in American Literature," *Michigan Quarterly Review* 28, no. 1 (1989): 1–34.

59. Omise'eke Natasha Tinsley, "Black Atlantic, Queer Atlantic: Queer Imaginings of the Middle Passage," *GLQ: A Journal of Lesbian and Gay Studies* 14, no. 2–3 (2008): 191–215, 193.

60. Cathy J. Cohen, "Deviance as Resistance: A New Research Agenda for the Study of Black Politics," *DuBois Review* 1, no. 1 (March 2004): 27–45, 39.

61. Ibid., 29. I do agree with Cohen that we have to consider the fact that not all acts of resistance end domination, but resistance is an irresolute process in itself. It can sometimes be the process by which Black people are more deeply ensnared in the processes of domination.

62. Dionne Brand, *A Map to the Door of No Return: Notes to Belonging* (Toronto: Vintage Canada, 2002), 18–19.

63. M. Jacqui Alexander, *Pedagogies of Crossing: Meditations on Feminism, Sexual Politics, Memory, and the Sacred* (Durham: Duke University Press, 2005), 288.

64. Ibid.

65. Linda Hutcheon, "Historiographic Metafiction: Parody and the Intertextuality of History," in *Intertextuality and Contemporary American Fiction,* ed. Patrick O'Donnell and Robert Con Davis (Baltimore: Johns Hopkins University Press, 1989), 3–32.

66. Bran Nicol, *The Cambridge Introduction to Postmodern Fiction* (Cambridge: Cambridge University Press, 2009), 17–30.

67. Hutcheon, "Historiographic Metafiction," 4.

68. Halberstam, *In a Queer Time and Place,* defines "queer time" as the "specific models of temporality that emerge within postmodernism once one leaves the temporal frames of bourgeois reproduction and family, longevity, safety/risk, and inheritance. . . . 'Queer space' refers to . . . new understandings of space enabled by the production of queer counterpublics" (6).

69. While I cannot claim as ambitious a project as the explication of the performativity of the punctuation of each text, I do agree with Brody (and Jones) regarding the aspects of performance that the creative use of text imbues on the pages of Black lesbian fiction. Jennifer DeVere Brody, *Punctuation: Art, Politics, and Play* (Durham: Duke University Press, 2008); Meta DuEwa Jones, *The Muse Is Music: Jazz Poetry from the Harlem Renaissance to Spoken Word* (Urbana: University of Illinois Press, 2011).

70. Halberstam, *In a Queer Time and Place.*

71. For a classic discussion of Black British history, see Peter Fryer, *Staying Power: The History of Black People in Britain* (London: Pluto Press, 1984). Although there are a growing number of books about Black presence in England, there still is very little written about Blacks in Scotland. See Philip D. Morgan and Sean Hawkins, *Black Experience and the Empire* (Oxford: Oxford University Press, 2004); and David Dabydeen, John Gilmore, and Cecily Jones, *The Oxford Companion to Black British History* (Oxford: Oxford University Press, 2010).

72. Hartman, "Venus in Two Acts," 12.

73. A. Timothy Spaulding describes the postmodern neo-slave narrative as a mode of fiction that "undermine[s] conventions of linearity and distinctions between past and present" in order to critique an ongoing legacy of slavery in contemporary U.S. race relations. I add that the neo-slave narratives and other fiction that I analyze mix temporalities in order to anachronistically place contemporary queer gender and sexual identities in the past. A. Timothy Spaulding, *Re-Forming the Past: History, The Fantastic, and the Postmodern Slave Narrative* (Columbus: The Ohio State University Press, 2005), 25.

74. Barbara Christian, "The Race for Theory," *Cultural Critique* 6 (1987): 52.

75. Both E. Patrick Johnson's *Sweet Tea* and Leon E. Pettiway's *Honey, Honey Miss Thang: Being Black, Gay, and on the Streets* (Philadelphia: Temple University Press, 1996) are rare examples of ethnographies that provide us with the voices of Black queer working-class and working-poor people.

76. Stuart Hall, "Cultural Identity and Diaspora," in *Theorizing Diaspora: A Reader,* ed. Jana Evans Braziel and Anita Mannur (Malden, MA: Blackwell Publishers, 2003), 237.

77. Ibid., 240.

78. Ntozake Shange, *For Colored Girls Who Have Considered Suicide When the Rainbow Is Enuf: A Choreopoem* (1975; New York: Scribner Poetry, 1997), 4.

79. Sylvia Wynter, "The Ceremony Must Be Found: After Humanism," *boundary 2* 12/13; 12, no. 3; 13, no. 1 (Spring–Autumn 1984): 19–70, 22.

80. Karin Knorr-Cetina, *Epistemic Cultures: How the Sciences Make Knowledge* (Cambridge, MA: Harvard University Press, 1999), 1.

81. Merrill, "Performing History," 68.

82. Scott, *Extravagant Abjection,* 165.

83. Ibid., 166

84. Gloria González-López, "Epistemologies of the Wound: Anzaldúan Theories and Sociological Research on Incest in Mexican Society," *Human Architecture: Journal of the Sociology of Self Knowledge* 4 (2006): 20, 21.

85. Higginbotham, "African American Women's History," 272.

86. I discuss the term "social death" in chapter 1 of this volume. For more on this, see Orlando Patterson, *Slavery and Social Death: A Comparative Study* (Cambridge, MA: Harvard University Press, 1982).

87. Angela Y. Davis, *Blues Legacies and Black Feminism: Gertrude "Ma" Rainey, Bessie Smith, and Billie Holiday* (New York: Vintage Books, 1999); Hazel V. Carby, "The Sexual

Politics of Women's Blues," in *Cultures in Babylon: Black Britain and African America* (London: Verso, 1999): 7–21.

88. Jill Dolan, "Utopia in Performance," *Theatre Research International* 31, no. 2 (July 2006): 163–73, 164.

89. Ibid.

90. Halberstam, *In a Queer Time and Place*.

91. José Esteban Muñoz theorizes the potential of performance to destabilize the audience in *Disidentifications: Queers of Color and the Performance of Politics* (Minneapolis: University of Minnesota Press, 1999).

92. The following novels, performance pieces, and short stories analyzed in this book have been gathered from a variety of difference resources including my own performance experience: "The Champagne Lady" is an unpublished short story by SDiane Adamz-Bogus that is archived at the Schomburg Center for Research in Black Culture; LaShonda K. Barnett, "Miss Hannah's Lesson" in *Callaloo and Other Lesbian Love Tales* (Norwich, VT: New Victoria Publishers, 1999); Dionne Brand, *In Another Place, Not Here* (New York, NY: Grove Press, 1996); *delta dandi* is, at the time of this writing, an unpublished performance piece by Sharon Bridgforth that I performed in at Fire and Ink: A Writer's Festival for GLBT People of African Descent in 2009 in Austin, TX (http://2009.fireand-ink.org/performances.html). I reference two published books by Bridgforth: *the bull-jean stories* (Austin, TX: RedBone Press, 1998) and *love conjure/blues* (Washington, DC: Red-Bone Press, 2004); Laurinda D. Brown, *The Highest Price for Passion* (Largo, MD: Strebor Books, 2008); Jewelle Gomez, *The Gilda Stories: A Novel* (Ithaca, NY: Firebrand Books, 1991); Jackie Kay, *Trumpet* (London: Picador Press 1998); and Cherry Muhanji, *Her: A Novel* (San Francisco, CA: Aunt Lute Books, 1990).

93. Sigmund Freud, "Mourning and Melancholia," in *The Complete Psychological Works of Sigmund Freud,* trans. and ed. James Strachey, vol. 14 (1957; New York: Vintage, 2001).

Chapter 1

1. Saidiya V. Hartman, *Scenes of Subjection: Terror, Slavery, and Self-Making in Nine-teenth-Century America* (New York: Oxford University Press, 1997). Hartman calls violence the "primal scene" wherein the slave is constituted (3).

2. According to *The Oxford Companion to African American Literature,* neo-slave narratives are contemporary works that depict the experiences of slavery in the Americas, representing "slavery as a historical phenomenon that has lasting cultural meaning and enduring social consequences." Ashraf H. A. Rushdy, "Neo-Slave Narrative," in *The Oxford Companion to African American Literature* (New York: Oxford University Press, 1997), 533. For more elaboration on the genre, see Ashraf H. A. Rushdy, *Neo-Slave Narratives: Studies in the Social Logic of a Literary Form* (New York: Oxford University Press, 1999).

3. There are two other pieces of fiction set in slavery and written by Black women that have woman-to-woman sexual relationships as their major concern: *The Salt Roads* by Nalo Hopkinson (New York: Warner Books, 2004); and "The Mistress and the Slave Girl" by Ann Allen Shockley, in *The Leading Edge: An Anthology of Lesbian Sexual Fiction,* ed. Lady Winston (Denver, CO: Lace Publishers, 1987). Both are intriguing pieces of fiction. The portion of *The Salt Roads* that is set partially on a slave plantation is most certainly about Black women's relationships with each other and deserves its own extended critical

examination in relationship to the rest of the chronologies and spiritual cosmologies at work in the novel. Ann Allen Shockley's short story is not discussed in this chapter because it is written from the perspective of the white mistress. However, it fits in well with "Miss Hannah's Lesson," as Shockley creates a world in which the white mistress utilizes her privilege within whiteness to emancipate her slave and set her up as her "lover" in a private northern cottage.

4. Saba Mahmood, "Feminist Theory, Embodiment, and the Docile Agent: Some Reflections on the Egyptian Islamic Revival," *Cultural Anthropology* 16, no. 2 (May 2001): 202–36, 208.

5. Hartman, *Scenes of Subjection*, 23.

6. Darieck Scott, *Extravagant Abjection: Blackness, Power, and Sexuality in the African American Literary Imagination* (New York: New York University Press, 2010), 163.

7. Mireille Miller-Young, "Putting Hypersexuality to Work: Black Women and Illicit Eroticism in Pornography," *Sexualities* 13, no. 2 (April 2010): 221.

8. Audre Lorde, "Uses of the Erotic: The Erotic as Power," in *Sister Outsider: Essays and Speeches* (Freedom, CA: Crossing Press, 1984), 57.

9. Ibid., 54

10. Although *The Erotic Life of Racism* was published after this chapter was written, both texts share a concern about the interconnectedness between the entanglements of anti-Blackness and queer desire. Sharon Patricia Holland, *The Erotic Life of Racism* (Durham: Duke University Press, 2012), 59.

11. Sylvia Wynter, "The Ceremony Must Be Found: After Humanism," *boundary 2* 12/13; 12, no. 3; 13, no. 1 (Spring–Autumn 1984): 27.

12. Ibid., 56.

13. Based on private interviews with Adamz-Bogus in October 2001, Gomez in May 2004, and Barnett in December 2004.

14. "The Champagne Lady" was written ca. 1988. It is currently in the collection of the Adamz-Bogus papers at the Schomburg Center for Research in Black Culture in New York. According to conversations with Adamz-Bogus in 2001, she originally conceived of the collection to deal with a different period in Black history.

15. At the time of our informal interview in 2004, LaShonda Barnett was completing a doctorate in history at the College of William and Mary. She originally wanted to write about woman-to-woman sexual relationships in slavery but was discouraged by a mentor who suggested that the research into plantation mistresses' diaries would take too long for a doctoral thesis project.

16. By the 1970s, feminist historians began to address the concept of slave resistance from the perspective of women, which reoriented historical attention to resistance as an embodied practice. See Angela Y. Davis, *Women, Race & Class* (New York: Random House, 1981); Paula Giddings, *When and Where I Enter: The Impact of Black Women on Race and Sex in America* (New York: Morrow, 1984); Deborah Gray White, *Ar'n't I a Woman? Female Slaves in the Plantation South* (New York: Norton, 1985); Jacqueline Jones, *Labor of Love, Labor of Sorrow: Black Women, Work, and the Family from Slavery to the Present* (New York: Basic Books, 1985); and Darlene Clark Hine, *Hine Sight: Black Women and the Reconstruction of American History* (Bloomington: Indiana University Press, 1994).

17. Gayl Jones, *Corregidora* (New York: Random House, 1975). Jones's main character, Ursa, describes the story of the slave owner, Corregidora, passed down through her maternal line in terms of violence and sexual pleasure. Similarly, Kara Walker's "Letter from a Black Girl" is irresolute in relation to the master: "Dear you duplicitous, idiot,

Worm, now that youve forgotten how you like your coffee and why you raised your pious fist to the sky, and the reason for your stunning African Art collection, and the war we fought together, and the promises you made and the laws we rewrote, I am left here alone to recreate my WHOLE HISTORY without benefit of you, my compliment, my enemy, my oppressor, my Love." Kara Walker, "Letter from a Black Girl," 1998, as cited in Adair Rounthwaite, "Making Mourning from Melancholia: The Art of Kara Walker," *Image [&] Narrative: Online Magazine of the Visual Narrative* 19 (November 2007), http://www.imageandnarrative.be/inarchive/autofiction/rounthwaite.htm. The "Black girls" in the neo-slave narratives and in Walker's letter are aggrieved but also love their oppressor.

18. Bernard W. Bell, *The Afro-American Novel and Its Tradition* (Amherst: University of Massachusetts Press, 1987).

19. Rushdy, *Neo-Slave Narratives.*

20. Elizabeth Ann Beaulieu, *Black Women Writers and the American Neo-Slave Narrative: Femininity Unfettered* (Westport, CT: Greenwood Press, 1999), 3–4.

21. Angelyn Mitchell, *The Freedom to Remember: Narrative, Slavery, and Gender in Contemporary Black Women's Fiction* (New Brunswick, NJ: Rutgers University Press, 2002).

22. Arlene R. Keizer, *Black Subjects: Identity Formation in the Contemporary Narrative of Slavery* (Ithaca, NY: Cornell University Press, 2004), 3–4.

23. Keizer, *Black Subjects,* 8.

24. Ibid., 9.

25. Scholarship that focused on slave commitment to heterosexual marriage and mo-nogamy was particularly emphasized in the 1970s and 1980s after the Moynihan Report stated that the root of African American problems was a historical lack of the father, us-ing the Sambo model of Black masculinity from Stanley M. Elkins, *Slavery: A Problem in American Institutional and Intellectual Life* (Chicago: University of Chicago Press, 1959). See also Herbert G. Gutman, *The Black Family in Slavery and Freedom, 1750–1925* (New York: Pantheon, 1976).

26. Cheryl Clarke, "Lesbianism: An Act of Resistance," in *This Bridge Called My Back: Writings by Radical Women of Color,* 2nd ed., ed. Cherríe Moraga and Gloria Anzaldúa (Latham, NY: Kitchen Table: Women of Color Press, 1983).

27. Ibid., 136.

28. Ibid.

29. Roderick A. Ferguson, *Aberrations in Black: Toward a Queer of Color Critique* (Minneapolis: University of Minnesota Press, 2004), 128.

30. Evelynn Hammonds, "Black (W)holes and the Geometry of Black Female Sexual-ity," *Differences: A Journal of Feminist Cultural Studies* 6, no. 2–3 (1994): 139.

31. Omise'eke Natasha Tinsley, "Black Atlantic, Queer Atlantic: Queer Imaginings of the Middle Passage," *GLQ: A Journal of Lesbian and Gay Studies* 14, no. 2–3 (2008): 196.

32. Hortense J. Spillers, "Mama's Baby, Papa's Maybe: An American Grammar Book," in *Black, White, and in Color: Essays on American Literature and Culture* (Chicago: Univer-sity of Chicago Press, 2003), 221.

33. Ibid.

34. Hartman, *Scenes of Subjection.* Hartman points out that according to custom and property law, slavery is founded on an "economy of enjoyment" (26). She also is concerned with the "dimensions of [white observers'] investment in and fixation with Negro enjoy-ment" in order to "grant the observer access to an illusory plentitude of fun and feeling" (34).

35. I ask this question to distinguish pleasure from the erotic (which we will explore later). In this chapter, the moment, pursuit, and anticipation of orgasm are tied to questions of political solidarity and unanimity.

36. Orlando Patterson, *Slavery and Social Death: A Comparative Study* (Cambridge, MA: Harvard University Press, 1982), 50.

37. Ibid., 38.

38. Ibid. Patterson defines this liminal status as on the outskirts of society, as being "in a limbo" as an institutionalized presence of absence, a presence of powerlessness that embodies the master's authority, will, and power (46).

39. Ibid., 52.

40. Ibid., 299–333.

41. Ibid., 303–4.

42. Ibid., 307.

43. Ula Y. Taylor, "Making Waves: The Theory and Practice of Black Feminism," *The Black Scholar* 28, no. 2 (Summer 1998): 27. For more on Black women denied femininity in white lesbian contexts see Audre Lorde, *Zami: A New Spelling of My Name* (Freedom, CA: Crossing Press, 1982).

44. A. Timothy Spaulding, *Re-Forming the Past: History, The Fantastic, and the Postmodern Slave Narrative* (Columbus: The Ohio State University Press, 2005), 2.

45. Spillers, "Mama's Baby, Papa's Maybe," 206–7.

46. See Elyce Rae Helford, "The Future of Political Community: Race, Ethnicity, and Class Privilege in the Novels by Piercy, Gomez, and Misha," *Utopian Studies* 12, no. 2 (Spring 2001): 124–42; and Shannon Winnubst, "Vampires, Anxieties, and Dreams: Race and Sex in the Contemporary United States," *Hypatia* 18, no. 3 (Fall 2003): 1–20.

47. However, as Ellen Brinks and Lee Talley have pointed out, Gomez complicates the desire for a "'pure' heritage or homeland," preferring instead to portray the displacement, alienation, and violent separation of Black people from their African past. Even as fragments, "these words and images of her mother's cultural tradition become the *symbolic property* that the slave owners cannot confiscate or control." Lee Talley and Ellen Brinks, "Unfamiliar Ties: Lesbian Constructions of Home and Family in Jeanette Winterson's *Oranges Are Not the Only Fruit* and Jewelle Gomez's *The Gilda Stories*," in *Homemaking: Women Writers and the Politics and Poetics of Home,* ed. Catherine Wiley and Fiona R. Barnes (New York: Garland, 1996), 159.

48. See Hartman, "Seduction and the Ruses of Power," in *Scenes of Subjection.*

49. Hartman, *Scenes of Subjection,* 112.

50. Winnubst, "Vampires, Anxieties, and Dreams," 15.

51. Talley and Brinks, "Unfamiliar Ties," 165.

52. Frantz Fanon, *Black Skin, White Masks,* trans. Charles Lam Markmann (New York: Grove Press, 1967), 60.

53. Marie-Louise Loeffler, "'Why White People Feel They Got to Mark Us?' Bodily Inscription, Healing and Maternal 'Plots of Power' in Jewelle Gomez's 'Louisiana 1850'," in *The Black Imagination: Science Fiction, Futurism and the Speculative,* ed. Sandra Jackson and Julie E. Moody-Freeman (New York: Peter Lang, 2011), 160.

54. Spaulding, *Re-Forming the Past,* 108.

55. Scott Bravmann, *Queer Fictions of the Past: History, Culture, and Difference* (Cambridge: Cambridge University Press, 1997), 116.

56. Alexis Pauline Gumbs, "Speculative Poetics: Audre Lorde as Prologue for Queer Black Futurism," in *The Black Imagination,* ed. Jackson and Moody-Freeman, 134.

57. Talley and Brinks, "Unfamiliar Ties," 166.

58. Winnubst, "Vampires, Anxieties and Dreams," 15.

59. Ibid., 11.

60. Ibid., 15.

61. Homi Bhabha discusses the colonized as being in a condition of aggression wherein they "want to take" the colonizer's place. *The Location of Culture* (London: Routledge, 1994), 44–45.

62. Nell Irvin Painter, *Sojourner Truth: A Life, a Symbol* (New York: Norton, 1996), 16–17.

63. Bhabha, *The Location of Culture.*

64. Hazel V. Carby, *Reconstructing Womanhood: The Emergence of the Afro-American Woman Novelist* (New York: Oxford University Press, 1987).

65. Ann DuCille, *The Coupling Convention: Sex, Text, and Tradition in Black Women's Fiction* (New York: Oxford University Press, 1993), 4.

66. The term "useful fiction" comes from Gayatri Spivak's "The Rani of Sirmur: An Essay in Reading the Archives," *History and Theory* 24, no. 3 (October 1985): 251. Spivak talks about the "useful fiction" that "texts or phenomena to be interpreted may answer one back and even be convincing enough to lead one to change one's mind" (251). In this example from neo-slave narratives, the stories present a deliberate fiction that Black women can be spared the destructive aspects of oppression through their liberating sexual choices. Spivak concludes that in fact a text cannot "'answer one back' after the planned epistemic violence of the imperialist project" (251). In the retelling of slavery, the realities of violence overtake the romance plot, rendering it impotent in repairing institutional brutality and relations of power.

67. Hartman, *Scenes of Subjection,* 112.

68. Fanon, *Black Skin, White Masks,* 45.

69. Ibid., 41.

70. Ibid.

71. Ibid.

72. She is "called," in the Althusserian sense, and interpellated into the "idea of reciprocal and collusive relations" with her mistress. Hartman stresses this idea of reciprocity that emerges through a discourse of seduction. However, in this case it is produced from a discourse of sisterhood. Hartman, *Scenes of Subjection,* 81. See Louis Althusser, "Ideology and Ideological State Apparatuses (Notes towards an Investigation)," in *Lenin and Philosophy and Other Essays* (New York: Monthly Review Press, 1971), 127–87.

73. Bhabha, *The Location of Culture,* 86.

74. Hartman, *Scenes of Subjection,* 57.

75. Fanon, *Black Skin, White Masks,* 60.

76. Ibid., 38.

77. Ibid., 68–69.

78. Ibid., 66, 69.

79. Hartman, *Scenes of Subjection,* 112.

80. Fanon, *Black Skin, White Masks,* 42.

81. Ibid., 45.

82. Ibid., 47.

83. For more on how women of color represent the nation see Andrew Parker et al., *Nationalisms and Sexualities* (New York: Routledge, 1992); and Caren Kaplan, Norma Alarcón, and Minoo Moallem, *Between Woman and Nation: Nationalisms, Transnational Feminisms, and the State* (Durham: Duke University Press, 1999).

84. Fanon, *Black Skin, White Masks,* 46n5.

85. Ibid.

86. Ibid.

87. Ibid., 47

88. Ibid.

89. Clarke, "Lesbianism: An Act of Resistance," 128.

90. Omise'eke Natasha Tinsley, *Thiefing Sugar: Eroticism between Women in Caribbean Literature* (Durham: Duke University Press, 2010), 152.

91. Lorde argues that "[t]he language by which we have been taught to dismiss ourselves and our feelings as suspect is the same language we use to dismiss and suspect each other . . . I must establish myself as not-you." Audre Lorde, "Eye to Eye: Black Women, Hatred and Anger," in *Sister Outsider,* 169.

92. Fanon, *Black Skins, White Masks,* 60; and David Marriott, "Bonding Over Phobia," in *The Psychoanalysis of Race,* ed. Christopher Lane (New York: Columbia University Press, 1998), 425.

93. Bill Ashcroft, Gareth Griffiths, and Helen Tiffin, *Post-Colonial Studies: The Key Concepts* (New York: Routledge, 2000), 170.

94. Marriott, "Bonding Over Phobia," 417.

95. Of course, this scene is resonant with Jacques Lacan's description of the "mirror stage" of development wherein the child recognizes itself in the mirror and forms an identification with an "ideal-I" that Lacan asserts "will forever remain irreducible for any single individual or, rather, that will only asymptotically approach the subject's becoming." In this case, Sarah's search for self in the visage of Miss Hannah is an act of misrecognition. Jacques Lacan, *Ecrits: The First Complete Edition in English,* trans. Bruce Fink (New York: Norton, 2006), 76.

96. Marriott, "Bonding Over Phobia," 421.

97. Hartman, *Scenes of Subjection,* 84.

98. Mutual pleasure between women is apparently outside the Black imagination. Sarah recalls that "[s]he'd heard many stories from Clara and the other women in the Big House. No story spoke of two women loving each other" (41). Barnett locates female–female desire and pleasure as external to Black experience, which helps explain why a white character is cast as the conveyor of sexual gratification.

99. Julia Kristeva, "About Chinese Women," in *The Kristeva Reader,* ed. Toril Moi (New York: Columbia University Press, 1986), 146–47.

100. For more on the refusal of Black maternity see Spillers, "Mama's Baby, Papa's Maybe."

101. Kristeva, "About Chinese Women," 146.

102. Patterson, *Slavery and Social Death,* 304.

103. Ibid.

104. Cheryl Harris, "Whiteness as Property," in *Critical Race Theory: The Key Writings That Formed the Movement,* ed. Kimberlé Crenshaw et al. (New York: New Press, 1995), 276–91.

105. Hartman, *Scenes of Subjection,* 79–112.

106. Mae G. Henderson, "Toni Morrison's *Beloved*: Re-Membering the Body as Historical Text," in *Toni Morrison's* Beloved: *A Casebook,* ed. William L. Andrews and Nellie Y. McKay (New York: Oxford University Press, 1999), 81.

107. Ibid., 83.

108. Harris, "Whiteness as Property," 281.

109. According to Heidegger, "only in perceiving and acting on things do we constitute ourselves as humans, just as only thereby do the things become things." Martin Heidegger, *What Is a Thing?* (Chicago: H. Regnery, 1967), 259. What is important here is the constitution of humanity through the distinction of the "thingness" of the other.

110. DuCille, *The Coupling Convention*. DuCille notes that women writers at the end of the nineteenth century reconfigure marriage as "utopian unions based on gender equality," as opposed to an institution based on deference to male authority (47).

111. Tinsley, "Black Atlantic, Queer Atlantic," 211.

112. Lorde, "Eye to Eye," 175.

113. Ibid., 160.

114. Ibid., 159, 174–75.

Chapter 2

1. Muñoz notes that counterpublic spaces are where Black queer subjects can emerge in connection, support, and creation of an entire community. José Esteban Muñoz, *Disidentifications: Queers of Color and the Performance of Politics* (Minneapolis: University of Minnesota Press, 1999).

2. For more on "blues epistemology" see Clyde Adrian Woods, *Development Arrested: The Blues and Plantation Power in the Mississippi Delta* (London: Verso, 1998).

3. The fact that this novel is set in the Midwest is an exciting departure in Black queer fiction. There is a lack of scholarship on the importance of the Midwest as a site of queer emergence. See Scott Herring, *Another Country: Queer Anti-Urbanism* (New York: New York University Press, 2010).

4. Enoch H. Page and Matt U. Richardson, "On the Fear of Small Numbers: A Twenty-First-Century Prolegomenon of the U.S. Black Transgender Experience," in *Black Sexualities: Probing Powers, Passions, Practices, and Policies*, ed. Juan Battle and Sandra Barnes (New Brunswick, NJ: Rutgers University Press, 2009), 57–81.

5. LeRoi Jones, *Blues People: Negro Music in White America* (New York: Morrow, 1963). Here Jones (*subsequently* Amiri Baraka) studies the influence of Black musical forms on the formation of a distinctly Black American identity.

6. I use the names Sunshine, Kali, or Sunshine/Kali depending on the main character's stage of development. This also requires some gender shifting throughout the chapter. When I discuss Sunshine before her transformation, I use female pronouns. When I refer to events that take place after the transformation to Kali, I use both male and female pronouns with a slash to indicate the character's dual gender.

7. Stewart E. Tolnay, "The Great Migration and Changes in the Northern Black Family, 1940 to 1990," *Social Forces* 75, no. 4 (June 1997): 1213–38.

8. Muhanji received a PhD from the University of Iowa in 1997.

9. Cherry Muhanji, Egyirba High, and Kesho Scot, *Tight Spaces* (San Francisco: Spinsters/Aunt Lute, 1987). This collection won the Before Columbus Foundation's American Book Award in 1988. I learned of *Her*'s autobiographical nature in a conversation with the author in April 2004. Her work is especially interested in the divisions created between Black women based on skin-color hierarchies. Throughout her published fiction, Muhanji's protagonists tend to be light-skinned women looking for acceptance and camaraderie in working-class African American communities.

10. *Her* is Muhanji's first novel and was published in a time now considered to be a renaissance for lesbian and gay literature. See Sonya L. Jones, ed. *Gay and Lesbian Literature since World War II: History and Memory* (New York: Haworth Press, 1997); and Robert McRuer, *The Queer Renaissance: Contemporary American Literature and the Reinvention of Gay and Lesbian Identities* (New York: New York University Press, 1997).

11. For a classic study of African American migration, see Robert B. Stepto, *From Behind the Veil: A Study of Afro-American Narrative* (Urbana: University of Illinois Press, 1970); and Lawrence R. Rodgers, "Paul Laurence Dunbar's 'The Sport of the Gods': The Doubly Conscious World of Plantation Fiction, Migration, and Ascent," *American Literary Realism 1870–1910* 24, no. 3 (Spring 1992): 42–57.

12. Farah Jasmine Griffin, *"Who Set You Flowin'?" The African American Migration Narrative* (New York: Oxford University Press, 1995). Griffin's stages of migration are consistent with earlier evaluations of African American migration in literature cited previously.

13. Ibid., 9.

14. Ibid.

15. Madhu Dubey, "Folk and Urban Communities in African American Women's Fiction: Octavia Butler's *Parable of the Sower*," *Studies in American Fiction* 27, no. 1 (Spring 1999): 103–28. Also see Hazel V. Carby, "The Sexual Politics of Women's Blues," in *Cultures in Babylon: Black Britain and African America* (London: Verso, 1999), 7–21.

16. Dubey, "Folk and Urban Communities," 104.

17. Ann DuCille, "Blues Notes on Black Sexuality: Sex and the Texts of Jessie Fauset and Nella Larsen," *Journal of the History of Sexuality* 3, no. 3 (January 1993): 418–44.

18. Angela Y. Davis, *Blues Legacies and Black Feminism: Gertrude "Ma" Rainey, Bessie Smith and Billie Holiday* (New York: Vintage Books, 1999), 79.

19. Passing women are people who were born female but pass as men in their daily lives. See Martin B. Duberman, Martha Vicinus, and George Chauncey, eds. *Hidden from History: Reclaiming the Gay and Lesbian Past* (New York: New American Library, 1989).

20. According to Charles Marsh, the term "beloved community" was popularized in the U.S. South during the 1960s civil rights movement as "the realization of the divine love in lived social relation." Charles Marsh, *The Beloved Community: How Faith Shapes Social Justice, from the Civil Rights Movement to Today* (New York: Basic Books, 2005), 2. Commonly, the term continues to be associated with a reified, nostalgic memory of poor and working-class African American southern communities of bygone eras.

21. Barbara Omolade, "Hearts of Darkness," in *Words of Fire: An Anthology of African American Feminist Thought,* ed. Beverley Guy-Sheftall (New York: New Press, 1995), 373. Also see bell hooks, *Ain't I a Woman: Black Women and Feminism* (Boston: South End Press, 1981).

22. Woods, *Development Arrested.* Woods states that plantation production "disfigures every nation, region, and ethnicity it touches" (271).

23. This arrangement to have children in order to preserve the farm is reminiscent of the imperative to "make generations" from Gayle Jones's classic novel *Corregidora.* The generations of offspring are a living, breathing archive of Black suffering and the physical and psychological pain of Black women.

24. Omolade, "Hearts of Darkness," 373. Omolade attributes this fierce sense of self-protection to many freed Black women in Reconstruction and beyond.

25. Ibid.

26. Ibid. Also see hooks, *Ain't I a Woman.*

27. Sylvia Wynter, "The Ceremony Must Be Found: After Humanism," *boundary 2* 12/13; 12, no. 3; 13, no. 1 (Spring–Autumn 1984): 27.

28. She makes reference to Hurston's dictate that "De nigger woman is de mule uh de world." Zora Neale Hurston, *Their Eyes Were Watching God* (1937; New York: Harper and Row, 1990), 14.

29. Lizzie and Laphonya's tale of excessive childbirth is a reference to the early migration story by Jessie Redmon Fauset, *Plum Bun: A Novel without a Moral* (New York: Frederick A. Stokes, 1929). Similarly, *Plum Bun* suggests that Black women must reject motherhood to save themselves from endless toil and domestic labor.

30. Woods, *Development Arrested;* and Jones, *Blues People.*

31. Tolnay, "The Great Migration," 1216. There is also some speculation about the drop in number of Black births after the wave of migration to the urban centers. This phenomenon is speculated to be associated with many factors related to housing, workload, and male eligibility. No one has suggested that Black women and men may have enjoyed more same-sex relationships in the North, thereby decreasing procreative sexual activity.

32. Jeanne F. Theoharis and Komozi Woodard, *Freedom North: Black Freedom Struggles outside the South, 1940–1980* (New York: Palgrave Macmillan, 2003), 6. Also see the discussion of the pathologization of Black migrants in Roderick A. Ferguson, *Aberrations in Black: Toward a Queer of Color Critique* (Minneapolis: University of Minnesota Press, 2004), 82–109.

33. Theoharis and Woodard, *Freedom North,* 7.

34. The term "New Negro" is used most often in reference to Alain Locke's pivotal anthology of essays and creative work by the same name. Alain Locke, *The New Negro* (New York: Atheneum, 1925).

35. George Chauncey, *Gay New York: Gender, Urban Culture and the Makings of the Gay Male World, 1890–1940* (New York: Basic Books, 1994); Marjorie B. Garber, *Vested Interests: Cross Dressing and Cultural Anxiety* (New York: Routledge, 1992); and Eric Garber, "A Spectacle in Color: The Lesbian and Gay Subculture of Jazz Age Harlem," in Duberman et al., *Hidden from History,* 318–31.

36. British filmmaker Inge Blackman and British writer Jackie Kay have created works that portray Harlem queer life while looking at their own connection to Black lesbian and gender-variant history diasporically. *B.D. Women,* directed by Inge Blackman (England, 1994; New York: Women Make Movies), DVD. Jackie Kay, *Bessie Smith* (New York: Absolute, 1997).

37. John D'Emilio, "Capitalism and Gay Identity," in *Powers of Desire: The Politics of Sexuality,* ed. Ann Barr Snitow, Christine Stansell, and Sharon Thompson (New York: Monthly Review, 1983), 100–113.

38. Carby, "The Sexual Politics of Women's Blues"; Davis, *Blues Legacies.*

39. The song's unabashed lyrics proclaim "Went out last night with a crowd of my friends / They must've been women 'cause I don't like no men / It's true I wear a collar and a tie / Make the wind blow all the while" (qtd. in Davis, *Blues Legacies,* 39). Rainey herself pushed the limits in her advertisement for the record which includes a drawing of a crossed-dressed woman in the act of seducing another woman (ibid.).

40. Davis, *Blues Legacies,* 19–20.

41. Saidiya Hartman, "Venus in Two Acts," *Small Axe* 12, no. 2 (June 2008): 12.

42. For more information see Robin D. G. Kelley, "Playing for Keeps: Pleasure and Profit on the Postindustrial Playground," in *The House Race Built: Black Americans, U.S. Terrain,* ed. Wahneema H. Lubiano (New York: Pantheon Books, 1997), 195–231. Kelley

suggests that there needs to be a more nuanced reading of poor Black people functioning through the alternative economy of illicit and illegal activity.

43. Frantz Fanon, *Black Skin, White Masks,* trans. Charles Lam Markmann (New York: Grove Press, 1967), 109.

44. Audre Lorde, *Sister Outsider: Essays and Speeches* (Freedom, CA: Crossing Press, 1984), 152.

45. Ibid., 156.

46. For Wintergreen a similar gender expedition begins in Paris in 1924 when she becomes a highly paid blues performer and ends in Berlin in 1939 when she is caught by Nazis and brutally beaten until she no longer has full control of her feet and legs. Wintergreen "sings the blues" for the lost connection between light- and dark-skinned Black women, for her lost career, and for the loss of her sexual relationship with Charlotte, Kali's mother-in-law.

47. See Judith Butler, *Gender Trouble: Feminism and the Subversion of Identity* (New York: Routledge, 1990), 138.

48. Feminine masculinity is often associated with effeminate gay men, but it is not exclusive to them.

49. Davis, *Blues Legacies;* McRuer, *The Queer Renaissance.*

50. An example of this diasporic connection is found in the film *B.D. Women* (1994) by Caribbean-born British filmmaker Inge Blackman. Blackman uses the visual representation of a Harlem speakeasy and the Ma Rainey song "B.D. Women" (bulldagger women) as reference points for her documentary on British Black lesbian history.

51. Transmasculine is a way to distinguish the transformation of female-bodied people to a male gender presentation. It refers to an individual who has been assigned female at birth but maintains masculine characteristics later in life. This includes a person who identifies as male but does not associate exclusively with transmen.

52. Hortense J. Spillers, "Mama's Baby, Papa's Maybe: An American Grammar Book," in *Black, White and in Color: Essays on American Literature and Culture* (Chicago: University of Chicago Press, 2003), 229.

53. *Her* was published in the same year as *Gender Trouble* and pushed the boundaries of the racial dialogue with and in queer theory. Butler, *Gender Trouble.*

54. Samuel A. Floyd, *The Power of Black Music: Interpreting its History from Africa to the United States* (New York: Oxford University Press, 1995), 96.

55. Ibid., 96–97.

56. Patricia Hill Collins, *Black Feminist Thought: Knowledge, Consciousness, and the Politics of Empowerment* (Boston: Unwin Hyman Press, 1990). Collins has defined the "safe space" as a social space wherein Black women can speak freely (95). These Black queer safe spaces appear in the novel as realms that allow for gender and racial signification to happen in the counterpublic bar culture. *Her* refigures the city as a place of both misery/industrial labor and play, highlighting the role of urban aesthetics to give language to the pleasure of the city.

57. Muñoz, *Disidentifications,* 146.

58. Portia K. Maultsby, "Africanisms in African American Music," in *The African Presence in Black America,* ed. Jacob U. Gordon (Trenton, NJ: Africa World Press, 2004), 39–83.

59. As I suggest in the introduction, the Black focus on propriety and regulating the public image stems from a desire to protect and defend the names of Black women in order to establish claims for citizenship.

60. Houston A. Baker, *Modernism in the Harlem Renaissance* (Chicago: University of Chicago Press, 1987), 33. Using Washington's example, Baker partially defines the "mastery of form" through his use of minstrel theater techniques in his Atlanta Exposition address. Baker quotes Booker T. Washington in *Up from Slavery,* which includes the Atlanta address. Washington's talent for employing stereotypical "darky" tropes enabled him to escape a "tight place" of impossible expectations and please his diverse audience. Baker contends that Washington demonstrated "in his manipulations of form that there are rhetorical possibilities for crafting a voice out of tight places" (33). However, what Washington said sacrificed African American political goals to a racist agenda. Charlotte's speech suggests that such sacrifices are necessary for African American survival. Baker discusses this in some detail in pages 25–36.

61. Baker, *Modernism,* 29.

62. Luisah Teish, *Jambalaya: The Natural Woman's Book of Personal Charms and Practical Rituals* (San Francisco: Harper and Row, 1985), 121–23.

Chapter 3

1. During the talk back of *Ring/Shout* at the University of Texas at Austin, February 20, 2011, Sharon Bridgforth described her previously published books—*the bull-jean stories* and *love conjure/blues*—as "performance novels," or texts that are written both to have a life on the page and to be read aloud or performed onstage.

2. M. Jacqui Alexander, *Pedagogies of Crossing: Meditations on Feminism, Sexual Politics, Memory, and the Sacred* (Durham: Duke University Press, 2005), 8.

3. Sharon Bridgforth, personal interview, February 2009. These concepts were reiterated in her performance of *Ring/Shout* at the University of Texas at Austin on February 20, 2011.

4. Omi Osun Joni L. Jones, Lisa L. Moore, and Sharon Bridgforth, eds., *Experiments in a Jazz Aesthetic: Art, Activism, Academia, and the Austin Project* (Austin: University of Texas Press, 2010), 6; and Bridgforth, interview. Bridgforth gains a tremendous amount of new information about the piece from the performance and the actors themselves. She then incorporates the information into subsequent revisions. She uses the art of improvisation or "spontaneous creation" in each performance. The script (or published book) does not contain stage directions, and through minimal rehearsal the actors and the director (conductor) find the music and movement. However, each participant is expected to bring his/her unique perspective to the embodiment of the work. Therefore, each performance is unpredictable and kinetic. Publication is not the end of the life of these texts, either. They have been performed, reinterpreted, and reworked in multiple ways after publication.

5. The Austin Project is a group of predominantly women of color (although there are a small number of white women and transmen of color who participate as well) who come together for eleven weeks to share in a writing workshop that is focused on the writing process.

6. Diana Taylor, *The Archive and the Repertoire: Performing Cultural Memory in the Americas* (Durham: Duke University Press, 2003).

7. Meta DuEwa Jones, "Jazz Prosodies: Orality and Textuality," *Callaloo* 25, no. 1 (2002): 78. Also see Meta DuEwa Jones, *The Muse Is Music: Jazz Poetry from the Harlem Renaissance to Spoken Word* (Urbana: University of Illinois Press, 2011).

8. Karla F. Holloway, *Moorings & Metaphors: Figures of Culture and Gender in Black Women's Literature* (New Brunswick, NJ: Rutgers University Press, 1992), 2.

9. Fred Moten, *In the Break: The Aesthetics of the Black Radical Tradition* (Minneapolis: University of Minnesota Press, 2003).

10. Hortense J. Spillers, "'The Permanent Obliquity of an In(pha)llibly Straight': In the Time of the Daughters and the Fathers," in *Black, White, and in Color: Essays on American Literature and Culture* (Chicago: University of Chicago Press, 2003), 230–50.

11. Sylvia Wynter, "The Ceremony Must Be Found: After Humanism," *boundary 2* 12/13; 12, no. 3; 13, no. 1 (Spring–Autumn 1984), 26.

12. Spillers, "Mama's Baby, Papa's Maybe: An American Grammar Book," in *Black, White, and in Color*, 207.

13. An essential part of West African spiritual practice is spirit possession. According to Phyllis Galembo, "Through possession, both the *lwa* and the community are affirmed. The people transcend their materiality by becoming spirits . . . the *lwa* communicate in a tangible way with the people, who during such times receive the best possible answers to pressing questions." Phyllis Galembo, *Vodou: Visions and Voices of Haiti* (Berkeley: Ten Speed Press, 1998), xxvii.

14. Sometimes Babaluaye, Orunmilla, or others are also listed with these spirits. Luisah Teish, *Jambalaya: The Natural Woman's Book of Personal Charms and Practical Rituals* (San Francisco: Harper and Row, 1985).

15. Teish, *Jambalaya*, 116.

16. See *Queering Creole Spiritual Traditions* wherein the author states that he interviewed Lorde about her relationship to Eleggua in 1986. Randy P. Conner with David Hatfield Sparks, *Queering Creole Spiritual Traditions: Lesbian, Gay, Bisexual, and Transgender Participation in African-Inspired Traditions in the Americas* (Binghamton, NY: Harrington Park Press, 2004), 242–44.

17. Henry Louis Gates Jr., *The Signifying Monkey: A Theory of African-American Literary Criticism* (Oxford: Oxford University Press, 1988).

18. LaMonda Horton-Stallings, *Mutha' Is Half a Word: Intersections of Folklore, Vernacular, Myth, and Queerness in Black Female Culture* (Columbus: The Ohio State University Press, 2007), 40.

19. Some critics have made the connection between the blues and West African religious practice in African American literature, for example, Thomas F. Marvin, "'Preachin' the Blues': Bessie Smith's Secular Religion and Alice Walker's *The Color Purple*," *African American Review* 28, no. 3 (Autumn 1994): 411–21. Marvin argues that "certain blues songs may be better understood in the context of West African belief" (412). He also goes as far as to suggest that the blues functions as a deity, stating that "the blues is a supernatural force that can take on human characteristics and possess its victims, just like a West African *orisha*" (413).

20. According to James Cone, "The blues are 'secular spirituals.' They are *secular* in the sense that they confine their attention solely to the immediate and affirm the bodily expression of black soul, including its sexual manifestations. They are *spirituals* because they are impelled by the same search for the truth of black experience." James H. Cone, *The Spirituals and the Blues: An Interpretation* (1972; Maryknoll, NY: Orbis Books, 1992), 100. Also see LeRoi Jones, *Blues People: Negro Music in White America* (New York: Morrow, 1963), 65.

21. Conjuration is an African American religious practice that brings together the West African religious characteristics of "the utility of sacred charms and the diversity of skills embodied by religious specialists." These specialists are used for purposes of divi-

nation and to access powerful supernatural forces. For more information see Yvonne Chireau, "Conjure and Christianity in the Nineteenth Century: Religious Elements in African American Magic," *Religion and American Culture: A Journal of Interpretation* 7, no. 2 (Summer 1997): 225–46, 228.

22. An analysis of the formal connections between the blues and West African music is beyond the scope of this project. For more on the relationship between the blues and African music see Gerhard Kubik, *Africa and the Blues* (Jackson: University Press of Mississippi, 1999).

23. A bigendered person is someone who identifies with both masculinity and femininity or a combination of genders. "The Other Bi: Bigender," *Bi Social Network,* accessed January 29, 2012, http://bisocialnetwork.com/the-other-bi-bigender/.

24. Audre Lorde, *Zami: A New Spelling of My Name* (Freedom, CA: Crossing Press, 1982), 7.

25. Gates, *The Signifying Monkey,* 37.

26. Ibid., 6.

27. Teish, *Jambalaya,* 113.

28. Galembo, *Vodou,* 40.

29. Judith Illsley Gleason, *Oya: In Praise of the Goddess* (Boston: Shambala Publishing, 1987), 1.

30. Teish, *Jambalaya,* 120.

31. The femme is also the spiritual leader of the *love conjure/blues Text Installation* performance piece.

32. For a discussion of queer mambos and houngan see Conner, with Sparks, *Queering Creole Spiritual Traditions,* 89–95.

33. Several of the words in the quoted text are spelled phonetically since Bridgforth writes in a Black southern dialect. Also, in accordance with conventions for quoting poetry, I use slashes to indicate line breaks when not quoting extensively.

34. *Lackawana Blues,* directed by George C. Wolfe (Los Angeles: HBO, 2005), DVD.

35. Suzan-Lori Parks, *Getting Mother's Body: A Novel* (New York: Random House, 2003).

36. Conner, with Sparks, *Queering Creole Spiritual Traditions,* 70.

37. Baba Ifa Karade, *The Handbook of Yoruba Religious Concepts* (York Beach, ME: Weiser Books, 1994), 27.

38. In Vodun, spiritual practices and the dialogue between drummers and dancers create the conditions to establish contact with ancestors and with deities called lwa. For more information see Gerdès Fleurant, *Dancing Spirits: Rhythms and Rituals of Haitian Vodun, the Rada Rite* (Westport, CT: Greenwood Press, 1996).

39. Bridgforth, interview.

40. Teish, *Jambalaya,* 118–19.

41. Previous performances of *delta dandi* included all-female casts.

42. Jones, Moore, and Bridgforth, eds., *Experiments in a Jazz Aesthetic,* 6.

43. Ibid., 6.

44. Ifi Amadiume, *Male Daughters, Female Husbands: Gender and Sex in an African Society* (London: Zed Books, 1987), 25–26.

45. Octavia Butler, *Kindred* (Garden City, NY: Doubleday, 1979).

46. Scott Knowles DeVeaux, *The Birth of Bebop: A Social and Musical History* (Berkeley: University of California Press, 1997), 224.

47. Farah Jasmine Griffin and Salim Washington, *Clawing at the Limits of Cool: Miles*

Davis, John Coltrane and the Greatest Jazz Collaboration Ever (New York: Thomas Dunne Books, 2008), 243.

48. Section 104 of the Ghanaian Criminal Code bans "unnatural carnal knowledge," which has been interpreted to mean same-sex relations. See Mark S. Luckie, "Somewhere over the Rainbow," in *Ghana: Somewhere Over the Rainbow* website, 2007, http://journalism.berkeley.edu/projects/mm/luckie/rainbow.html.

49. Pat Ogden et al., "Including the Body in Mainstream Psychotherapy for Traumatized Individuals," *Psychologist-Psychoanalyst* 15, no. 4 (Fall 2005): 19–24.

Chapter 4

1. Diane Wood Middlebrook, *Suits Me: The Double Life of Billy Tipton* (Boston: Houghton Mifflin, 1998).

2. The following is a selected bibliography of Jackie Kay's published work. Poetry: *That Distance Apart* (London: Turret Press, 1991), *The Adoption Papers* (Highgreen, Wales: Bloodaxe Books, 1991), *Other Lovers* (Highgreen, Wales: Bloodaxe Books, 1993), *Three Has Gone* (London: Blackie Press, 1994), and *Off Colour* (Highgreen, Wales: Bloodaxe Books, 1998). Fiction: *Bessie Smith* (Bath, England: Absolute Press, 1997), *Trumpet* (London: Picador, 1998), *Why Don't You Stop Talking* (London: Picador, 2002), and *Wish I Was Here* (London: Picador, 2006). Kay is also an accomplished playwright. She has published two of the few Black lesbian plays in print and is most noted for *Chiaroscuro* (London: Methuen, 1986) and *Twice Over,* in *Gay Sweatshop: Four Plays and a Company* (London: Methuen, 1989).

3. Inge Blackman, personal interview, London, 2002.

4. *B.D. Women,* directed by Inge Blackman (England, 1994; New York: Women Make Movies), DVD. The statement that "sometimes you have to make your own history" is also a quote from Cheryl Dunye's 1996 film *The Watermelon Woman* (New York: First Run Features, 2000), DVD. Blackman indicates in her interview that she considers African American lesbian filmmakers to be in dialogue with her work.

5. Alan Rice, "'Heroes across the Sea': Black and White British Fascination with African Americans in the Contemporary Black British Fiction by Caryl Phillips and Jackie Kay," in *Blackening Europe: The African American Presence,* ed. Heike Raphael-Hernandez (New York: Routledge, 2004), 228.

6. Alice Walker, "As You Wear: Cross-Dressing and Identity Politics in Jackie Kay's *Trumpet," Journal of International Women's Studies* 8, no. 2 (February 2007): 35–43; Victoria R. Arana, "Clothing the Spirit: Jackie Kay's Fiction from *Trumpet* to *Wish I Was Here,"* *Women: A Cultural Review* 20, no. 3 (2009): 250–61; Tracy Hargreaves, "The Power of the Ordinary Subversive in Jackie Kay's *Trumpet," Feminist Review* no. 74 (2003): 2–16.

7. Frantz Fanon, *Black Skin, White Masks,* trans. Charles Lam Markmann (New York: Grove Press, 1967), 151–52.

8. Kay, *Trumpet,* 200.

9. This term is from Sigmund Freud's *The Interpretation of Dreams* wherein he describes the psychosexual dynamics of the patriarchal nuclear family in order to map the development of neurosis. Freud's description of the relationship between fathers, mothers, and sons has become the Western model of the "family." Sigmund Freud, *The Interpretation of Dreams,* trans. A. A. Brill (New York: Macmillan, 1913).

10. Fanon, *Black Skin, White Masks,* 143.

11. Hortense J. Spillers, "Mama's Baby, Papa's Maybe: An American Grammar Book," in *Black, White and in Color: Essays on American Literature and Culture* (Chicago: University of Chicago Press, 2003), 204.

12. See Minnie Bruce Pratt, *S/He* (Ithaca, NY: Firebrand Books, 1995). See also Loree Cook-Daniels, "Trans-Positioned," first published in *Circles Magazine,* June 1998 (*TransPartners Project* website, http://www.elspethbrown.org/sites/default/files/imce/cook-daniels_trans-positioned1998_0.pdf). This brief essay takes the reader through the female-to-male transition process from the perspective of lesbian partners and also gives insight into the difference between being with a transman and being with a butch (masculine female) lover. Cook-Daniels says that most lesbians' partners appreciate their lover's butchness but are often unprepared for their partners' transition to being male: "what they prize is masculinity wrapped in a woman's body, masculinity as displayed by a man often feels totally different" (2).

13. In the chapter titled "Right of Death and Power over Life," Foucault discusses the mechanisms of biopower in a "normalizing society" (144). Sex became a "standard for the disciplines and a basis for regulations" (146) so that "power" could be "organized around the management of life" (147). Michel Foucault, *The History of Sexuality*, trans. Robert Hurly, vol. 1 (New York: Vintage Books, 1988).

14. Michel Foucault et al., *Society Must Be Defended: Lectures at the Collège De France, 1975–76* (New York: Picador, 2003). In her book *Terrorist Assemblages*, Jasbir Puar discusses how the relationships of queer people of color to biopolitics are just beginning to be explored. Puar engages both Foucauldian biopolitics and Mbembe's necropolitics in order to articulate the position of South Asian and Middle Eastern queers caught between unexpected biopolitical and necropolitical impulses toward life and death, respectively. *Trumpet* (and other texts analyzed in this volume) gives some indication of where further examination is needed in how the Black queer body is uniquely positioned in relation to these state impulses. Jasbir K. Puar, *Terrorist Assemblages: Homonationalism in Queer Times* (Durham: Duke University Press, 2007); Achille Mbembe, "Necropolitics," *Public Culture* 15, no. 1 (Winter 2003): 11-40.

15. Homi Bhabha, *The Location of Culture* (London: Routledge, 1994), 35.

16. I am using the term "gender reassignment" to highlight the Home Office assertion that "biological sex . . . cannot be changed." British Home Office, Report of the Interdepartmental Working Group on Transsexual People (April 2000), 3, *Social Care Online,* accessed November 15, 2012, http://www.scie-socialcareonline.org.uk.

17. Binding is the act of using ace bandages or other material to flatten or "bind" breasts into a flat chest.

18. Home Office, Report, 5. The report is issued by the British Home Secretary and was submitted to the Scottish Parliament, the Northern Ireland Assembly, and the National Assembly for Wales for review and consideration.

19. Ibid., 3. Transpeople are carefully tracked through the reporting of psychiatric care and medical procedures. According to the statistics of the British Home Office and the National Health Service, there were only "250 to 400 female to male transsexual people" in all of the United Kingdom in 2000 (3). However, this number does not include people whom the state cannot "see," which includes those who do not seek psychiatric treatment specifically for Gender Identity Disorder and those who do not have reassignment surgeries. For more on Gender Identity Disorder see American Psychiatric Association, *Diagnostic and Statistical Manual of Mental Disorders: DSM-IV-TR,* 4th ed., text revision (Washington, DC: American Psychiatric Association, 2000).

20. Home Office, Report, 3. The phrase "opposite biological sex" is crucial to the state's definition of a transsexual as one who is "really" one sex but has a medical condition that drives him/her to live as another. In this view, there are only two legitimate immutable sexes, and surgery and hormone treatment change only the social gender category of an individual, which is also bifurcated and fixed. People who identify as both male and female, or neither, or who do not change themselves through hormones or surgery, are not considered for recognition by the state at all.

21. Ibid., 6.

22. Ibid.

23. Ibid., 5. The law is detailed in its insistence that surgical gender re-assignment is a precondition for recognition of gender identification "opposite" from that assigned at birth in each of these instances, including the registration or re-registration of individual sex at birth, marriage, incarceration, and parental responsibilities.

24. Ibid., 9-10. In matters relating to children and parents, "if a person undergoes gender reassignment their position as 'father' or 'mother' would continue to depend on their birth sex" and on the fact that the child has some biological tie to the parent (10). Curiously, adoption of a child where neither parent is a biological parent (as in the case of Joss and Millie) is not specified in the report.

25. For more information see Judith Butler, *Gender Trouble: Feminism and the Subversion of Identity* (New York: Routledge, 1990), and *Bodies That Matter: On the Discursive Limits of "Sex"* (New York: Routledge, 1993).

26. Marjorie B. Garber, *Vested Interests: Cross Dressing and Cultural Anxiety* (New York: Routledge, 1992), 16.

27. Bhabha, *The Location of Culture,* 35.

28. See Foucault, *The History of Sexuality.*

29. I take my definition of the state from Wendy Brown, who says that it is the prerogative dimension of "legitimate arbitrary power in policy making and legitimate monopolies of internal and external violence in the police and the military" which "marks the state as a state." Wendy Brown, *States of Injury: Power and Freedom in Late Modernity* (Princeton: Princeton University Press, 1995), 176. For a discussion of biopower and the biopolitical state as having the power to legitimize authority over the regulation and control of given populations, see Foucault, *The History of Sexuality.*

30. Gregor McLennan, David Held, and Stuart Hall, *The Idea of the Modern State* (Philadelphia: Open University Press, 1984), 15.

31. For more on "genital classification" see Joshua Gamson, *Freaks Talk Back: Tabloid Talk Shows and Sexual Nonconformity* (Chicago: University of Chicago Press, 1998), 153.

32. Ibid., 154.

33. Ibid.

34. Ibid., 141.

35. Edd McCracken, "Black Affronted; Edd Mccracken Reveals That Many Blacks in Scotland Still Feel the Chill of Pernicious Racism, yet Hope That an Exhibition on Black Culture Could Help Instil a Greater Understanding of a Troubled Past," *Sunday Herald* (Scotland), October 12, 2003.

36. Tomás Monterrey, "A Scottish Metamorphosis: Jackie Kay's *Trumpet,*" *Revista Canaria de Estudios Ingleses* no. 41 (2000): 180.

37. David Marriott, *On Black Men* (New York: Columbia University Press, 2000), 13. Neither Marriott nor the theorists cited below are concerned about the Black female child's

or Black women's encounter with premature death, or what happens when someone witnesses their denigration. However, their work here is valuable in understanding Colman's profound loss of self when he encounters his father's female physicality.

38. Ibid., 9.

39. Ibid., 15.

40. Ibid.

41. "*Imago*" is a term that refers to the images perpetuated through someone else's desires. In *Black Skin, White Masks,* Fanon describes the imago of Black masculinity in the white imagination. See Fanon, *Black Skin, White Masks,* 61, 161n25, 169. Gilroy discusses the predominant framing of Blacks as inherently criminal through the image of the Black male mugger in Britain. Paul Gilroy, *"There Ain't No Black in the Union Jack": The Cultural Politics of Race and Nation* (Chicago: University of Chicago Press, 1987), 74.

42. Of course, although this fact is rarely acknowledged, Black women also are criminalized in the eyes of a racist society, and they face the possibility of racialized and sexualized brutality every day from within and outside their homes and families.

43. Mercer argues that Black men do not have access to the role of patriarchal breadwinner, and thus the only avenue of identification is their penises. Kobena Mercer, *Welcome to the Jungle: New Positions in Black Cultural Studies* (New York: Routledge, 1994).

44. T. Denean Sharpley-Whiting, *Frantz Fanon: Conflicts and Feminisms* (Lanham, MD: Rowan and Littlefield, 1998). As Lewis Gordon states, "To be desired by a black woman is denigrated as a presumed desire. . . . [B]lacks desire to be desired by whites." Lewis R. Gordon, *Bad Faith and Antiblack Racism* (New York: Humanity Books, 1995), 101.

45. Gordon's chapter titled "Effeminacy: The Quality of Black Beings" is very much about the quality of the Black male's closeness to femininity. He says, "From the standpoint of an antiblack world, black men are nonmen–nonwomen, and black women are nonwomen–nonmen. This conclusion is based on our premise of whites—white men and white women—being both human, being both Presence, and our premise of blacks, both black men and women, being situated in the condition of the 'hole,' being both Absence. This dichotomy poses a gender question concerning black men and a metaphysical one concerning black women" (124). Why would this not pose a gender question for Black women? There is a tacit acceptance that "women are holes" in a misogynist world, leaving Black women outside of consideration. He asks, "If blackness is a hole, and women are holes, what are white women, and what are black men in an antiblack world" (124)? He concludes that "antiblack racism is therefore intimately connected to misogyny" (125). It seems more the case that misogyny and anti-Black racism coform each other, and that Black masculinity is predicated on the separation between the two, such that Black manhood can be paired with white womanhood in an effort to ascertain a racialized philosophy of gender. Gordon, *Bad Faith and Antiblack Racism.*

46. Ibid., 127.

47. Ibid., 124.

48. Ibid., 127.

49. Fanon, *Black Skin, White Masks,* 165.

50. I would like to thank Zakiyyah Jackson for pointing out to me that the mother is a phobic object in psychoanalytic terms.

51. Fanon, *Black Skin, White Masks,* 170.

52. Ibid.

53. Ibid., 151.

54. See Spillers, *Black, White, and in Color: Essays on American Literature and Culture;* and Brown, *States of Injury.*

55. Jacques Lacan, *Ecrits: The First Complete Edition in English,* trans. Bruce Fink (New York: Norton, 2006), 75–81.

56. Marriott, *On Black Men,* 96.

57. Ibid., 98.

58. Ibid., 96–97.

59. Gordon, *Bad Faith and Antiblack Racism,* 127.

60. Monterrey, "A Scottish Metamorphosis," 172.

61. Ibid.

62. Marriott, *On Black Men,* 95.

63. Ibid.

64. Ibid., xiv.

65. Sharon Bridgforth, "Preface" *the bull-jean stories* (Austin, TX: RedBone Press, 1998).

66. Stuart Hall, "Cultural Identity and Diaspora," in *Theorizing Diaspora: A Reader,* ed. Jana Evans Braziel and Anita Mannur (Malden, MA: Blackwell Publishers, 2003), 237.

67. Ibid., 240.

68. Spillers, "Mama's Baby, Papa's Maybe," 229.

69. For examples of African American jazzmen constructed as womanizers and abusers, see Miles Davis and Quincy Troupe, *Miles, the Autobiography* (New York: Simon and Schuster, 1989). Charles Mingus's autobiography, *Beneath the Underdog,* describes a world of African American jazz through a language of sexism and misogyny. Charles Mingus, *Beneath the Underdog: His World as Composed by Mingus* (New York: Knopf, 1971). Pearl Cleage's now infamous essay "Mad at Miles" reveals the behind-the-scenes of domestic violence in the relationship between Davis and Cicely Tyson in *Deals with the Devil, and Other Reasons to Riot* (New York: Ballantine, 1993).

70. Marriott, *On Black Men,* 44.

71. Ibid., 55.

72. Joss is a combination of masculine and feminine that is underscored in jazz history through the artistic collaboration of Miles Davis and John Coltrane. Farah Jasmine Griffin and Salim Washington describe Davis as cool, hip, "self-assured, sexy and stylish" (145), and Coltrane as "humble and gentle" (146). Griffin and Washington argue that Davis and Coltrane had "conflicting styles of masculinity" (147) that worked in cooperation with each other. Like a beautiful composition, these conflicting styles also come together in the character of Joss. Farah Jasmine Griffin and Salim Washington, *Clawing at the Limits of Cool: Miles Davis, John Coltrane and The Greatest Jazz Collaboration Ever* (New York: Thomas Dunne Books, 2008).

73. Paul Gilroy, *The Black Atlantic: Modernity and Double Consciousness* (Cambridge, MA: Harvard University Press, 1993), 85.

74. These terms, originally applied to "the repetition of heterosexual constructs within sexual cultures both gay and straight," come from Butler, *Gender Trouble,* 31. Or we could say that Black cultural expression is not restricted to the born-Black individual, as white men and a variety of other races have copied Black masculinity to a varying degree of success, from the days of Blackface to the present.

75. Fred Moten, *In the Break: The Aesthetics of the Black Radical Tradition* (Minneapolis: University of Minnesota Press, 2003), 160.

76. For more on "racial castration" see David L. Eng, *Racial Castration: Managing Masculinity in Asian America* (Durham: Duke University Press, 2001).

77. Gilroy, *The Black Atlantic,* 85.

78. Ibid.

79. Rice, "Heroes across the Sea," 229.

80. Moten, *In the Break,* 161.

81. Ibid., 174.

82. Ibid., 161.

83. Ibid.

84. Ibid., 160.

85. Ibid., 151.

86. Moten, *In the Break,* describes Black "feminization" as a process of "invagination," as an attempt to depathologize the association of the feminine with Blackness. He describes this condition as being in "the sexual cut."

87. See Gilroy, *The Black Atlantic,* for his discussion of the ways in which certain Black music comes to symbolize Black masculinity.

88. A. Lâmia Gülçur, "Resistance and Reinvention of the Subject in Jackie Kay's *Trumpet,*" *Ethnic Studies Review* 29, no. 1 (Summer 2006): 101–11, 108.

89. Monk was known for his eccentric behavior as well as the off-beat innovations of his music. See Robin D. G. Kelley, *Thelonious Monk: The Life and Times of an American Original* (New York: Free Press, 2009).

90. Spillers, "Mama's Baby, Papa's Maybe," 228.

91. Ibid.

92. Ibid., 229.

Chapter 5

1. This argument can be found across academic works, including the following: Orlando Patterson, *Slavery and Social Death: A Comparative Study* (Cambridge, MA: Harvard University Press, 1982), 58; St. Clair Drake, *Black Folk Here and There: An Essay in History and Anthropology* (Los Angeles: Center for Afro-American Studies, University of California, 1987); Robin D. G. Kelley and Tiffany Ruby Patterson, "Unfinished Migrations: Reflections on the African Diaspora and the Making of the Modern World," *African Studies* 43, no. 1 (April 2000): 11–45; and Brent Hayes Edwards, *The Practice of Diaspora: Literature, Translation, and the Rise of Black Internationalism* (Cambridge, MA: Harvard University Press, 2003).

2. Marlon M. Bailey, "Rethinking the African Diaspora and HIV/AIDS Prevention from the Perspective of Ballroom Culture," in *Global Circuits of Blackness: Interrogating the African Diaspora,* ed. Percy C. Hintzen, Jean Muteba Rahier, and Felipe Smith (Chicago: University of Illinois Press, 2010), 96–126.

3. Audre Lorde, *Sister Outsider: Essays and Speeches* (Freedom, CA: Crossing Press, 1984), 53.

4. For a primer on the 1979 revolution and its causes, see Maurice Bishop and Steve Clark, *Maurice Bishop Speaks to U.S. Workers: Why the U.S. Invaded Grenada* (New York: Pathfinder Press, 1983).

5. I am careful not to suggest that the novel takes up the identity "lesbian" to define Elizete and Verlia's relationship. As Greg A. Mullins notes, Brand "de-links the logic that

would associate same-sex desire with sexual identity" and instead gives us a relationship that is not co-opted by the terms of Western politics. Greg A. Mullins, "Dionne Brand's Poetics of Recognition: Reframing Sexual Rights," *Callaloo* 30, no. 4 (Fall 2007): 1100–1109, 1104.

6. Homi K. Bhabha, "The World and the Home," *Social Text* no. 31–32 (1992): 144.

7. See Achille Mbembe, "Necropolitics," *Public Culture* 15, no. 1 (Winter 2003): 21; and Membe, *On the Postcolony* (Berkeley: University of California Press, 2001).

8. Omise'eke Natasha Tinsley, "Black Atlantic, Queer Atlantic: Queer Imaginings of the Middle Passage," *GLQ: A Journal of Lesbian and Gay Studies* 14, no. 2–3 (2008): 191–215.

9. See "Invasion of Grenada," *Economic & Political Weekly* 18, no. 44 (October 29, 1983): 1587; Gail R. Pool, "Culture, Language and Revolution in Grenada," *Anthropologica* 36, no. 1 (1994): 73–107; M. J., "U.S. Invasion of Grenada," *Social Scientist* 12, no. 1 (January 1984): 74–77.

10. Runaway slave Harriet Jacobs asks, "Why does the slave ever love?" Toni Morrison also asks the question through her fictional character Baby Suggs, who determines that it is too dangerous to love—so much so that she focuses instead on pieces of cloth and on colors to avoid facing the crushing heartbreak of loss. Harriet A. Jacobs, *Incidents in the Life of a Slave Girl, Written by Herself*, 1861, ed. Jean Fagan Yellin (Cambridge, MA: Harvard University Press, 1987); Toni Morrison, *Beloved* (1987; New York: Vintage Books, 2004).

11. The folktale of the captured African slaves who flew back home is in the young adult book *The People Could Fly: American Black Folktales*, told by Virginia Hamilton and illustrated by Leo and Diane Dillon (New York: Knopf Books for Young Readers, 1985). It is also referenced in *Daughters of the Dust* as a particularly Igbo story. *Daughters of the Dust*, directed by Julie Dash (1991; Kino Video, 2000), DVD.

12. Paul Huebener, "'No moon to speak of': Identity and Place in Dionne Brand's *In Another Place, Not Here*," *Callaloo* 30, no. 2 (Spring 2007): 623, 624.

13. Mbembe, "Necropolitics," 40.

14. Brand gives us an opportunity to extend some of Mbembe's work to consider suicide as a consequence of state control of life and the threat of physical death with regard to gender that is undertheorized by critical race theorists; see also Mbembe, *On the Postcolony*.

15. Lorde, *Sister Outsider*, 58.

16. Ibid.

17. Frantz Fanon, *Wretched of the Earth*, 1961, trans. Constance Farrington (New York: Grove Press, 1963), 201.

18. Darieck Scott, *Extravagant Abjection: Blackness, Power, and Sexuality in the African American Literary Imagination* (New York: New York University Press, 2010), 32.

19. Fanon, *Wretched of the Earth*, 47–48.

20. Frantz Fanon, *Black Skin, White Masks*, trans. Charles Lam Markmann (New York: Grove Press, 1967), 60.

21. Fanon, *Wretched of the Earth*, 47.

22. Ibid., 52.

23. Ibid., 53.

24. Nikki Giovanni, "Poem for Aretha," in *Women Working: An Anthology of Stories and Poems*, ed. Nancy Hoffman and Florence Howe (Old Westbury, NY: Feminist Press, 1979), 42–45.

25. Che Guevara, "Man and Socialism" (speech), 1965, transcript, *The Che Guevera Archives* website, accessed November 24, 2012, www.hey-che.com.

26. bell hooks, *Salvation: Black People and Love* (New York: William Morrow, 2001), 9.

27. Ibid.

28. For more on the separation of love and radical politics—and the possibility of unifying them—see Chela Sandoval, *Methodology of the Oppressed* (Minneapolis: University of Minnesota Press, 2000); bell hooks, *Salvation: Black People and Love;* bell hooks, *Communion: The Female Search for Love* (New York: William Morrow, 2002).

29. Audre Lorde, *Sister Outsider,* 162.

30. Hortense J. Spillers, "Mama's Baby, Papa's Maybe: An American Grammar Book," in *Black, White and in Color: Essays on American Literature and Culture* (Chicago: University of Chicago Press, 2003), 206–7.

Epilogue

1. Toni Morrison, "Rootedness: The Ancestor as Foundation," in *Black Women Writers (1950–1980): A Critical Evaluation,* ed. Mari Evans (New York: Anchor Books, 1984), 339–45, 344.

2. M. Jacqui Alexander, *Pedagogies of Crossing: Meditations on Feminism, Sexual Politics, Memory, and the Sacred* (Durham: Duke University Press, 2005), 289.

3. The question of which deaths inspire Black insurrection was particularly pertinent at the time of the writing of this book, as the fatal police shooting of Mark Duggan in the Tottenham section of London was the catalyst for massive protests across London that eventually spread through England. See "England Riots: Maps and Timeline," *BBC News UK,* August 15, 2011, http://www.bbc.co.uk/news/uk-14436499; "Protests in London," *The Express Tribune with the International Herald Tribune* (Pakistan), August 8, 2011, http://tribune.com.pk/story/226875/protests-in-london/.

4. Obama was pictured with members of the Byrd and Shepard families during the ceremony when the bill was signed into law. See "A Hopeful Sign for Equality: Historic Hate Crimes Legislation Becomes Law," *ACT on Principles* blog, accessed October 23, 2010, http://www.actonprinciples.org/2009/10/29/a-hopeful-sign-for-equality-historic-hate-crimes-legislation-becomes-law-aop-lgbt-hatecrimes/. The video and text of President Obama's remarks made at the ceremony can be found on the White House website: "Remarks by the President at Reception Commemorating the Enactment of the Matthew Shepard and James Byrd, Jr. Hate Crimes Prevention Act," *The White House* website, October 28, 2009, http://www.whitehouse.gov/the-press-office/remarks-president-reception-commemorating-enactment-matthew-shepard-and-james-byrd-.

5. Matthew Shepard Hate Crimes Prevention Act, S. 909, 111th Cong. (2009), http://hdl.loc.gov/loc.uscongress/legislation.111s909.

6. Ibid.

7. The bill states, "For generations, the institutions of slavery and involuntary servitude were defined by the race, color, and ancestry of those held in bondage. Slavery and involuntary servitude were enforced, both prior to and after the adoption of the 13th amendment to the Constitution of the United States, through widespread public and private violence directed at persons because of their race, color, or ancestry, or perceived race, color, or ancestry. Accordingly, eliminating racially motivated violence is an important means of eliminating, to the extent possible, the badges, incidents, and relics of slavery and involuntary servitude." Ibid.

8. Eric Stanley, "Near Life, Queer Death: Overkill and Ontological Capture," *Social Text* 29, no. 2 107 (Summer 2011): 10.

9. Gail Williams O'Brian, "Return to 'Normalcy': Organized Racial Violence in the Post–World War II South," in *Violence in America: Protest, Rebellion, Reform,* ed. Ted Robert Gurr, vol. 2 (Newbury Park, CA: Sage Publications, 1989), 231–54.

10. In June 2009 the prosecutor claimed that there was not enough evidence to pursue murder charges against the two men accused of McClelland's death. A truck driver came forward and said that he may have hit McClelland. Charges were subsequently dropped and investigations are ongoing. See "Texas: Call For a Federal Inquiry Into a Dragging Death." *The New York Times,* June 9, 2009, LexisNexis; and *The New York Times,* July 21, 2009, p. A16, New York Edition.

11. "Full Duty to be Restored," *The New York Times,* February 27, 1987, http://www.nytimes.com/1987/02/27/nyregion/full-duty-to-be-restored.html.

12. "One Year After Acquittal in Sean Bell Shooting, Lives Remain in Limbo," *The New York Times,* April 24, 2009, http://www.nytimes.com/2009/04/25/nyregion/25bell.html.

13. "Officer Guilty in Killing that Inflamed Oakland," *The New York Times,* July 8, 2010, http://www.nytimes.com/2010/07/09/us/09verdict.html and "Shooting unarmed black man nets former policeman two years in prison" *National Post (The Financial Post)* (Canada). November 6, 2010, LexisNexis.

14. "Second Annual Report on Discrimination and Hate Crimes Against Transgendered People in Illinois," February 1997, *It's Time, Illinois* website, http://www.genderadvocates.org/reports/report97a.html#96-16.

15. Mandy Carter, "Still No Freedom Rainbow for Trans People of Color," *Colorlines.com,* February 7, 2001, http://colorlines.com/archives/2011/02/transgender_discrimination_study.html.

16. "Memphis Police Beat Transsexual—Caught on Tape," YouTube video, 3:58, posted by "mbatwo," June 18, 2008, http://www.youtube.com/watch?v=pJ2cLyblhpc. For more about interpellation see Louis Althusser, "Ideology and Ideological State Apparatuses (Notes Towards an Investigation)," in *Lenin and Philosophy and Other Essays* (New York: Monthly Review Press, 1971).

17. "Homicide Victim Identified as Transgendered Person, Duanna Johnson," *abc24.com,* November 10, 2008, http://www.abc24.com/news/local/story/Homicide-Victim-Identified-as-Transgendered/CX278wImn0ygMyufj8owGA.cspx.

18. "Memphis Police Beat Transsexual."

19. Lewis R. Gordon, *Bad Faith and Antiblack Racism* (New York: Humanity Books, 1995).

20. Gordon expounds on Fanon's thought in the following: "Fanon has unmasked the reasoning. The world has a duality of good and evil that eventually situates itself as powerful and weak, oppressor and oppressed. It defies 'nature' to place power in the hands of evil; therefore those with power, those who oppress, must not really be evil. Those who are oppressed must be evil; on some level, they must *deserve* their oppression." Gordon, *Bad Faith and Antiblack Racism,* 107

21. Paisley Currah, "Stepping Back, Looking Outward: Situating Transgender Activism and Transgender Studies—Kris Hayashi, Matt Richardson, and Susan Stryker Frame the Movement," *Sexuality Research and Social Policy: Journal of the NSRC* 5, no. 1 (2008): 93–105, 99.

22. LeRoi Jones, *Home: Social Essays* (New York: William Morrow, 1966).

23. M. Jacqui Alexander describes this struggle with colonialism as a "psychic residue" created by the "racialized psychic impasse of colonization." Namely, the colonizer has determined that the "natives" are incapable of governing themselves partially because of an innate hyper- and aberrant sexuality, and then the neocolonial state managers struggle to prove them wrong by policing sexuality. Alexander, *Pedagogies of Crossing*, 45.

24. "Malawi Gay Couple who 'married' Face Harsh Prison Sentences," *The Guardian*, May 14, 2010, http://www.guardian.co.uk/world/2010/may/14/malawi-homosexual-couple-face-prison.

25. "Same-Sex Couple Stir Fears of a 'Gay Agenda,'" *The New York Times*, February 13, 2010, http://www.nytimes.com/2010/02/14/world/africa/14malawi.html.

26. Achille Mbembe, *On the Postcolony* (Berkeley: University of California Press, 2001); Alexander, *Pedagogies of Crossing*.

27. Scott Long, director of the Lesbian, Gay, Bisexual, and Transgender Rights Program for Human Rights Watch, recently stated that Victorian laws permeated African politics. "Uganda Newspaper Publishes 'Gay List,' Calls For Their Hanging," *CNN.com*, October 10, 2010, http://www.cnn.com/2010/WORLD/africa/10/20/uganda.gay.list/index.html.

28. "Malawi Gay Couple Get Maximum Sentence of 14 Years," *BBC.co.uk*, May 20, 2010, http://www.bbc.co.uk/news/10130240.

29. "Same-Sex Couple," *The New York Times*.

30. "Malawi Government Pleased with Homosexual Couple Conviction," *Voice of America* website, May 17, 2010, http://www.voanews.com/english/news/africa/southern/Butty-Malawi-Gay-Verdict-React-Thotho-19may10-94221744.html.

31. "Same-Sex Couple," *The New York Times*.

32. "Thousands Attend First Anti-Gay Protests in Ghana," GhanaWeb, June 4, 2010, http://www.ghanaweb.com/GhanaHomePage/NewsArchive/artikel.php?ID=183484.

33. "Inter-Religious Organisation condemns Gay and Lesbian Film Fest," *Kaieteur News Online*, June 29, 2010, http://www.kaieteurnewsonline.com/2010/06/29/inter-religious-organisation-condemns-gay-and-lesbian-film-fest/. This controversy is reminiscent of the uproar that occurred over the International Book Fair in South Africa in the 1990s.

34. Plays: Ed Bullins, "Clara's Ole Man," in *Ed Bullins: Twelve Plays and Selected Writings*, ed. Mike Sell (Ann Arbor: University of Michigan Press, 2006); Cheryl L. West, *Jar the Floor* (New York: Dramatists Play Service Inc., 2002); Shirlene Holmes, *A Lady and a Woman*, in *Amazon All Stars: Thirteen Lesbian Plays, with Essays and Interviews*, ed. Rosemary Keefe Curb (New York: Applause, 1996); Michelle Parkerson, *Loving Eunice;* Hanifah Walidah, *Straight Black Folks' Guide to Gay Black Folks* (2003); Sharon Bridgforth, *delta dandi*, dir. Sharon Bridgforth (Austin: Women and Their Work Visual and Performing Arts Organization, January 9, 2009); Renita Martin, *It Is the Seeing*, dir. Renita Martin (Amherst, MA: New World Theatre, July 13, 2007); Renita Martin, *Blue Fire on the Water*, dir. Renita Martin (New York: The LGBT Community Center, April 30, 2009); Renita Martin, *Five Bottles in a Six Pack*, dir. Renita Martin (San Antonio: Sterling Houston Theatre at Jump-Start Organization, May 27, 2005); Renita Martin, *Lo She Comes;* Renita Martin, *No Parking*, dir. Renita Martin (Minneapolis: The Jungle Theatre, 2000); Micia Mosely, *Where My Girls At?* dir. Micia Mosley (Washington, DC: Hip Hop Theatre Festival at Studio Theatre, July 8, 2010).

35. Films: *Pariah*, directed by Dee Rees (New York: Focus Features, 2011), DVD; *Still Black: A Portrait of Black Transmen*, directed by Kortney Ryan Ziegler (Aliso Viejo, CA: Blackstar Media, 2008), DVD; *black./womyn. Conversations with Lesbians of African De-*

scent, directed by Tiona M[cClodden] (Philadelphia: 2010), DVD; *Badass Supermama,* directed by Etang Inyang (San Francisco: Frameline, 1996), DVD; *Butch Mystique,* directed by Debra A. Wilson (Oakland, CA: Moyo Entertainment, 2003), DVD; *Living with Pride: Ruth Ellis @ 100,* directed by Yvonne Welbon (Chicago: Our Film Works, 1999), DVD; *A Litany for Survival: The Life and Work of Audre Lorde,* directed by Michelle Parkerson and Ada Gay Griffin (New York: Third World Newsreel, 1995), DVD; *U People: LGBT Rockumentary,* directed by Hanifah Walidah and Olive Demetrius (2008), DVD; *Chasing the Moon,* directed by Dawn Suggs (1990), short film; *The Watermelon Woman,* directed by Cheryl Dunye (1996; New York: First Run Features, 2000), DVD; *Mississippi Damned,* directed by Tina Mabry (2009; Los Angeles, CA: Morgan's Mark, 2010), DVD.

36. Activist Organizations: Audre Lorde Project, www.alp.org; Society Against Sexual Orientation Discrimination (SASOD), a Guyana-based organization dedicated to eradicating the discrimination of queer people, www.sasod.org.gy; Jamaica Forum for Lesbians, All-Sexuals, and Gays (JFLAG), Jamaica's first human rights organization dedicated to serving the country's gay and lesbian community, www.jflag.org; ALLGO, an organization servicing the needs of Texan queer people of color through cultural arts, health, and advocacy programs, www.allgo.org; Southerners on New Ground (SONG), a southern regional organization promoting the rights of the working class, immigrants, people of color, and the LBGTQ community, www.southernersonnewground.org; None on Record, an audio-based documentary project that collects and organizes the stories of queer people from the African continent and the diaspora, www.noneonrecord.com; Mobile Homecoming, in which project conductors Julia Wallace and Alexis Pauline Gumbs tour the United States in an environmentally sustainable mobile home, documenting the stories of Black LBGTQ communities, www.mobilehomecoming.org/; Forum for the Empowerment of Women (FEW), South Africa, http://www.few.org.za/; Sexual Minorities Uganda, http://sexualminoritiesuganda.net; Steven G. Fullwood, founder of the Black Gay and Lesbian Archive at the Schomburg Center for Research in Black Culture, reflects on ideas of Black queerness, stevengfullwood.org/; Ajamu X, a fine art photographer and queer community activist who dedicates himself to collecting and preserving the cultural, political, and historical contributions of the Black LBGTQ community of Britain, http://rukus.org.uk/introduction/; New York Public Library Black Gay and Lesbian Archive, http://www.nypl.org/archives/4117.

37. One organization collecting such testimonials is the Coalition Advocating for Inclusion of Sexual Orientation (CAISO). See "CAISO Informational Brochure 2010," http://gspottt.files.wordpress.com/2010/07/caiso-brochure.pdf; and Melissa Dassrath, "CAISO—Seeking equal rights for gays, lesbians," *Newsday* (Trinidad and Tobago), August 9, 2009, http://www.newsday.co.tt/features/0,105248.html.

38. See "U.S. Co-Sponsors High Level Panel on LGBT Rights at United Nations in Geneva," http://geneva.usmission.gov/2010/09/17/lgbt-panel/.

39. Matt Richardson, "Our Stories Have Never Been Told: Preliminary Thoughts on Black Lesbian Cultural Production as Historiography in *The Watermelon Woman,*" *Black Camera* 2, no. 2 (Spring 2011): 100–113.

40. David L. Eng and David Kazanjian, *Loss: The Politics of Mourning* (Berkeley: University of California Press, 2003).

INDEX

BLACK PERFORMANCE AND CULTURAL CRITICISM SERIES
Valerie Lee and E. Patrick Johnson, series editor

The Black Performance and Cultural Criticism series includes monographs that draw on interdisciplinary methods to analyze, critique, and theorize black cultural production. Books in the series take as their object of intellectual inquiry the performances produced on the stage and on the page, stretching the boundaries of both black performance and literary criticism.

The Queer Limit of Black Memory: Black Lesbian Literature and Irresolution
MATT RICHARDSON

Fathers, Preachers, Rebels, Men: Black Masculinity in U.S. History and Literature, 1820–1945
EDITED BY TIMOTHY R. BUCKNER AND PETER CASTER

Secrecy, Magic, and the One-Act Plays of Harlem Renaissance Women Writers
TAYLOR HAGOOD

Beyond Lift Every Voice and Sing: The Culture of Uplift, Identity, and Politics in Black Musical Theater
PAULA MARIE SENIORS

Mutha' Is Half a Word: Intersections of Folklore, Vernacular, Myth, and Queerness in Black Female Culture
L. H. STALLINGS

Prisons, Race, and Masculinity in Twentieth-Century U.S. Literature and Film
PETER CASTER